THE GOTHAM LIBRARY
OF THE NEW YORK UNIVERSITY PRESS

The Gotham Library is a series of original works and critical studies. Devoted to significant works and major authors and to literary
topics of enduring importance, Gotham Library texts offer the
best in literature and criticism.

Comparative and Foreign Language Literature:
Robert J. Clements, Editor

Comparative and English Language Literature:
James W. Tuttleton, Editor

AMERICAN THEORIES OF THE NOVEL: 1793–1903

SERGIO PEROSA

New York University Press
New York *and* London
1983

All quotations from *The Art of the Novel: Critical Prefaces* by Henry James,
ed. by Richard P. Blackmur, copyright 1934, 1962 Charles Scribner's Sons
are used with the permission of Charles Scribner's Sons.

Library of Congress Cataloging in Publication Data

Perosa, Sergio.
American theories of the novel, 1793–1903.

(The Gotham library of the New York University Press)
Includes bibliographical references and index.
1. Criticism—United States—History—19th century.
2. American fiction—19th century—History and
criticism.   3. Fiction.   I. Title.
PS74.P47   1983   801'.953'0973   83-11484
ISBN 0-8147-6585-8

*Clothbound editions of New York University Press book are Smyth-sewn
and printed on permanent and acid-free paper.*

To
Agostino Lombardo,
in long friendship

CONTENTS

FOREWORD

When I am tempted, on occasion, to ask myself why we should, after all, so much as talk about the novel, the wanton fable, . . . I seem to see that the simplest plea is not to be sought in an attempted philosophy, in any abstract reason for our perversity or for our levity. The real gloss upon these things is reflected from some great practitioner, some concrete instance of the art, some ample cloak under which we may gratefully crawl.

Henry James, *The Lesson of Balzac*

THIS STUDY aims to trace the origin, growth, and interaction of American theories of the novel as they developed in the nineteenth century. It attempts to capture and to outline their early appearances, first formulations, and steady progress. It deals, as it were, with theories in the making. The book does not offer, then, a theoretical approach or an overall theoretical interpretation: it is concerned with historical development.

A pattern emerges. We move from post-Revolutionary considerations of how to naturalize the novel in America to discussions of historical fiction leading to variously motivated exaltations of the freedom of romance and open forms. After the Civil War the question of realism becomes of central importance. It shapes the debate in the 1870s and 1880s; it gives Henry James a starting point and a guiding principle, it promotes the idea of the "art of fiction", reaching fruitful combinations with other literary theories, from local color to impressionism to romance. The second half of the century closes, symmetrically with the first, with a renewed vindication of the value of romance. Contrary to accepted views, at least in theoretical terms, realism and romance seem to contend for equal status during the century: romance is never fully severed from its realistic matrix; realism is being constantly qualified and modified by a tendency or urge to blend with romantic and symbolic modes. This realization provides one of the main themes of the book. Also symmetrically, in both the first and the second halves of the century two important writers disclaim the very form of the novel—Edgar Allan Poe asserting the superiority of the tale, Mark Twain extolling storytelling over fiction writing. This attitude, which is also found in magazine writers, provides an undercurrent, in dialectical opposition to the urge to create the Great American Novel.

Most of the theories I deal with were propounded and debated by the novelists themselves, as is quite natural. A good deal of attention is therefore devoted to their views and conceptions. But I have restricted myself to their *expressed* views—in essays, letters, prefaces, in some cases in the novels themselves—and I have not attempted to relate their theories to their practice. When they are not at cross-purposes, theory and practice, particularly with artists, often follow divergent paths; to study their relation would have resulted in a different kind of book. My aim is to identify, analyze, and discuss as clearly as possible the range and the implications of their theoretical formulations as such. A good deal of attention is also devoted to the views and opinions of essayists, literary critics, and magazine writers. They not only provide the background, texture, and historical continuity of much that was discussed during the century but often a revealing counterpart to what practicing novelists thought of their craft as well.

In both cases a major feature emerges forcefully: much of the theorizing has an empirical and a practical rather than a philosophical or a purely theoretical bias. This tendency is also prominent in English theories of the eighteenth and nineteenth centuries, and it seems to distinguish English and American from, say, German or French theories. My analysis therefore often tends to deal with questions that are properly those of *poetics* rather than of pure theory—specific questions of novel writing and novel making rather than generalizations on the nature, function, and purpose of the novel. Much as I may have emphasized theoretical formulations as opposed to specific points of poetics, I would have betrayed and misrepresented the nature of my material if I had distinguished too nicely general theories from specific applications. This empirical and practical bias is, after all, an advantage, not a weakness of Anglo-American conceptions of fiction.

To some considerable extent, during the period treated in this work, theories of fiction in America had to do with a particular problem that became a central concern. This was the obsessive question of an *American* novel; that is, the question of the ways and means—indeed, of the possibility itself—of creating a distinct American novel in a country that was so closely linked, from a cultural point of view, with England, and shared its language. This was an unprecedented, touchy, and all-important problem in terms of cultural, national, and political definition. It loomed large throughout the century; it reappeared with periodic insistence; and it conditioned and qualified most of the issues and the outcomes. No mere question of label, of course, but one of substance, it involved the very existence, nature, and form of the American novel. This is particularly true of the first half of the century, which dealt so often with the question of the suitability of American materials to fictional exploitation, offering a whole range of responses—from dejected laments over the lack of materials to boisterous vindications of their richness.

Much as that specific question may blur or divert the basic theoretical question—that of the novel as such—it would have been impossible to ignore its importance. It may in fact serve the purposes of a crucial distinction. While in the first half of the century we are mainly confronted with theories of the *American novel*, it is only after the Civil War that we find what can be properly termed *American theories* of the novel—theories that eschew the question of Americanness and contribute originally to a conception of the novel in its own right, regardless of its national application. Here the contributions of writers such as Henry James, William Dean Howells, Hamlin Garland, and Frank Norris testify to achieved maturity and full independence.

The case of James, spanning as he does the second half of the last century and the beginning of our own, posed a problem of selection. I have chosen to deal with the theories he elaborated as a nineteenth-century writer, and to restrict to an appendix the views he expressed in the next century. This is meant to indicate that he bridges the gap and embodies the continuity between nineteenth- and twentieth-century theories of fiction. On the other hand, his Prefaces have been analyzed and discussed so often that it seems superfluous to deal with them at length here. Moreover, they provide an example of a general theory proliferating into numberless points of poetics: for once, it has been deemed preferable to consider James's essential contribution to a general theory of fiction, where a strong realistic interest blends beautifully with an acute sense of the artistic nature and potentialities of the novel.

In most chapters I start with a brief exposition of coeval theoretical discussions of the novel in England (in one obvious case, in France). This is not meant to suggest in any way a dependence of American theories on English models, or their "imitation" by American writers. Rather, the aim is to provide the proper context for the discussion and definition of American theories, which acquire relevance and originality when seen against the European background as they confront themselves with their English counterparts. This seems to me a point of historical and methodological correctness. Those discussions were carried on in America with keen awareness of, and constant reference to, English and European texts—often taking issue with them, subjecting them to close scrutiny and modifications, but making the most of them for purposes of definition (increasingly so toward the end of the century).

Second, it seems to me that once the years of discovery are over any consideration of American literature that does not take into account its close connection with English and European (as well as American) cultural contexts is bound to prove limited, parochial, and sterile. A fruitful reconsideration of its characteristics, achievements, and successes—something we expect in the 1980s—has everything to gain and nothing to lose from the application of this method.

Within the chapters, I have chosen to make the authors speak as much as possible for themselves. I have not refrained, I trust, from the task of analysis, commentary, and elucidation; but I believe that an ounce of example *is* worth tons of generalities, and after making my points I have let the writers speak in their own voices. Quotes are therefore extensively woven into the text. Given the wealth of primary sources, I have had to be drastically selective, sticking to the main line of my argument, throwing into relief the important innovators, and dealing summarily with those rehashing accepted views. I have also tried to make this a readable work, addressing myself to the general reader as well as to the specialist. I believe that I have not compromised scholarship, but I have preferred quick references and rapid suggestions to elaborate analyses. Clarity of outline and foreshortening—"the art of figuring synthetically," as James called it—have been my goal and guiding principle.

As far as I know, there is no book dealing with this subject in a systematic way: there are valuable studies of single authors, movements, and magazines of particular periods, but no overall view such as the one attempted here. I have made use of secondary sources rather sparingly, when strictly needed. Notes are therefore kept to a minimum; references are to texts that are more easily available.

* * *

I wish to acknowledge the help provided over a number of years by grants from the American Council of Learned Societies, the Italian Consiglio Nazionale delle Ricerche, and the J. F. Kennedy Center of the Free University of Berlin. These grants allowed me to spend protracted periods in the United States, England, and Berlin; to collect and check primary and secondary sources, particularly back files of magazines and out-of-the-way publications; and to discuss and test my views with American and European colleagues. The facilities provided by Bobst Library at New York University, Firestone Library at Princeton University, and the J. F. Kennedy Center Library at the Free University of Berlin proved particularly useful. I am very grateful to William Boelhower for his unfailing assistance with the typescript, and to Peter Shaw for valuable suggestions. In the final stages of the writing, much was owed to the kindness of Jean and Gladys Delmas.

Ca' Foscari, November 1982   S. P.

PART I

1.

NEW SETTINGS FOR
THE NOVEL

————•—•————

I

IN COLONIAL AMERICA there was no real discussion
of fiction. First, up to the Revolutionary War there was
hardly a sense of a national culture as distinct from, and
independent of, England. Second, Puritans and utilitarian
rationalists alike (I am thinking of Benjamin Franklin) were
deeply suspicious of fiction. For the former it was frivolous,
morally reprehensible, and harmful; for the latter, a waste
of time.[1] It made girls dream of impossible things; it kept
boys away from profitable work. Above all, it offered a de-
ceitful escape into a nonexistent world—a world of idleness
or pure desire—that was false in itself and led to inevitable
ruin in real life.

Eighteenth-century England had elaborated an articulate
prototheory of the novel.[2] The first impact in America was
an impressive series of negative reactions, disclaimers, and
refusals. These became particularly strong toward the end

of the century when the novel was established in Europe (especially in Germany) as the romantic genre par excellence and when in the United States the first "native" American novels began to appear. The number and vehemence of the attacks may indicate that it was a desperate fight against a conquering enemy—the more its spreading influence was felt, the greater the call for defense. But it is nonetheless significant that the first attitude we encounter was couched in mostly negative terms.

C. Harrison Orians has analyzed this attitude in detail.[3] Novels were considered as pernicious trash: they were declared false, immoral, useless; they formed bad mental habits; they were calculated "to dissipate, to corrupt, to destroy." Novel reading was beneath the dignity of the human mind, a disreputable amusement; it prevented a proper application to serious pursuits, such as history or science. Especially among the young fair sex, novels developed idle thoughts, a proneness to sentiment; they became instruments of seduction. They influenced the passions or corrupted the heart; by extinguishing high or virtuous feeling and robbing "the common incidents of life of half their charms," they led to vice. "They create, for their unfortunate votaries, momentary scenes of unreal bliss, only to be followed by a long—long night of woe; they twist the understanding into every obliquity of distortion." Timothy Dwight, Noah Webster, and Nathaniel Appleton Haven joined Dr. Benjamin Rush and countless magazine writers in their vociferous opposition to novels. There is no doubt that part of this opposition was due to the fact that novels and romances reflected or propounded the levity and vices of the mother country, the false splendors of a social world that had no bearing on, or counterpart in, America: republican sternness and virtue must have nothing to do with such aristocratic frivolities.[4]

Early theories of fiction in America must therefore be read against this background, and they appear understandably in a defensive or apologetic mood. Magazines not joining in the outcry (like Joseph Dennie's *Port Folio*) or serious writers applying themselves to fiction (like Charles Brockden Brown) first directed their efforts to a defense of both its truthfulness and its morality. But they were also confronted at once with a new, unprecedented question: the question of the suitability of American settings and conditions for the novel. Since the very beginning the debate on the novel intermingled with the wider question of the very possibility of fiction writing in America: Would the New World allow, favor, or prevent the writing of novels, given its social as well as geographical peculiarities? The question ran through the whole nineteenth century; it colored, conditioned, and sometimes perverted the growth and development of American theories of the novel. It was an undercurrent that constantly threatened to become the mainstream.

II

The first move was to emphasize truthfulness. When Susanna Haswell Rowson, one of the earliest novelists, called her novel *Charlotte: A Tale of Truth,* she reverted to a seventeenth-century stereotype that had originated with Daniel Defoe but that was commonly and preeminently found in various contemporary subtitles. The novel was to be considered "as not merely the effusion of Fancy," but as a reality; being "anxious for the happiness of the sex whose morals and conduct have so powerful an influence on mankind in general," she would convey no wrong idea to their heads nor a corrupt one to their hearts (1791 Preface). As is here implied, the second move was to stress a moral purpose (or excuse). In the short Preface to his *The Power of Sympathy* (1789), William Hill Brown, another of the earliest novelists, avowed that "the dangerous Consequences of Seduction are exposed, and the Advantages of Female Education set forth and recommended"; Caroline Matilda Warren (in her Preface to *The Gamesters: or, Ruins of Innocence,* 1805) wrote of "instruction offered under the similitude 'of a story.' "

These claims (or disclaimers) were traditional, almost a commonplace, and are quoted here as indications of the obvious reaction to the prevailing climate of censure and opposition surrounding the novel. This might also account for Hugh Henry Brackenridge's rather startling Introduction to his multivolume *Modern Chivalry* (1793). His book was to be simply a model of style ("orthography, choice of words, idiom of phrase, and structure of sentence"); it would "consider language only, not in the least regarding the matter of the work," the "idea." Given this one purpose, and "being a book without thought, or the smallest degree of sense, it will be useful to young minds, not fatiguing their understandings, and easily introducing a love of reading and of study." When insisting that "I shall consider myself, therefore, as having performed an acceptable service, to all weak and visionary people, if I can give them something to read without the trouble of thinking," Brackenridge was of course being ironical, so as to expose the fallacy of the widespread prejudice against the novel. In this, as well as in other matters, he was a follower of Henry Fielding, of the picaresque tradition of the novel, just as the other two early novelists previously quoted, Susanna Rowson and William Hill Brown, followed in the steps of Samuel Richardson and the epistolary-sentimental school.[5] A third, more recent kind—Gothic fiction, which would develop into a typically American genre—was "naturalized" in America by Charles Brockden Brown, a novelist who also proved the first American theorist of the novel of some standing.

Brown defended the novel against abstract or prejudiced criticism. As he wrote in a short essay in dialogue form: "Those who condemn novels, or fiction, *in the abstract,* (continued the lady) are guilty of shameful absurdity and inconsistency. They are profoundly ignorant of human nature; the brightest of whose properties is to be influenced more by example than by precept: and of human taste; the purest of whose gratifications is to view human characters and events, depicted by a vigorous and enlightened fancy. . . . They condemn every thing which has gained the veneration of the world in all ages." Though not all novels are declared ingenious and beneficial, "A profligate novel is an extreme rarity," and

> They who prate about the influence of novels to unfit us for solid and useful reading, are guilty of a double error: for in the first place, a just and powerful picture of human life in which the connection between vice and misery, and between felicity and virtue is vividly portrayed, is the most solid and useful reading that a moral and social being (exclusive of particular cases and professional engagements) can read; and in the second place, the most trivial and trite of these performances are, to readers of certain ages and intellects, the only books which they will read. If they were not thus employed, they would be employed in a way still more trivial or pernicious.

Novels thus reveal the mechanism of life and provide a useful kind of middlebrow reading. Their popularity depends on "the tameness and insipidity of common life"; tired of this, we pick up history, but are put off by its forbidding gravity and dignity: "Finding, therefore, but scanty amusement in these grave and regular performances, where it is absolutely necessary that nothing should be related but what is true, and no ornaments appended which did not belong to the original fact, we fly for relief from the sameness of real life to the composition called novels[.] In them we find common things related in an uncommon way, which is precisely the remedy we have been seeking to vary our amusements."

In the last line Brown was echoing a romantic concept (Samuel Taylor Coleridge's definition of William Wordsworth's poetry), but he moved further in postulating a correction of the flat aspects of life and reality on the part of the novel. Fiction is "the art of making much out of little";

we are led into "worlds of a new creation"; and we fall "under the dispensations of a romantic imagination." A danger was represented here by the excesses so often exemplified by romances and horror stories, which proliferated in opposition to actual life; so Brown added many sobering thoughts. Romantic life and love would eventually prove as insipid as the progress of ordinary life; readers would then revert to the pages of history, which contain as much variety, instruction, and surprise, even if "the events which surprise us are always true, or at least probable."

With a strain if not a background of romantic aesthetics, Brown was very sensitive to the question of *effect* and of the reader's response (anticipating here, as well as elsewhere, Edgar Allan Poe): "The eloquence of any narrative relates to that propriety in it by which it fastens the attention, awakens the passion, and illuminates the imagination of the reader. That writer is eloquent who creates distinct images of characters and objects and the circumstances of events which are requisite to constitute the picture, and by clothing them in language always perspicuous, and *sometimes* ornamental."[6] But he proved particularly significant when entering into details. The novel "aims at the illustration of some important branches of the moral constitution of man"; if it relates "extraordinary and rare" incidents, "the solution will be found to correspond with the known principles of human nature" ("Advertisement" to *Wieland,* 1798). This idea was not only in accordance with Ann Radcliffe's well-known fictional device of the *explained supernatural* (which Brown indeed followed to a great extent in his fiction); it was also a way of getting to "the latent springs and occasional perversions of the human mind." Brown stressed and advocated here a very important feature, which would prove of the highest importance in nineteenth-century American fiction: the novel as a spring to, or a key for, the inner life. Elsewhere (in the Preface to *Edgar Huntly,* 1799), he wrote of the novel's interest for "the most wonderful diseases or affections of the human frame" and faced the question of American materials with startling ingenuity.

He had already maintained, in a letter, that "there is no sphere, however limited, in which human nature may not successfully be studied, and in which sufficient opportunities are not afforded for the exercise of the deepest penetration." In that letter he had written of novels as of "verbal portraitures" and had insisted on their accuracy, minuteness, and thoroughness of description: careful observation would prove as important as invention. In the Preface to *Edgar Huntly* he postulated the idea of the novelist as "moral painter," who was to face the challenge provided by the novelty and sparseness of the American scene where, if properly sought and expressed, "the sources of amusement to the fancy and instruction to the heart" were "as numerous and inexhaustible" as in Europe. A transposition of elements was necessary, however, and Brown went on to propose his well-known recipe for the naturalization of the Gothic novel in America: "Puerile superstition and exploded manners, Gothic castles and chimeras, are the materials usually employed for this end. The incidents of Indian hostility, and the perils of the Western wilderness, are far more suitable: and for a native American to overlook these would admit of no apology."

This meant stressing local settings, local events, and local color, as well as envisaging or introducing an archetype— on the one hand, nature as an American substitute for, or alternative to, history; on the other, the Indian as a tangible and recognizable ghost, the white man's foil or alter ego, if not (as he would later become) the dark side of his conscience. This anticipation was borne out by the fact that in his conception of the Gothic and the romance Brown went in every sense deeper.

When he set out to draw in an essay dealing specifically with this topic a carefully worked-out distinction between history and romance, Brown began with accepted and fairly obvious views: "one dealt in fiction and the other in truth"; one was a picture of the *probable* and certain, of what *might* have happened, while the other described "what never had existence." He then continued: "The observer or experimentalist, therefore, who carefully watches, and faithfully enumerates the appearances which occur, may claim the appelation of historian. He who adorns these appearances with cause and effect, and traces resemblances between the past, distant, and future, with the present, performs a different part. He is a dealer, not in certainties, but probabilities, and is therefore a romancer." The distinction, however, became charged with latent meanings and important implications as Brown went on: the romancer "will go to the origins of things, and describe the centrical, primary, and secondary orbs composing the universe, as masses thrown out of an immense volcano called *chaos;*" he will arrange the objects of his observation in *clusters,* dispose them in *strata.* He will report what influences are at work, describe *modes* rather than facts; he will deal not so much with human actions as with the *motives* leading to actions, with the connections between actions. "If history relates what is true, its relations must be limited to what is known by the testimony of our senses"; where only space and time connect the facts, we are bound by the need for evidence. But Brown asked: "How wide, then, if romance be the narrative of mere probabilities, is the empire of romance? This empire is *absolute and undivided over the motives and tendencies of human actions*" (my italics).[7]

This view seems to me of crucial importance at this stage. At the very outset of American theorizing we are confronted with the clearest claim for the width and depth of romance.[8] Romance is not merely descriptive but heuristic; dealing not so much with the world of facts as of *motivations,* it is a means and a way to the hearts of men. By distinguishing it from history—and indeed severing its link with history, and the social world of mere facts—Brown was setting his seal at the beginning of what would prove a long tradition, opening the way for Poe and Nathaniel Hawthorne. For Poe, in a well-known dictum, "terror is not of Germany, but of the soul"; Hawthorne would significantly write of his "allegories of the heart."

III

When proposing that the wilderness should take the place of Gothic stage properties, Brown faced the all-important question of American materials, a question that ran through the whole nineteenth century and for half a century was in danger of restricting American theorizing to a debate on the very possibility of American fiction. Especially at the beginning, when it intermingled with the pleas and claims for American literary nationalism, the debate was often heated and confused. If seen in its gradual development, however, it allows a clear understanding of the difficulties, the risks, and the proposed ways not only of "naturalizing" fiction in America but of distinguishing American novels from their contemporary European or British counterparts. The question is thus not an idle one. It touches on the very roots of literary expression in a country stemming out of an established culture and using its same language. As in Canada and Australia at a later stage, it is only partly or at the very beginning a question of literary nationalism; it soon becomes a question of subtle literary distinction. Answers are often polemical, sometimes blurred or confused, but they allow a better focusing on the peculiarities of fictional expression in general, and in America in particular.

One of the first points to be debated was that of the scantiness and thinness of American materials. As early as in 1819, in a discussion of Charles Brockden Brown, Edward Tyrell Channing (Boylston Professor of Rhetoric and Oratory at Harvard) stressed that point, and in particular the lack in America of romantic associations. In many ways he anticipated future theoretical statements of Hawthorne and

James. America's busy streets are considered unsuitable for wonders and adventures; if deserted, they produce no awful sense; actions that are esteemed great are the useful rather than the heroic. The want of romantic associations in American scenes and persons is strongly felt by readers: "The writer then who frames a story to call forth extraordinary and violent interest, and lays the scene amongst ourselves, must encounter the difficulty of creating an illusion, where his events and characters are broad exceptions to all we witness or should expect, and where our imaginations are kept from wandering, and from deceiving us into a faint conviction of reality." If, moreover, the contemporary novel gives an increased and nearer knowledge of the state of society and of mankind, and does so by representing "what exists" and by appealing "to men's observation and daily experience," it faces in America the almost insurmountable difficulty of a lack of clearly defined classes and, consequently, of manners. "Our state of society at present," Channing continued, "offers very imperfect materials for the novel." The peculiarity of the lower class "would not be found in character so much as in vulgarity of manners," while the higher classes may offer splendor and luxury but "little of the exclusive spirit of an established order." One is, then, left with an amorphous middle order, "composed of sensible, industrious, upright men, whose whole experience seems at war with adventure." They were "exactly fitted to make society secure and prosperous," free from wild superstitions though affected by prejudices: "With such a class of men, we should find more instruction than entertainment, more to gratify our kind feelings and good sense than to fill our imaginations."

For the purpose of a domestic, contemporary story, chances were, then, rather poor:

> In every class amongst ourselves there are fine subjects for the moral and satirical observer, which have already called forth much grave and light rebuke, and many short, lively

sketches of domestic manners, national customs and individual singularities. But our common every-day life hardly offers materials as yet for a long story, which should be full of interest for its strong and infinitely various characters, fine conversation and striking incident, for conflicting pretensions and subtle intrigues in private life, and which should all appear to be exactly in the ordinary course of things, and what every one would feel to be perfectly true, without being obliged to verify it by particular and limited applications.[9]

Channing's views were to some extent echoed by a novelist, James Kirke Paulding, who noted the scarcity in America of "traditionary lore to warm the heart or elevate the imagination" but stressed that "wherever there are men, there will be materials for romantic adventure" and saw with relief the liberation from the "antiquated machinery" of Gothic superstition. "The best and most perfect works of imagination appear to me to be those which are founded upon a combination of such characters as every generation of men exhibits, and such events as have often taken place in the world and will again." Paulding wisely acknowledged that "these probable and consistent fictions are by far the most difficult to manage," but he put forth an interesting plan for what he termed "Rational Fictions." Granted the impossibility—or indeed the end—of romance in America, the most must be made of a typical attitude of sound rationality that lay at the bottom of the experience of the New World. Misled by bad models from foreign countries, American novelists could now develop what would seem like a peculiarly national form of novel—borrowed from nature, local in attachments, warm in feeling. Paulding, however, seems to waver between this view and a concept of higher realism or present-day romance peculiar to Americans, as borne out by his statement on "Rational Fictions": "the wild and terrible peculiarities of their intercourse, their adventures, and their contests with the savages [are] amply sufficient for all the purposes of those higher works of imagination which may be called Rational Fictions."

This was confirmed by a later letter of his, where he identified the cause of, and indeed the best chance for, a national literature with the West:

> I have always looked for something new or original in the literature of the West, and have seldom been disappointed. It seems to me that if we are ever to have a national literature, characterisk [*sic*] and original it will grow up far distant from the shores of the Atlantic where every gale comes tainted with the moral, political, and intellectual corruption of European degeneracy, and where the imitative faculty seems exercised to the exclusion of all others.

He repeated there a declaration of faith in science and went on to speak highly of "the History and Geography of the vast Valley of the Mississippi" as an unexhausted field of inquiry for the novelist. But he was against the idea of a historical novel and seemed rather to lean toward a view of the mythological foundation of fiction that would combine with its truthfulness:

> I do not think authentic History a proper basis for a novel. Tradition, or that species of History which belongs to the fabulous ages, or at least to a very remote period of obscurity, I should think much better. It would allow of alterations, additions and embellishments, without violating the sanctity of truth for what nobody believes, and suffer no injury by being combined with fiction. . . . A writer of fiction may avail himself of historical characters and events, but I think the prevalence of Historical novels of late years, has impaired the dignity of history, and injured the cause of truth.[10]

The depiction of the drama of human life and of exciting manners seemed eventually a higher commitment: Henry Fielding rather than Walter Scott, therefore, provided a better model for Paulding, who thus joined in the contemporary debate on the comparative value of the domestic and historical novels.

This question of American materials was given a great deal of attention in the pages of the *North American Review* in the 1820s and 1830s. In an essay of 1822, William Howard Gardiner did not share the widespread skepticism on their suitability for fiction: "We have long been of opinion that our native country opens to the adventurous novel-writer a wide, untrodden field, replete with new matter admirably adapted to the purposes of fiction." Granted the newness of American civilization, the uniformity of its social life and the sobriety of its character, the sad utility of its manner and the lack of ruins, "gorgeous palaces and cloud-tapped towers," historical and romantic associations, Gardiner was of the opinion that these would constitute shortcomings for the novel only if the principle of generality prevailed, that is, if "characters of fiction should be descriptive of classes and not of individuals." But he opposed the idea—ultimately neoclassical—[11] that a hierarchical, classified, and generalized society would be better suited for fiction, and wrote in favor of the principle of individuality, so well suited to American conditions. While denying "that there is not in this country a distinction of classes," he chose rather to stress the fact "that in no one country on the face of the globe can there be found a greater *variety of specific character*" (my italics). This variety was to be found in New England and Virginia, in the Connecticut peddler or the boatman from Kentucky, in the Dutch burgomaster and the Pennsylvania settler, in the white savage roaming in the West and the red native of the wilderness. "It would be hard indeed out of such materials, so infinitely diversified," Gardiner went on, "if nothing can be fabricated."

Here he ran a definite risk—as is often the case in such statements—not only of overvaluing regionalism and local color but of identifying them with the realistic depiction of contemporary life. Still, even "for the higher order of fictitious compositions," where the lack of romantic elements would be strongly felt, Gardiner had a positive answer. He envisaged a kind of modern romance that would not only deal with a comparatively recent past (much in the manner of Scott's *Waverley*) or the wilderness (which Gardiner evoked in an impassioned way) but would freely roam in the open, unfettered regions of the mind: "it matters little in regard to these mere creations of the brain, in what earthly region the visionary agents are supposed to reside." If in dealing with the lack of superficially romantic aspects in America Gardiner struck a pre-Jamesian tone, he was very positive in his proposals for a modern historical romance (on three great epochs: "the times just succeeding the first settlement—the era of the Indian wars . . . —and the revolution"), and in his view of its inherent narrative freedom.

The novelist John Neal also denied, explicitly or implicitly, the absence of suitable American materials and declared himself in favor of a novel of contemporary life. In a series of fragmentary and idiosyncratic statements—which, however, acquire some degree of consistency—[12] he ended up by finding or suggesting a possible answer in regionalism. He was for the depiction of "natural characters," for dealing with "mere men and women of the world," and he found a suitable homogeneity of character in New England, particularly in "Brother Jonathan"—a local as well as a representative character. He felt that effective portrayal of character involving real people was of prime importance; in this sense western characters, as well as the Indians, would offer good chances—the first for localism, the second as "the last of a people who have no history." Neal joined here the ranks of those advocating the romantic possibilities of America, but his enunciations were more specific than usual in terms of fictional rendering. He insisted on the readers' emotional responses to literary stimuli, which work on the brain (when artificial), the blood (through poetry and nature), and the heart (through the realistic manifestations of another heart, through sympathy and emotion). The realm of fiction was this last one, where we are affected by the direct representation of human action; hence Neal's interest in the specificity and naturalness of character. Thus, he subordinated plot and incident to the portrayal of character (better, for fictional purposes, if under stress or trial) and wished minor figures subordinated to one central character, so as to attract the undivided sympathy of the reader.

Neal also went into technical details: the writer must not betray his plot in advance, in order to allow the reader his full vicarious experience, just as he must not provide the reader with information unknown to the character, in order to establish the proper author-reader relation and to favor the proper reader-character identification. Just because of his interest in the psychological response of the reader John Neal was all for a realistic setting, and for realistic dialogue, hence his advocacy of Yankee speech to express the New England character, of "the real *spoken* language" to be incorporated in the novel. A forerunner of Poe in his insistence on the question of the reader's response, Neal was a transitional figure also in his view of the fictional value of contemporary life as well as of recent history.

In a similar way the poet William Cullen Bryant, in an essay in the *North American Review,* wrote in favor of a novel of contemporary and domestic life, decked in sober and simple colors, one that avoided going back to the infancy of the country, to the colonial feuds or the War of Independence, and that did without adventures of the romantic kind. Owing to the familiarity of the setting, characters, and incidents, this was a more difficult task. Bryant found, however, neither mediocrity of character nor a lack of social classes in America, which proved good for both the romance and the familiar or local novel. "Wherever there are human nature and society, there are subjects for the novelist. The passions and affections, virtue and vice, are of no country. . . . Everywhere has nature her features of grandeur and beauty," he wrote. The novel of manners could eschew intrigue and adventure and rely on the enterprise and exertion of contemporary men, engaged in business and practical activities, and thus attain a greater degree of truthfulness. "Distinctions of rank are nothing, and difference of character is everything," Bryant insisted (in accordance with John Neal).[13] The depiction of democratic Americans, among other things, one must here note, served the purposes of an underlying, widespread anti-British attitude, which was particularly felt in these years; conversely, we witness the emergence of a view of the American character as detached, free from plot constrictions, unfettered by history or society, that would prove a distinguishing trait—almost a stereotype—of American fiction.

A distrust for the wilderness as setting, and for the Indian ("this bronze noble of nature") as fictional character was also poignantly expressed by another reviewer in the *North American Review*, Grenville Mellen, in 1828: "there is a barrenness of the novelist's peculiar circumstance in the life of a savage . . . there is not enough in the character and life of these poor natives to furnish the staple of a novel. The character of the Indian is a simple one, his destiny is a simple one, all around him is simple." Raw nature itself can offer only scant nourishment for fiction, which must rely on "variations of life that give interest and grace to the works of fancy." The spirit of the age "demands, for the most part, descriptions of real life, and the display of characters who talk and act like ourselves or our acquaintance"; and if the American past is thin, the wilderness barren, and contemporary society rather uniform and monotonous, Mellen's answer to the question of materials was a strikingly new one, such as we would find expressed over the years in Henry James:

> We belong as a people to the English school of civilization. It is not necessary that the scene of an American work of imagination should be laid in America. It is enough that it represent our character and manners either at home or abroad. Whatever of romance, or tradition, or historical fact England may boast, as material for her novelists and poets, rightfully belongs as well to us as to herself.[14]

In his polemical attitude toward the Indian as fictional character, Mellen joined in the controversy raging in those years on the historical novel (and the American romance). It is significant, however, that the question of the American materials, so badly put and inconsistently debated in these early years, should receive such an early and poignant disclaimer. The question obviously had not so much to do with the particular materials used as with the particular point of view assumed by the novelist, as later theorists would recognize. Grenville Mellen deserves credit for an early and radical acknowledgment: "It is the author, not his theatre or his matter, that nationalizes his work." The controversy, naturally enough, went on for most of the nineteenth century, and with fruitful and original developments: it could not, and probably should not, be rooted off until full confidence and a degree of internationalism was reached by American fiction. James Fenimore Cooper joined in at this stage, and, as he provides a useful transition to a discussion of the further question (examined in the next chapter) of the naturalization of the historical novel, it is worthwhile considering him at the close of this chapter.

In spite of his gallant and successful efforts in the field of the American historical novel, Cooper expressed his distrust of American materials in the Preface to *The Red Rover* (1827: "the history of this country has very little to aid the writer of fiction") and in *The Heidenmauer* (1832), where he reiterated the by then common lament on the lack of antiquities, ruins, fortresses, or castles in America. But it was in *Home as Found* (1838), conceived in a mood of bitterness and resentment at his compatriots, that he vented his most open denunciation of the mediocrity of the American scene as being devoid of distinct and salient features in terms that anticipate Hawthorne and James: "this country, in its ordinary aspects, probably presents as barren a field to the writer of fiction, and to the dramatist, as any other on earth; we are not certain that we might not say the most barren." This prevented success in fiction, and it was therefore "a desperate undertaking, to think of making anything interesting in the way of a *Roman de Société* in this country." Regional specificity seemed to Cooper nothing but provincialism, and he emphasized there that the lack of a social center fostered homogeneity rather than variety, while preventing a common standard in manners and language. "Every man, as a matter of course, refers to his own particular experience. . . . As a consequence, no useful stage can exist."[15] Given these formidable obstacles in the path of the novel of manners in America, Cooper found a way out that was to be frequently followed in the future as well, that is, a recourse to romance as a liberating experience. In his case, however, this liberation was also a backward leap into the past; it became an experience and a naturalization of the historical novel. In other words, we are brought back to the fact that in these early years of theorizing about the novel the question of American materials was indissolubly mingled with the question of the historical novel; and this, in turn—just because of the doubts so often expressed on the suitability of American materials—was strictly connected in America with an almost irresistible pull toward the romance.

NOTES

1. They are in fact two sides of the same coin: see Nathaniel Hawthorne's "The Custom House" chapter in *The Scarlet Letter* (1850).

2. See *English Theories of the Novel: Eighteenth Century,* ed. Walter F. Greiner (Tübingen: Niemayer, 1970); *Novel and Romance, 1700–1800: A Documentary Record,* ed. Ioan Williams (New York: Barnes and Noble, 1970); and my own *Teorie inglesi del romanzo 1700–1900* (Milan: Bompiani, 1983).

3. C. Harrison Orians, "Censure of Fiction in American Romances and Magazines 1789–1810," *PMLA,* 3 (1937): 195–214. See also Jean-Marie Bonnet, *La critique littéraire aux Etats-Unis, 1783–1837* (Lyon: Presses Universitaires, 1982), pp. 97–156 (chapter 4: "Le discours critique sur le roman"), and bibliography.

4. The attitude toward novel reading was more liberal in the South than in New England. The success and diffusion of Walter Scott brought most of these prejudices to an end in the North as well. See Bonnet, *La critique littéraire* (also for quotes).

5. For these early developments, see Henri Petter, *The Early American Novel* (Columbus: Ohio State University Press, 1971), and Leslie Fiedler, *Love and Death in the American Novel* (New York: World Publishing, 1960). The subtitle of William H. Brown's second novel, *Ira and Isabella* (1807), was, however, "A Novel Founded on Fiction"; the preface developed the idea ("I lament the want of *machinery* in modern novels . . . I grieve for the extinction of the *eastern manner*") and stressed the imaginative quality of fiction writing. See Bonnet, *La critique littéraire*, pp. 130–33.

6. Charles Brockden Brown, "Novel Reading," *Literary Magazine* (March 1804); reprinted in *Essays und Rezensionen von Charles Brockden Brown*, hrg. Alfred Weber, *Jahrbuch für Amerikastudien*, 6 (1961): 235–36; "On the Cause of the Popularity of Novels," *Literary Magazine* (June 1807), in *Jahrbuch für Amerikastudien*, pp. 267–69; "Parallel between Hume, Robertson and Gibson," *Monthly Magazine* 1 (May 1799), in *Jahrbuch*, pp. 174–78.

7. Charles Brockden Brown's letter to Henrietta G., undated, in David Lee Clark, *Charles Brockden Brown: Pioneer Voice of America* (Durham, N.C.: Duke University Press, 1952), pp. 98–99; "The Difference Between History and Romance," *Monthly Magazine* 2 (April 1800), in *Jahrbuch für Amerikastudien*, pp. 185–87. In his review of Robert Southey's *Joan of Arc* (*Jahrbuch*, p. 280), Brown wrote against consecrating one's powers "to the embellishment of childish chimeras and vulgar superstitions," and distinguished fictitious from true narratives: the former could be either verse or prose. But he insisted on "supplying with judicious hand, the deficiencies of history, in the statement of motives and the enumerations of circumstances; fashioning falsehood by the most rigid standard of probability and suggesting to the readers beneficial truths, is the sublimest province that can be assigned to man." On Brown's ideas, see Warner B. Berthoff, " 'A Lesson of Concealment': Brockden Brown's Method in Fiction," *Philological Quarterly* 37 (1938): 45–57.

8. In the second part of his Preface to *The Asylum* (1811), called a short essay on the novel, after a quick historical survey Isaac Mitchell distinguished the romance from the novel, but in rather traditional terms. The romance had to do with violent adventures and heroic facts and was therefore giving way to the newer genre of the novel (which was severely criticized for being based on seduction, and hence being morally dangerous). For Mitchell, however, fiction must not copy life as it is, but represent it as it could be. He kept to a middle ground, distinguishing the two genres but was uneasy with both and wished to set limits to both, rather than "liberate" either. Also, in stylistic terms, "the language should be of

the middle class," neither soaring to sublimity nor sinking to dull inelegance. See Bonnet, *La critique littéraire*, pp. 135–39.

9. For ease of reference, quotes are from *The Native Muse: Theories of American Literature from Bradford to Whitman*, ed. Richard Ruland (New York: Dutton, 1976), pp. 118–22.

10. The essay originally appeared in *Salmagundi*, 2d ser., 2 (1820); see also Ruland, ed., *The Native Muse*, pp. 132–34; the letter is printed in Ralph M. Aderman, "James Kirke Paulding on Literature and the West," *Notes and Queries* 27 (1955): 97–101. For Paulding's view of romance and the West, see also his *Westward Ho!* (New York: Harper, 1832), pp. 55–57. His views were criticized by Daniel Drake in his *Discourse on the West*, originally a lecture delivered at the Union Literary Society of Miami University, September 23, 1834 (Cincinnati: Truman & Smith, 1834); ed. Perry Miller (Gainsville, Fla.: Scholars Facsimiles Reprints, 1955).

11. See Scott Elledge, "The Background and Development in English Criticism of the Theories of Generality and Particularity," *PMLA* 62 (1947): 147–82; Houghton W. Taylor, " 'Particular Character': An Early Phase of a Literary Evolution," *PMLA* 60 (1945): 161–74. For Gardiner's essay, see Ruland, ed., *The Native Muse*, pp. 186–90, and G. Harrison Orians, "The Romance Ferment after *Waverley*," *American Literature* 3 (1931): 408–21.

12. See John Neal, *American Writers*. A series of papers contributed to *Blackwood's Magazine* (1824–25), ed. Fred L. Pattee (Durham, N.C.: Duke University Press, 1937); his "Unpublished Preface" to his *Rachel Dyer* (1828) and the first pages of his *Otter-Bag* (1829). See also Benjamin Lease, "Yankee Poetics: John Neal's Theory of Poetry and Fiction," *American Literature* 24 (1953): 505–19.

13. See Bryant's review of Mrs. Sedgwick's *Redwood* in the *North American Review* 20 (1825), also in Ruland, ed., *The Native Muse*, pp. 212–19.

14. In a review of Cooper's *The Red Rover*, the *North American Review* 17 (1828), also in Ruland, ed., *The Native Muse*, pp. 206–9.

15. James Fenimore Cooper, *Home as Found* (New York: Capricorn Books, 1961), pp. xxvii–xxix. For the period, see also David H. Hirsh, *Ideas in the Early American Novel* (The Hague: Mouton, 1971).

2.
THE HISTORICAL NOVEL AND
THE AMERICAN ROMANCE

I

THE IMPULSE behind a theory of the historical novel was of course provided by Walter Scott and the debate that had developed in England and was spreading in Europe. In America, it was once more a question of how to naturalize the genre.

Maria Edgeworth, in the Preface to *Castle Rackrent* (1800), had already placed the novelist's main interest in the revelation of the domestic aspects of public figures: in going behind the scenes of bygone days, the novel was to be "a memoir," with concessions to the vernacular and the picturesque (later on she would oppose the romantic character to figures drawn with "Dutch" realism). Lady Morgan, in the Preface to her novel *O'Donnel* (1814), saw the novel as a mirror of the times and as the best history of nations, which could offer arbitrary models while leaving abstractions to poets and philosophers. Walter Scott had originally shared in the rediscovery of, and the enthusiasm for, medieval romance, which he saw as "the abstract and brief chronicle of the time," loose, rambling, and desultory, "just a necklace of beads" but close to the sublime. He first theorized on the modern romantic poem, then on historical fiction: the connection between history and romance was present both in his theory and in his practice from the beginning.

The romantic poem, as he wrote in his Preface to *The Bridal of Triermain* (1813), was "a fictitious narrative, framed and combined at the pleasure of the writer; beginning and ending as he may judge best;" it was "free from the technical rules of Epée," and set in either remote ages or the present, in which "the author is absolute master of his country and its inhabitants, and everything is permitted to him, excepting to be heavy or prosaic." The stress was on absolute freedom; its only·measure, organic growth. At the same time, Scott was deeply interested in the Gothic novel. In his introduction (1813) to Horace Walpole's *The Castle of Otranto* he maintained that Walpole's object was to write the ancient romance "with the accurate display of human character and contrast of feelings and passions which is, or ought to be, delineated in the modern novel." In his review of *Frankenstein* (1818) he was to distinguish between sensational and serious romance. This particular origin of his theories must be kept in mind. In the General Preface to the Waverley novels (1829) he avowed that he had wished to start his writing career with a "tale of chivalry, which was to be in the style of *The Castle of Otranto,* with plenty of Border characters and supernatural incident."[1]

His choice of the historical novel, as expressed in the first chapter of *Waverley* (1814), was by exclusion. "Neither a romance of chivalry nor a tale of modern manners, with heroes neither in iron nor on heels," neither properly Gothic nor sentimental, the novel would refer neither "to antiquity so great as to have become venerable" nor to "scenes which are passing daily before our eyes" but to a period "sixty years since," a middle ground between yesterday and today, romance and contemporary life. In an eighteenth-century manner, Scott spoke not only of "the great book of Nature" but also of "throwing the force of narrative upon the characters and passions of the actors" (whose bearings remain the same throughout the ages), rather than on manners.

Elements of romance, on which in 1824 he wrote a well-known essay for the *Encyclopaedia Britannica*—where he insisted on its canonical difference from the novel, and on its general attributes of the marvelous and the uncommon rather than simply of love and chivalry—elements of romance color most of his desultory and not always profound or well-argued theories. He emphasized the need for atmosphere and adventure, the picturesque and the sensational, the prevalence of character over plot (Preface to John Galt's *The Omen,* 1826), evanescent hues. He had no great opinion of the novelist ("I was far from considering him high in literary rank," Preface to *The Abbot,* 1820), but he tended to see him as a poet, to whom "the quality of imagination is absolutely indispensable," and who must possess the power of examining and embodying human character and passion, of describing what he feels with acuteness. When speaking of the historical background or setting, Scott stressed the need for an adherence to the ageless canons of human nature and to intermediate or contemporary manners and language (Dedicatory Epistle prefixed to *Ivanhoe,* 1819). In his *Lives of the Novelists* he wrote about almost all his predecessors, but he never really faced the crucial relation between history and fiction, which was his great bequest to the modern world of letters. George Lukacs saw in him the first novelist to establish a link between fictional characters and great historical movements, between man and the unity of the sociohistorical life ("deriving the particular behaviour of men from the historical characteristics of the age"), which opened the way to the nineteenth-century novel.[2] In fact, Scott is closer to the romance both in theory and in practice. He was attracted by and valued Jane Austen's—as well as Daniel Defoe's—everyday realism, nature and life seen in ordinary circumstances, not as *belle nature;* but he could never write a novel of that kind. His truest achievement was in liberating the poetic—and romantic— potentialities of the novel, in fostering its organic form rather than its mechanical construction. His true heritage, at least in English-speaking culture, lay in the realm of romance.[3]

II

One more aspect was to appeal to America: Scott's national bias, his deliberate illustration of the national, local, and characteristic features of Scottish life and manners, in terms of both geography and speech. Here was a direction that could be picked up in the new country, one that by-passed the question or the dread of an adherence to English models. There was skepticism, as we have seen, as to the suitability of the New World materials, given a lack of antiquity and ruins, of heroic and magnificent historical deeds. William Tudor and John Knapp joined with John Bristed and Walter Channing in doubting the possibility of an American historical novel; and the laments concerning the lack of fictional elements in America that were touched upon in Chapter 1 had a great deal to do with the challenge raised by the new forms of historical fiction; just as William Howard Gardiner's or William Cullen Bryant's optimistic views in the pages of the *North American Review* also met that challenge. The natural grandeur of America was even felt to be superior to Scott's Scottish scenery, and the fact that he had stressed a recourse to a recent rather than a remote past offered a good chance to domesticate his kind of fiction. Colonial New England, the wilderness (including the Indian wars), and the Revolution more than met that challenge:[4] it was left to James Fenimore Cooper to provide both the examples and a remarkable body of theories to validate this contention.

Cooper expressed his ideas in more than fifty prefaces

and occasional writings or passages. His views altered significantly during the thirty years of his writing career, changing from a preference for a truthful representation of reality to a "naturalization" of the historical novel that inclined
heavily toward the romance. At first, in a period of sincere
patriotism, Cooper declared himself in favor of a mild descriptive realism. In the first Preface to *The Spy* (1821) he
wrote ironically of the common setting and the ordinary incidents he adopted against romantic temptations ("in short,
we were compelled to let the yellow-haired girl choose her
own suitor, and to lodge the Whartons in a comfortable,
substantial, and unpretending cottage"). In the 1823 Preface to *The Pioneers* he insisted that he had endeavored to
confine himself strictly to the reviewers' injunction to be in
"keeping" (as the phrase then went), that is, respectful of
nature: "This is a formidable curb to the imagination . . .
but under its influence I have come to the conclusion, that
the writer of a tale, who takes earth for the scene of its
history, is in some degree bound to respect nature." Therefore, there would be no gods or goddesses, spooks or witches
in his book. In the Preface of the same year to *The Pilot* he
further distinguished the privileges of the historian and the
writer of romances: "the latter is permitted to garnish a
probable fiction, while he is sternly prohibited from dwell-
ing on improbable truths"; he will offer "scenes" of life and
traits of people. Cooper admitted to following in the steps
of Tobias Smollett in his attempt to paint what the British
novelist had properly termed "a large diffuse picture." In
chapter 9 of this novel he attacked the Gothic and sentimental schools, claiming that the writer's "business is solely
to treat of man, and this fair scene on which he acts; and
that not in his subtleties and metaphysical contradictions,
but in his palpable nature."[5]

According to a widespread tendency of this period,
Cooper was more concerned with the delineation of character and setting than with plot construction (see, e.g., his
1827 Preface to *The Prairie*). Still, although a deviation from

strict historical truth and some freedom in the delineation, attitude, and disposition of figures were permissible, it would be a mistake to mix too much of the real with the "purely ideal" (1834 Preface to *The Water Witch*). All this, in spite of the lack (or at least the dubious consistency) of American materials, on which Cooper insisted on many occasions (some of which were noted at the end of the previous chapter), and that could jeopardize not only the attempts but the very possibility of the historical romance in the United States.

"Perhaps there is no other country," he wrote in the Preface to *Lionel Lincoln* (1832), "whose history is so little adapted to poetical illustration as that of the United States of America." There is neither a dark nor even an obscure period in the American annals: "nothing is left for the imagination to embellish"—in America the circumstances themselves are opposed to the success of the writer who selects customs and events from different ages. We shall find similar sentences in Hawthorne and James, which is perhaps why Cooper became an expatriate in England for so many years. In spite of all this, however, he was the one who "naturalized" the historical novel in America; and this was made possible by a change in attitude and perspective that gradually led him to emphasize the role of imagination rather than observation and the portrayal of the "ideal" rather than of the real in fiction.

Although declaring himself in favor of historical documentation, of the examination of records, and of the faithful depiction of facts—even if not averse to mild anachronisms and to "an occasional departure from strict historical veracity," especially on the question of names and language—Cooper was brought to realize the value of the imagination and of the ideal by a study of Walter Scott. A "powerful and voluminous" author, Scott seemed to him to be deficient in ultimate moral aim, though still capable of raising the novel "as near as might be, to the dignity of the epic." With a "just estimate of men," his was the art of *vraisemblance* and the power of imagination (though possibly not creative genius). In any case, "he threw so much seeming reality around his pictures, that even those who ought to have known better, were frequently puzzled to distinguish between the true and the false."[6] *Seeming reality* is the key term, and the aim to which Cooper appears to have turned: it indicated a middle ground between the real and the imagined which moved away from facts toward epic grandeur. Something of the kind must have loomed large in his mind as he proceeded toward the completion of his *Leatherstocking* cycle.

As is well known, on the level of the novels themselves Cooper engaged in a characteristic transposition, which was never openly discussed, whereby the frontier—the setting (or stage) of white-Indian warfare—took the place of the Scottish border, where so many battles between the English and the Scottish were fought. The wilderness also became the crucial place where nature and civilization met, often in tragic or deadly antagonism; in this perspective, moreover, the Indian lost the features or the connotations of the villain, which had been attributed to him by Charles Brockden Brown and Robert Montgomery Bird, for instance, and more often than not took on the attributes of the noble savage. To proceed with the assumed or suggested analogies, the West could be presented as a counterpart of the Scottish Highlands; in this view it took on idyllic connotations and was turned into a sort of earthly paradise, the seat of a new Golden Age.

Little of this was expressed theoretically, though on many occasions—notably in his 1833 Preface to *The Wept of Wishton-Wish*—Cooper discussed the features and the potentialities of the Indian as character. On the theoretical level, however, Cooper prepared himself for the ingenious naturalization of those Scottish or European elements by gradually identifying the distinguishing traits of fiction as its *general* faithfulness to nature, rather than its mere adherence to facts or living models. In his later Preface to *The Pioneers* (1832), he emphasized that the tale was "purely a fiction.

The literal facts are chiefly connected with the natural and artificial objects." The character of Leatherstocking was a creation, and Cooper regretted not having drawn "still more upon fancy" (though he admitted that "the picture would not have been in the least true, without some substitutes for most of the other personages"). He went even further in his 1850 Preface to the same novel:

> As this work professes, in its title-page, to be a descriptive tale, they who will take the trouble to read it may be glad to know how much of its contents is literal fact, and how much is intended to represent a general picture. The Author is very sensible that, had he confined himself to the latter, always the most effective, as it is the most valuable, mode of conveying knowledge of this nature, he would have made a far better book. But in commencing to describe scenes, and perhaps he may add characters, that were so familiar to his own youth, there was constant temptation to delineate that which he had known, rather than that which he might have imagined. This rigid adhesion to truth, an indispensable requisite in history and travels, destroys the charm of fiction; for all that is necessary to be conveyed to the mind by the latter had better be done by delineations of principles, and of characters in their classes, than by a too fastidious attention to originals.

In stressing the "general picture" and the "delineation of principles, and of characters in their classes" rather than "a too fastidious attention to originals," Cooper not only adhered to a well-established eighteenth-century view but moved toward a theory of fiction as representing the general or the ideal, which was bound to foster and betray elements of romance. "This rigid adhesion to truth . . . destroys the charm of fiction," we read here. In the 1844 Preface to *Afloat and Ashore* he had already written: "Every thing which can convey to the human mind distinct and accurate impressions of events, social facts, professional peculiarities, or past history, whether of the higher or more familiar character, is of use. All that is necessary is, that the pictures should be true to nature, if not absolutely drawn from living sitters." He had concluded: "This is the greatest benefit of all light literature in general, it being possible to render that which is purely fictitious even more useful than that which is strictly true, by avoiding extravagances, by portraying with fidelity, and, as our friend Marble might say, by 'generalizing' with discretion." But at midcentury, in the General Preface to the *Leatherstocking Tales*, he wrote openly of the "poetical view of the subject," while his hero was presented as "purely a creation" that ideally embodied the better qualities of nature as well as of civilization.

"The idea of delineating a character that possessed little of civilization but its highest principles as they are exhibited in the uneducated, and all of savage life that is not incompatible with these great rules of conduct, is perhaps natural to the situation in which Natty was placed. . . . On the other hand, removed from nearly all the temptations of civilized life, placed in the best associations of that which is deemed savage, and favorably disposed by nature to improve such advantages, it appeared to the writer that his hero was a fit subject to represent the better qualities of both conditions, without pushing either to extremes." Natty Bumppo was, moreover, seen as the free, unencumbered exhilarated hero, escaping from the restrictions and ties of reality, urged by the wish to roam and experience Life, which was usually associated with romance:

> A leading character in a work of fiction has a fair right to the aid which can be obtained from a poetical view of the subject. It is in this view, rather than in one more strictly circumstantial, that Leather-Stocking has been drawn. The imagination has no great task in portraying to itself a being removed from the every-day inducements to err, which abound in civilized life, while he retains the best and simplest of his early impressions; who sees God in the forest; hears him in the winds; bows to him in the firmament that o'ercanopies all; submits to his sway in a humble belief of his justice and mercy; in a word, a being who finds the impress of the

Deity in all the works of nature, without any of the blots produced by the expedients, and passion, and mistakes of man.

Traits of *vraisemblance* are left—for instance, weaknesses are
mixed with his qualities. And, if the Indian appears too good
to be true, Cooper's final answer reveals to what extent he
had moved in the direction of romance:

> It is the privilege of all writers of fiction, more particularly
> when their works aspire to the elevation of romances, to pre-
> sent the beau-idéal of their characters to the reader. This it
> is which constitutes poetry, and to suppose that the red man
> is to be represented only in the squalid misery or in the de-
> graded moral state that certainly more or less belongs to his
> condition, is, we apprehend, taking a very narrow view of an
> author's privileges. Such criticism would have deprived the
> world of even Homer.

By choosing the wilderness and the red man, nature rather
than society, the ideal rather than the real, Cooper led historical fiction fully into the realm of romance. Homer, rather
than Walter Scott, looms large in the background. The *beau
idéal* is by definition inseparable from romance; where you
have one, you are bound to have the other. Thus Cooper,
in a very crucial and significant way, transformed historical
fiction from a study of documented reality to the expression
of a poetical, ideal truth, hovering in a realm of pure fantasy, which was already identified or identifiable with romance.

III

The idea that the Indians would provide distinctive romantic material, indeed the very source of romance, was
often held in those early years. One writer maintained that
their history would "undoubtedly form the classic lore of
American literature"; another that "their superstitions fur-

nished abundant food to an imagination inclined to the sombre and terrible." Their superstitions could be "successfully employed to supersede the worn-out fables of Runic mythology." The Indians were pronounced "admirable instruments of romance" and were "admirably calculated to form an engine of great power in the hands of some ingenious romancer"—thus, on various occasions, in the pages of the *North American Review*. Elsewhere it was maintained that "if a writer of this country, wishes to make its history or its traditions the subject of romantic fiction . . . he must go back to the aborigines."[7]

Cooper's *The Last of the Mohicans* provided the example, while writers such as John Neal or John Greenleaf Whittier joined in the view. It is against this optimistic consideration of local history as romance that disclaimers such as the one expressed by Grenville Mellen and discussed in Chapter 1 are to be read. There the voice of fact and contemporary life spoke against the tendency to romanticize. A writer of the West like James Hall also thought that the new territories would furnish materials for fresh adventures rather than romance, and Cooper himself must at one point have despaired of his Indians as romantic material and turned therefore to European historical subjects in *The Bravo* or *The Heidenmauer*.[8] Toward the midcentury he was greeted as the American historical romancer (thus in the *Southern Literary Messenger*: "He has shown that ivied walls, time-worn castles and gloomy dungeons were not necessary to make a world of romance, that the war of the revolution rivaled, in romantic interest, the wars of the crusades; that the Indian warfare equally with the turbaned Saracen, was the theme of the romancer"). And it was in the South that his expressed or implied theories of historical fiction were developed and extended fully in the direction of romance by William Gilmore Simms.

From the beginning Simms showed a marked preference for romance. His works, he wrote in a letter, were *"romances, not novels,"* thus involving "sundry of the elements of heroic poetry." In a review of Cooper he expressed a poor opinion of the so-called social life novel: "In works of this class, the imagination can have little play. The exercise of the creative faculty is almost entirely denied. The field of speculation is limited; and the analysis of minute shades of character, is all the privilege which taste and philosophy possess, for lifting the narrative above the province of mere lively dialogue, and sweet and fanciful sentiment. . . . Writers of much earnestness of mood, originality of thought, or intensity of imagination, seldom engage in this class of writing."[9] In his 1835 "Advertisement" to *The Yemassee* he distinguished between the novel and the romance: his was "an American romance"; and "Modern romance is the substitute which the people of today offer for the ancient epic" (a point to which we shall return).

Quite contrary to early Cooper, he preferred works that were "imaginative, passionate, metaphysical"; he often declared himself in favor of the supernatural, against the mere reproduction of the actual (which could be as unbelievable as the former). "The ideal is nothing more than the possible real," he wrote in an essay on Edward Bulwer-Lytton. "To show the real as it is, is the subordinate but preliminary task of genius. It is the holding the mirror up to the common nature. To contrast with this image of the real, such as it may become, is the holding the mirror up to the universal nature." It was specifically when dealing with the question of history for the purposes of art that Simms couched his view of historical fiction in the typical terms of romance: "A certain degree of obscurity, then, must hang over the realm of the romancer. The events of history and of time, which he employs, must be such as will admit of the full exercise of the great characteristic of genius—imagination. He must be free to conceive and to invent—to create and to endow;—without any dread of crossing the confines of ordinary truth, and of such history as may be found in undisputed records." His only laws are those of good taste and probability, and as for his subjects:

That twilight of time, that uncertainty of aspect and air in history, which so provokes curiosity, and so encourages doubt—that moving, morning hour, grey and misty, which precedes and follows the dawn, but melts away, with all its vague outlines and wondrous shadows, in the broad bright blaze of the perfect day—or that other kindred period, at its close, when the imperfect shadows reappear, and, in the obscurity of the twilight, once more leave fancy free to her sports, and imagination to his audacious dreams and discoveries;—these are the periods of time, in history, which, illustrated by corresponding periods of light and darkness, afford to the poet or the artist of a nation the proper scope for his most glorious achievements.[10]

We shall find similar views expressed by Hawthorne, although in a rather negative way. Not so with Simms. In the 1840s, when he wrote these essays and matured as a romancer, he joined the "Young America" group of literati and pronounced himself strongly in favor of literary nationalism. In his essay "Americanism in Literature" he dealt with the possible effects of a democracy on literature much in the way of de Tocqueville. He insisted that one should write *"from* one's people"; and that "to write *from* a people, is to *write* a people—to make them live—to endow them with a life and a name." This could be done in America; and if the task was made difficult by the great social mobility and the fluctuating criteria of American society, one had to turn for inspiration to its skies and its natural objects—woods and streams, dense forests and deep swamps—and to its historical infancy. Then came the crucial statement: "In this, and from such impressions, the simplest records of a domestic history, *expand into the most ravishing treasures of romance"* (my italics).[11]

There is nothing in the short history of America that cannot be used for historical fiction. Almost everything, in fact, is already decked in romantic lines and offers chances for a free fictional treatment. If there is reason for fear and trembling, or for doubt, on account of its thinness and pro-

pinquity—"Genius dare not take liberties with a history so
well known"—Simms's proposed solution in his essay "Ben-
edict Arnold as a Subject for Fictitious Story" was rather
linear. "Materials even so unpromising as these", he argued,
"if they cannot furnish themes for the epic and dramatic
poet," are suitable to the lyric and the romance, which is
gradually seen as a modern compendium of various genres
and "susceptible of far more various employment than any."
Pliant and more universal in its appreciation of readers, entering more readily into the general sense, the prose romance has superseded other genres (specifically, poetry and
the drama) owing to its "larger flight" and its lack of constrictions. The conclusion of Simms's essay is an impassioned plea for romance:

> how very superior are the privileges of the prose romancer.
> His realm is wider and more various in its possessions. His
> wing is more excursive. He possesses a right of way into re-
> gions in which other artists possess not—by reason of their
> own self-made impediments—even a right of entrance. The
> laws by which he is bound are less rigid and restraining. He
> may be tragic or comic as he pleases. He may depict in ac-
> tion, or describe in narrative as best suits his purpose. He
> may employ dialogue in such portions of his work as suggests
> the use of dramatic materials, and, when the action subsides,
> be simply narrative and descriptive. . . . He is neither lim-
> ited by localities nor by time;—nor bound, as in the case of
> the dramatist, to concentrate his interest upon the fortunes
> of some one conspicuous personage. He may carry his story
> through a period of many years,—may conduct his actors into
> many countries,—may indulge in numerous digressions,—may
> require the sympathies of his audience for many persons at
> the same time, and does not need to hazard his strength upon
> those events only which conduce to the catastrophe. In brief,
> the art of the novelist enables him to conform his writings
> more nearly to the form and aspect of events as they really
> happen, than can ever be the case with the dramatist and
> poet,—and this very conformity to nature is a source of vast
> freedom and flexibility. His laws are not only less arbitrary

than those of other artists, but his privileges combine, in turn, those of all the rest. He may contend with the painter in the delineation of moral and natural life,—may draw the portrait, and colour the landscape, as tributary to the general *vraisemblance* which is his aim. He may view [*sic*] with the poet in the utterance of superior sentiment and glowing illustration and description; with the dramatist in his dialogue and exciting action; with the historian and philosopher, in his detail and analysis of events and character.[12]

The romance is here seen as closer to nature and human reality, and indeed Simms's view becomes a eulogy for its "latitude" in a pre-Hawthornesque way and a recognition, in pre-Jamesian terms, of its "great form." It was due to this impassioned recognition that Simms was led to see the romance, not only as the proper form for historical fiction, but as an enhancement of, and a substitute for, history. Hence the great relevance of his propositions in a period of crucial discussions, not only about the possibilities of American fiction, but about the potentialities, the role and the forms of historical fiction in general (and in other countries as well).

The historian must be, and often is, an artist. His objects are "not simply truths of time, but truths of eternity": he also deals with the great moral truths, he is not a chronicler but must have recourse to imagination. Yet, as Simms put it, "it is the artist only who is the true historian." Simms cited two main reasons for this, which he saw significantly combined in the prince of historical novelists, Walter Scott: "Scott's [and, by extension, the romancer's] uses of skeleton history have been to furnish it with life and character, to reclothe its dry-bones, and to impart a symmetry and proportion to its disjointed members, which, otherwise, were . . . unnatural and formless."

First, then, the romancer fills the gaps and provides those details that the historian ignores or overlooks or cannot deal with; the romancer's task, though of less dignity and grandeur, is of more delicacy and variety, more attractive in bringing us "to a familiar acquaintance with the graces of the family circle, the nice sensibilities of the heart, the growth of the purest affections." The romancer deals not with the study of mere facts but with the study of motives, and his inquiries "conduct him into the recesses of the individual heart." Even if the historian's realm is that of conjecture, "the province of the romancer, if its boundaries be not yet generally recognized, at least leave him large liberties of conquest. . . . The liberties of conjecture which are accorded to the historian, become, in his case, liberties of creation. . . . We permit the historian to look from his Pisgah into the land of equal doubt and promise; but the other is allowed to enter upon its exploration and to take formal possession of its fruits." Or, as Simms wrote in a letter, the romancer has "the free use which the imaginative mind may make of that which is unknown, fragmentary and in ruins— the *debris* of history."

This leads directly to the second point. The artist (the romancer) is the only true historian because "it is he who gives shape to the unhewn fact, who yields relation to the scattered fragments—who unites the parts in coherent dependency, and endows, with life and action, the otherwise motionless automata of history."[13] Just as the fiction writer is thus wedded to history, historical fiction is put under the redeeming and enhancing shield of romance—with all the advantages, and some of the disadvantages, of such a proposition for the state of contemporary American fiction, especially in the South.

These two threads of Simms's theory, however, are worth pursuing, once the American brand of historical romance has been amply established. In his later and revised Preface (1853) to *The Yemassee,* Simms expanded on the superiority of the modern historical romance over the novel. The former he saw as "the substitute which the people of the present day offer for the ancient epic" and as differing "much more seriously from the English novel than it does from the epic and the drama, because the difference is one of material, even more of fabrication." The romance's difference from the novel was determined on usual grounds: it does not deal with "common and daily occurring events," with "character in ordinary conditions of society," and it is "of loftier origin than the Novel. It approximates the poem." Though romance could be seen as "an amalgam of the two," (i.e., the novel and the poem), its standards were those of the epic. Here Simms stressed both its poetic character—its wild and wonderful ambience, its swift pace—*and* its control of form and unity of design: "It invests individuals with an absorbing interest—it hurries them rapidly through crowding and exacting events, in a narrow space of time—it requires the same unities of plan, of purpose, and harmony of parts, and it seeks for its adventures among the wild and wonderful. It does not confine itself to what is known, or even what is probable. It grasps at the possible." The "latitude," as far as subjects and situations is concerned, is here tempered by the need for structural and thematic form: this is perhaps why Simms called his novel "the natural romance of our country" (where, incidentally, the difficulty was not in the lack, but rather in the abundance, of the material itself).[14]

Elsewhere Simms had emphasized that the structure of the romance demanded extraordinary events, startling incidents that "require constantly to rise in their excitements in order to produce the proper effects," so that its standards were those of the drama: "Scene follows scene; act, act, events crowd upon the heels of events" in ever increasing speed up to the denouement. He had recognized the superiority of character over plot, and that the hero of romance must be neither subject to events nor subordinate to other figures. Such a hero was indeed to be better seen—as in Cooper—in isolation, in the wilderness rather than in society. While stressing the delineation of character ("one of the most important requisites in modern romance and novel writing") and the analysis of passions—indeed, of "the heart in some of its obliquities and perversities"—Simms was,

however, among the few in his time who emphasized the
"constructive faculty"—what he described as "that careful
groupings of means to ends, and all, to the one end of the
dénouément, which so remarkably distinguished the genius
of Scott, and made all the parts of his story fit as compactly
as the work of the joiner." With pre-Jamesian images and
analogies, Simms insisted on the writer as joiner and builder:
"the perfecting of the wondrous whole—the admirable
adaption of means to ends—the fitness of parts,—the propriety of the action—the employment of the right materials,—and the fine architectural proportions of the fab-
ric,—these are the essentials which determine the claim of
the writer to be the BUILDER!" [15]

From these, as well as from other statements of his, a case
could be made for Simms as a close forerunner of James in
questions of fictional theory. He wrote, for instance, that
the morality of a writer was in proportion to truthfulness,
and he even envisaged the potentialities of a fictional narrator or limited point of view.[16] What matters here, however, is, on the one hand, Simms's decided vindication of
the *romantic* quality of historical fiction in America, and of
the freedom and "latitude" inherent in romance; and, on
the other hand, his recognition, unusual for the times, of
the problems of narrative construction. The two aspects
might appear to be contradictory: one points directly to
Hawthorne (on whom Simms wrote perceptively, with a
preference for *The Marble Faun*); the other, to James. But
both confirm Simms's importance in the development of
American theories of the novel. In his later years, after the
delusions and disappointments of the Civil War, he was to
harden his nationalism and his southern allegiance. He
maintained that American literature should embody "genius of the RACE identified with PLACE" and that sectionalism
would guarantee a truly national literature. "To be *national*
in literature, one must need be *sectional* . . . he who shall
depict *one section* faithfully, has made his proper and sufficient contribution to the great work of *national* illustration,"

he had written as early as 1856, and was to harp often on this point.[17] This points, however, to the concerns and preoccupations of a later period: Simms's contribution was mainly in the advocacy of the historical romance, and the romance in general, to which we shall turn shortly.

IV

Before moving on to the next chapter, however, at least two significant oppositions to the general trend must be briefly noted. In his Preface to his novel *Meredith* (1831), James McHenry saw the historical romance as impeded or at least made particularly difficult by the implicit need for accuracy. "To construct a tale purely from the workings of my own imagination, would be comparatively easy. Invention would furnish me with materials at will," he wrote. But in composing "a romance of an historical character" (connected in particular with the Revolution), he felt that "the excursion of fancy must be circumscribed within the limits, not of probability only, but of consistency with well-known facts." Although the author could invent and embellish incidents, characters, and scenes, he could not do so arbitrarily according to his own will or caprice; he had to conform with "transactions already recorded, manners, customs and characters already delineated . . . Public events must not be distorted, their dates must not be changed, nor the places where they occurred erroneously described." Accuracy was needed in all these details: "Hence the peculiar labour and difficulty of writing the historical romance." For McHenry, therefore, the historical romance could enjoy no real freedom of fancy or "latitude" of approach; it could not be, properly speaking, a romance.[18]

In his Preface to the first edition of *Nick of the Woods* (1837), Robert Montgomery Bird stripped the theme of the American Indian of all romantic premises and connotations and qualified the romance of the wilderness and of the for-

est with sober observations. He noted that "a peculiarly romantic interest has ever been attached to the name and history of Kentucky,—the first region of the great ultramontane
Wilderness penetrated by the *Saggenah,* or Englishman."
Together with Simms, he considered Daniel Boone and the
pioneers' sagas particularly suitable for fictional, and indeed
romantic, treatment:

> The ramblings of the solitary Boone, in whose woodland ad-
> ventures we recognize the influence of the wild passion, as
> common on the American frontier as in the poet's closet,—
>
> > To roam for food, and be a naked man,
> > And wander up and down at liberty,—
>
> and the fierce strife of those who followed in his paths with
> the lords of the forest, are chapters in its annals which, if
> they be not themselves poetry, are productive of all the ef-
> fects of poetry on the minds of the dreamy and imaginative.

Yet, apart from the romantic charm, these subjects had a
serious interest, those men were mostly drawn from "the
humbler spheres of life"; and their success could offer "the
philosophic examiner . . . an illustration of the efficacy of
the republican spirit in enlarging the mind and awakening
the energies" of men who would have been kept in darkness
and insignificance under another political faith. The wilderness, then, had a political lesson rather than mere romance
to offer. In much the same way, the Indian was drawn by
Bird in "hues darker than are usually employed by the
painters of such figures." For him—and his opposition to
Cooper in this respect was well known—the "North American savage" did not appear as a "gallant and heroic person-
age" and could hardly be used as a "hero" of romance: "we
look into the woods for the mighty warrior, 'the feather-
cinctured chief,' rushing to meet his foe, and behold him
retiring, laden with the scalps of miserable squaws and their
babes."

This idea was repeated in even stronger terms in Bird's

Preface to the revised, Redfield Edition of his novel (1853). In spite of the glowing tints of "the history of early Western civilization," he claimed that "if he drew his Indian portraits with Indian ink, rejecting the brighter pigments which might have yielded more brilliant effects, and added an 'Indian-hater' to the group, it was because he aimed to give, not the appearance of truth, but truth itself—or what he held to be truth—to the picture." At the time, Bird maintained, the genius of René de Chateaubriand and of Cooper "had thrown a poetical illusion over the Indian character." The red men were presented "as the embodiments of grand and tender sentiment—a new style of the beau-ideal." For Bird, however, the conceptions of Atala and Uncas were "beautiful unrealities and fictions merely, as imaginary and contrary to nature as the shepherd swains of the old pastoral school of rhyme and romance." For his purposes, he had confined himself to "real Indians," desiring "his delineations in this regard as correct and true to nature as he could." The same principle applied to his startling depiction of an "Indian hater," although Bird also admitted here that it was sufficient for him "to be sustained in such a matter by poetical possibility."[19]

Much of this second Preface was devoted to the controversy over two contrasting ways of presenting the Indian. Yet Bird's conception deserves at least a brief notice because, contrary to established practice, he was one of the few who wanted historical fiction linked to a realistic, rather than a romantic, basis, and thus provided a counterstatement, if not a countercurrent, to the prevailing attitude. The climate of the times, and the trend of most representative theorists, as we have seen, favored historical, as well as general, romance.

NOTES

1. See Walter Scott, *Essays on Chivalry and Romance, and the Drama* (London, 1888); *On Novelists and Fiction,* ed. Ioan Williams (New York: Barnes

and Noble, 1958); Gillian Beer, *The Romance* (London: Methuen, 1970); Arthur Johnston, *Enchanted Ground* (London: The Athlone Press of the University of London, 1964), chap. 7.

2. See George Lukacs, *Der historische Roman* (Berlin: Aufbau Verlag, 1957); Avron Fleishman, *The English Historical Novel* (Baltimore: The Johns Hopkins Press, 1971).

3. The critic William Hazlitt took him on immediately on that point, writing of the historical romance as bearing witness to, and offering the best illustration of, past customs and manners. Another Scotsman, John Galt, defined the novel as "theoretical history." Moving toward the mid century, the novelist Edward Bulwer-Lytton provided the best theoretical body on the historical romance: it is the most direct way of portraying historical and social manners, but it must eschew both antiquarianism and Dutch "still lifes." More important than manners, however, are the passions and characters of men, which are immutable and with which fiction can deal in a slightly exaggerated way. Man is universal, and so character is more important than plot; organic form is better than plot; the "science of the heart" is more crucial than structure. The romance is almost a substitute for the drama, though (following Goethe and Schiller) the romancer is given more freedom and latitude in the game. Psychological analysis, the portrayal of broad backgrounds and dramatic climaxes are subservient to a representation of the *beau idéal*. See William Hazlitt, "On the English Novelists," in *The Complete Works*, ed. P. P. Howe (London: Dent, 1930–34), vol. VI, pp. 106–32; Keith M. Costain, "Theoretical History and the Novel: The Scottish Fiction of John Galt," *English Literary History* 43 (1976): 342–65; Harold H. Watts, "Lytton's Theories of Prose Fiction," *PMLA* 50 (1935): 274–89. Lytton's ideas are to be kept in mind for some developments of the American historical romance, for which see below.

4. See G. Harrison Orians, "The Romance Ferment after *Waverley*," *American Literature* 3 (1931): 410–16. He also quotes the critical reassurances offered by critics such as Sands, Grimke, Winne and Walsh ("This land is full of materials"). In his Introduction to *The Spectre of the Forest* (1823), James McHenry also stressed the historical potentialities of the wilderness: "The difficulty arose not from the scarcity but from the abundance of materials which every period of the history of this new and interesting country offered" (quoted in the above essay by Orians, p. 417). A very interesting prize essay by Isaac Appleton Jewett, "Themes for Western Fiction," *Western Monthly Magazine* 2 (1833): 574–88, listed with care, consideration and youthful enthusiasm the various topics offered by "the broad valley of the Mississippi" and the "wilderness of the West" for "poetic prose": the Arcadia of the primitive settlers and the original scenery; the thrust and industry of the pioneers; Indian hostility and

border warfare; the boatmen (and their humor); "the character of the aboriginal proprietors of this territory"; present institutions, and so on. All these were presented as themes for "the Genius of Romance." One further reason why Scott appealed to Americans was his idea, expressed in the Preface to *Waverley,* that "It is from the great book of Nature, the same through a thousand editions, . . . that I have venturously essayed to read a chapter to the public." See Perry Miller, "The Romance and the Novel," *Nature's Nation* (Cambridge: Harvard University Press, Belknap Press, 1967), pp. 241–78.

5. On these points, see Arvid Shulenberger, *Cooper's Theory of Fiction: His Prefaces and Their Relation to the Novels* (Lawrence: The University Press of Kansas, 1955). See also Cooper's 1826 Preface to *The Last of the Mohicans:* the reader expecting to find "an imaginary existence" would be disappointed.

6. In a review of John Gibson Lockhart's *Life* of Scott (1838), quoted in Shulenberger's *Cooper's Theory of Fiction,* pp. 51–53.

7. Orians, "The Romance Ferment after *Waverley,*" pp. 418–21 (for further documentation as well: the border struggles of the western continent were seen as valuable substitutes for the period of chivalry in Europe by Increase Niles Tarbox).

8. Ibid., pp. 421–26 (p. 427 for the quote that follows).

9. See Edd Winfield Parks, *William Gilmore Simms as Literary Critic* (Athens: The University of Georgia Press, 1960), pp. 11–12, and William Gilmore Simms, *Views and Reviews in American Literature, History and Fiction,* ed. C. Hugh Holman (Cambridge: Harvard University Press, Belknap Press, 1962), p. 259.

10. Parks, *William Gilmore Simms,* pp. 13–17; Simms, *Views and Reviews,* pp. 56, 59–60 and 76 ("the poet and romancer are only strong where the historian is weak, and can alone walk boldly and with entire confidence in those dim and insecure avenues of time which all others tremble when they penetrate; having arrived at the conclusion that, in the employment of historical events, for the purposes of art in fiction, a condition of partial obscurity and doubt in history being that which leaves genius most free to its proper inventions, is the one which is most suitable for its exercise").

11. See Simms, *Views and Reviews,* pp. 12, 17. In his essay on Cooper, Simms wrote of "self-dependence" and "self-reference" (a felicitous expression) in the arts and mental resources (p. 266); in the first issue of the *Southern Quarterly Gazette* (September 1828), which he coedited, he had already extolled the native genius and the value of American scenery.

12. Simms, *Views and Reviews,* pp. 74–75. "View" in the last sentence must be a misprint for "vie."

13. Ibid., pp. 36, 42–45 ("True Uses of History"), and Parks, *William Gilmore Simms*, p. 17 and passim.

14. For ease of reference, the relevant parts of the Preface are also in *The Theory of the American Novel,* ed. George Perkins (New York: Holt, Rinehart and Winston, 1970), pp. 38–41.

15. Parks, *William Gilmore Simms*, pp. 14–15 (a controversial review of *Uncle Tom's Cabin*) and Simms, *Views and Reviews*, pp. 260–61, 265.

16. Parks, *William Gilmore Simms*, p. 15 (1856 Preface to *Richard Hurdis:* "The hero tells, not only what he himself performed, but supplies the events, even as they occur, which he yet derives from the reports of others. . . . The hero and the author, under the plan, become identical.")

17. Ibid., chap. 5 ("Nationalism and Sectionalism"), pp. 89–104 (pp. 99–100 for quote).

18. See Jean-Marie Bonnet, *La critique littéraire aux Etats-Unis, 1783–1837* (Lyon: Presses Universitaires, 1982), pp. 154–55.

19. Robert Montgomery Bird, *Nick of the Woods* (Macy-Masius: The Vanguard Press, 1928), pp. 7–9 (1837 preface); *Nick of the Woods,* ed. Curtis Dahl (New Haven: College and University Press, 1967), pp. 31–35 (1853 Preface).

3.
THE AMERICAN ROMANCE
AND
NEW FORMS OF FICTION

I

A REMARKABLE INFLUENCE in the direction of the abstracting and idealizing qualities of romance (both historical and general) was represented by the theories of Edward Bulwer-Lytton. The English novelist, so active and popular between 1825 and 1875, was one of the few to face theoretically various aspects of fiction in a period when the main British novelists—from Charles Dickens to William Makepeace Thackeray—appeared rather reluctant to take up and discuss its theoretical grounds. Lytton began with a consideration of historical fiction and moved on to discuss the nature and the potentialities of the novel in a way that provides a link between the early-nineteenth-century ideas of Scott and the later question of realism as taken up, for instance, soon after midcentury by George Eliot and George

Henry Lewes. Owing to his popularity, and to the kind of historical romance that he practiced (*The Last Days of Pompeii* may suffice as an indication), Lytton was presented as a possible model in America as well. Cooper may have echoed him, and Simms wrote about him extensively and perceptively. He himself wrote enthusiastically on Hawthorne, and since some of his ideas provide a useful background to the kind of romance that was theorized and practiced by Hawthorne and Herman Melville and that became the distinguishing mark as well as the glorious achievement of mid-nineteenth-century America, they are briefly summarized here for purposes of documentation and comparison.

In an early article, "The Critic" (1838), Lytton had emphasized the importance of ideal or abstract configurations: "For the Ideal consists not in the imitation, but the exalting of Nature; and we must accordingly inquire, not how far it resembles what we have seen so much as how far it embodies what we can imagine." In the same year, in the important essay, "On Art in Fiction," he had considered the Historical Romance as concerned with the delineation of manners, that is, concerned with social as well as historical customs. It had to avoid antiquarianism as well as "Dutch copies of the modern still life"; it was to make historical figures human. The passions and the character of man, however, were more important than manners, and there lay the most enduring interest of fiction—in the emotions as they work on the individual, in sentiment as the unifying principle of a book. A worthy conception in moral as well as in literary terms was a prerequisite and condition of success: there Shakespeare was superior to Scott.

Lytton dealt with various technical aspects of the romance—manners, passions, terror versus horror, singularity of effect, even what the French seventeenth century would have called *bienséances*—but he emphasized the universality of man and hence the predominance of character over plot, the organic form of sentiment that determined the story line even without too much concern for structure, and above all "the science of the heart" displayed by the *struggle* of emotions. Thus, the novel, or indeed the romance, became a modern substitute for the drama; hence the insistence with which Shakespeare is offered as a model for the fiction writer (the model will be at work in Melville), and Elizabethan drama is evoked for its rhetoric and "charged" emotions. Moreover, in the wake of Goethe's and Friedrich Schiller's ideas, a greater freedom, flexibility, and "latitude," flashbacks and multiple catastrophes, a more casual mechanism and a looser conduct of events are granted to the romancer, who can excel in psychological analysis: "Conduct us to the cavern of the heart, light the torch, and startle and awe us by what you reveal," Lytton enjoins the fiction writer.[1]

Another advantage of the fiction writer over the dramatist is that he can depict settings and scenery; hence the novel (or the romance) as "picture," and above all their inherent possibility of alternating between background painting and *scènes à faire,* psychological analyses and dramatic contrasts—that is, of their combining illustration and dramatic features. It would require too much space and possibly be misleading to discuss Lytton's theories in detail here; some, however, are very relevant with respect to their American counterparts or American developments. In the long Dedicatory Epistle to *The Last of the Barons* (1843), he saw *fiction* as the soul of historical *facts;* to fiction "is permitted that liberal use of Analogical Hypothesis which is denied to History" and which "seeks to detect and to guess the truth." He was drawn by a "twilight time" (it seems like an obsession with theorists at this time), but distinguished between the Familiar, the Picturesque, and the Intellectual kinds of imaginative writing according to the presence, in the third kind, of the Ideal. In a later essay, "On Certain Principles of Art in Works of Imagination," collected in his *Caxtoniana* (1863), Lytton openly wrote of the study of human nature as identified with the representation of the *beau idéal* and of the nonmimetic, metaphysical character of this representation ("To create in the reader's mind images which do not exist in the world"—almost a sort of "rival creation"). Narrative fiction, whether in verse or prose, provides an escape, "for the moment, out of this hard and narrow positive world in which we live"; it is not an exact imitation of what is called Nature, but bestows on its features "that which nature does not possess—viz., *the mind and the soul of man.* . . . The great artist deals with large generalities, broad types of life and character."

It was a program for unequivocal romance writing; furthermore, Lytton openly expanded on the *symbolic* potentialities of such writing. An added interest "is that of the process and working out of a symbolic purpose interwoven with the popular action. Instead of appending to the fable a formal moral, a moral signification runs through the whole fable, but so little obtrusively, that, even at the close, it is to be divined by the reader, not explained by the author." This was to be found in Goethe's *Wilhelm Meister,* but to us it sounds almost like a description of Hawthorne's purpose and practice in fiction; in fact, Lytton applied it to Hawthorne's *Transformation* (the British title of *The Marble Faun*). This "double plot," as Lytton termed it, was "wholly unknown" (though with some exceptions) to former masters of the novel; moreover, it was to be clearly distinguished from allegory. "This duality of purpose—[which] unites an interior symbolical signification with an obvious popular interest in character and incident" had to merge "the two into an absolute unity at the end."[2]

With these words Lytton characterized, ahead of time, the type of symbolism that colored and indeed imbued American romance in its highest forms, just as his former definitions provide the perfect background and the best link for a proper appreciation of its peculiarities. Some of his statements are almost identical with Hawthorne's well-known propositions: "To prose fiction there must always be conceded an immense variety in the mode of treatment—a bold licence of loose capricious adaptation of infinite materials to some harmonious unity of interest . . . an intelligent criti-

cism must always allow a latitude to artistic prose fiction
which it does not accord to the dramatic, nor indeed to any
other department of imaginative representation of life and
character."[3]

II

Romance seemed originally to be inherent in the American experience, a consequence of the predominance of the
wilderness over society. It was felt to appertain to its places
and its history, to its settlers and pioneers, its builders of a
"brave new world." But romance was also seen and proposed in negative terms as a shortcut or a way out of the
American lack of social characteristics and historical connotations: it was imposed by the mere fluidity and amorphous-
ness of its daily life, by its absence of recognizable degrees,
signs, hierarchies. In this sense, romance had or acquired a
quality of escapism; it was or could become an escape from
the world and society, from the visible and the ordinary. It
led to realms of legend and fable—or into the dark recesses
of forests and troubled consciences. It began to represent
more and more an experience of estrangement, of exaltation or suffering, which somehow reflected the very essence
of the new continent, of its people and of its artists.

This romantic dislocation involved, as we have seen, historical fiction (from Cooper to Simms) as well as its characters: whether the pioneer or the settler, both alone in the
immensity of the wilderness, the republican or the revolutionary hero, the free, democratic man facing the open
spaces and the grand chances of the New World. Someone,
like Marshall Tufts in the subtitle of, and Introduction to,
his *Shores of Vespucci: or Romance without Fiction* (1835), saw
the romance as factual and as little fictitious as possible. But
the prevailing tendency was to see it as an escape or a flight
from the actual, going above or beyond or inside—and this
is the qualifying point—human experience.[4] This was the

direction indicated by Lytton and that was thoroughly pursued by Nathaniel Hawthorne.

For Hawthorne, too, idealization was the "fact" and Samuel Johnson's Uttoxeter the "crust."[5] Hawthorne's notion of life, of art, and of fiction was Platonic and transcendental, and it colored or possibly determined his particular view (and practice) of romance. F. O. Matthiessen and others have shown his basic links with transcendentalism. "Everything, you know, has its spiritual meaning, which to the literal meaning is what the soul is to the body," Hawthorne had one of his characters say in a short story. And in the original draft of "The Old Manse" he had noted that "I am half convinced that the reflection is indeed the reality—the real thing which Nature imperfectly images to our grosser sense. At all events, the disembodied shadow is nearest to the soul." The work of the fiction writer turned toward that realm of shadows and reflexes, which was more and more often identified with the realms of romance: a moonlit, neutral territory (as he wrote in a well-known passage in "The Custom House," the introductory chapter to *The Scarlet Letter*), "somewhere between the real world and fairy-land, where the Actual and the Imaginary may meet."[6] Hawthorne explored that middle- or meeting-ground both theoretically and in countless sketches or stories on the theme of the artist, where he was eager to show both the need for, and the dangers of, that escape into the middle ground of evasion and reflexes, shadows and mysterious presences. One thing is sure, and it seems to underlie Hawthorne's conception of fiction and romance: they are one, both exalting and depressing, triumphing and condemning, in that they remove us from the actual and lead into a higher or deeper world, which becomes more real than reality itself. Hawthorne's conception of fiction and romance began as a *pis aller* and disclaimer of virtue or value; it then turned into a view and exaltation of another world, another realm, a *natura altera,* which is created by art and therefore superior to—or at least an alternative to—life. He sometimes wavered, just like some of his characters, between these two conceptions and these two worlds, ill at ease in one, suspicious of the other. The sum of his views was, however, in the direction of a removal from the actual, whether cherished by the artist or imposed by circumstances.

He was very cautious in his 1851 Preface to his early *Twice-Told Tales:* self-mockingly and apologetically, from a distance of years and acquired experience he wrote of an attenuation of tones ("the pale tint of flowers that blossomed in too retired a shade") and of allegory "even in what purport to be pictures of actual life . . . not always so warmly dressed in its habiliments of flesh and blood." He recognized "an effect of tameness," the need for the book "to be read in the clear, brown, twilight atmosphere in which it was written"; if opened in the sunshine, its pages might become blank. Although poorly successful attempts, in Hawthorne's well-known phrase, "to open an intercourse with the world," his early sketches and tales appeared to him not only the work of a person in retirement but at least partly removed from the world; in retrospect, "his pleasant pathway among realities seems to proceed out of the Dreamland of his youth, and to be bordered with just enough of its shadowy foliage to shelter him from the heat of the day." Removal, retirement, shelter: in "The Old Manse," the extended sketch that opens his second collection of tales, *Mosses from an Old Manse,* Hawthorne wrote openly that "there were circumstances around me which made it difficult to view the world precisely as it exists" and that "hobgoblins of flesh and blood were attracted thither." In the semiserious or half-mocking editor's preface to "Rappaccini's Daughter," when speaking of M. de L'Aubépine (i.e., himself), Hawthorne stressed his midway position or uncertain stance: he generally contented himself "with a very slight embroidery of outward manners,—the faintest possible counterfeit of real life." Only occasionally would a breath of nature "find its way into the midst of his fantastic imagery" and make us feel "yet within the limits of our native earth."[7]

The fiction writer, then, inhabits a middle zone between heaven and earth, reality and abstraction, life and fancy, sign and allegory (Hawthorne's predilection for the allegorical mode needs no expatiation here); and there the specific nature and role of the American romance is defined. In "The Custom House" sketch already referred to, Hawthorne wrote first of the moonlight quality of romance and then of a kind of spiritual transformation wrought on ordinary objects by that particular atmosphere: "Moonlight, in a familiar room, falling so white upon the carpet, and showing all its figures so distinctly,—making every object so minutely visible, yet so unlike a morning or noontide visibility,—is a medium the most suitable for a romance-writer . . . [all the details in the room], so completely seen, are so spiritualized by the unusual light, that they seem to lose their actual substance, and become things of intellect. Nothing is too small or too trifling to undergo this change." Hence Hawthorne's idea of the "neutral territory" of romance, "where the Actual and the Imaginary may meet, and each imbue itself with the nature of the other. Ghosts might enter here, without affrighting us." These snow forms summoned up by fancy were to be converted into warmer and livelier characters, but the writer worked by "glancing at the looking-glass" and beholding "the smouldering glow of the half-extinguished anthracite, the white moon beams on the floor, and a repetition of all the gleam and shadow of the picture, with one remove further from the actual, and nearer to the imaginative." If in such a condition, Hawthorne went on, a man "cannot dream strange things, and make them look like truth, he need never try to write romances."[8]

In this long and winding introductory chapter to *The Scarlet Letter* (1850) the question of romance seemed basically a question of external atmosphere and mental attitude or disposition on the part of the writer. In the more specific Preface to *The House of the Seven Gables* (1851), the romance is distinguished from the novel in terms of its greater freedom and "latitude" in the choice of materials as well as of form:

> When a writer calls his work a Romance, it need hardly be observed that he wishes to claim a certain latitude, both as to its fashions and material, which he would not have felt himself entitled to assume had he professed to be writing a Novel. The latter form of composition is presumed to aim at a very minute fidelity, not merely to the possible, but to the probable and ordinary course of man's experience. The former— while, as a work of art, it must rigidly subject itself to laws, and while it sins unpardonably so far as it may swerve aside from the truth of the human heart—has fairly a right to present that truth under circumstances, to a great extent, of the writer's own choosing or creation. If he think fit, also, he may so manage his atmospherical medium as to bring out or mellow the lights and deepen and enrich the shadows of the picture. He will be wise, no doubt, to make a very moderate use of the privileges here stated, and, especially, to mingle the Marvellous rather as a slight, delicate, and evanescent flavor, than as any portion of the actual substance of the dish offered to the public. He can hardly be said, however, to commit a literary crime even if he disregard this caution.

The first is a traditional eighteenth-century distinction and looks forward to James's conception of the "unencumbered" quality of romance; the last point is almost a commonplace. But two aspects are worth emphasizing: Hawthorne's insistence on the mellow lights and deep shadows that are necessary to the "atmospheric medium" and his passing, though crucial, remark that the romance must not "swerve aside from the truth of the human heart" (of which hereafter). He went on with more personal and revealing observations. Granted its immunities, the romance is such because of its attempt "to connect a bygone time with the very present that is flitting away from us"; it has a moral purpose, but inherent rather than explicit: "when romances do really teach anything . . . it is usually through a far more subtile process than the ostensible one." He had considered it hardly worthwhile, therefore, "to impale the story with its moral as with an iron rod,—or rather, as by sticking a pin through a butterfly,—thus at once depriving it of life, and causing it to stiffen." The romance, in the specific case, can have an actual locality and historical connections; yet, there is a notable danger in bringing its "fancy-pictures almost into positive contact with the realities of the moment." Hawthorne is very clear in disclaiming descriptions of local manners and in stressing that he is "appropriating a lot of land which has no visible owner, and building a house of materials long in use for constructing castles in the air." Not only are the personages of his own making or mixing; he sees the romance as "having a great deal more to do with the clouds overhead than with any portion of the actual soil of the county of Essex."[9]

There may be an element of shyness and of self-defense at work here (as so often in Hawthorne). Yet the romance is removed as much as possible not only from actuality but from its geographical and historical connections or connotations. In spite of Hawthorne's deep historical awareness, his theory makes of romance not only a free form and a medium for the free play of fancy and imagination but a vehicle—and here his importance is crucial—for the exploration and expression of "the truth of the human heart." If anything, Hawthorne's conception tends to become a conception of *psychological* romance. The definition is his own. In his Preface ("To Horatio Bridge," 1851) to *The Snow Image* he wrote of "burrowing, to his utmost ability, into the depths of our common nature, for the purposes of psychological romance"—admittedly a "dusky region" but certainly a most important, new ground of inquiry for the "fiction-monger."[10]

The removal of romance from actuality was confirmed by Hawthorne in his second, articulate discussion of the characteristics of the genre in his Preface (1852) to *The Blithedale*

Romance. Here it was all the more significant in that germ
and setting, characters and events of that self-styled romance were inspired by actual facts: the Brook Farm social-
ist experience in which Hawthorne himself had taken part.
In spite of this, however, he insisted that the characteristic
of his romance was "merely to establish a theatre, a little
removed from the highway of ordinary travel, where the
creatures of his brain may play their phantasmagoric antics,
without exposing them to too close a comparison with the
actual events of real lives." One of the privileges of the romancer was that his works are not "put exactly side by side
with nature"; he is allowed not only "latitude" but also "a
licence with regard to every-day probability, in view of the
improved effects." For the first time in his theorizing, however, Hawthorne put forth the idea that that atmosphere of
fairyland and of strange enchantment so crucially needed
by the romancer was lacking in America: "In its absence,
the beings of imagination are compelled to show themselves
in the same category as actually living mortals; a necessity
that generally renders the paint and paste-board of their
composition but too painfully discernible."[11]

It would seem, therefore, that at this stage that meeting
ground of fiction and reality on which Hawthorne had insisted so much as typical of romance were a sort of sad necessity, a *pis aller,* for the American writer, given the so often
lamented lack of legendary or fairy connotations of the
country. He indeed proceeded in this direction, and in his
third, later discussion of romance, in the 1859 Preface to
The Marble Faun, he saw it as usual as "a fanciful story,
evolving a thoughtful moral," free from the need to portray
contemporary manners, but with a new, surprising slant.
Romance he saw now as the realm of poetry and antiquity,
and more and more he identified it with a legendary or fairy
land where actualities need not be insisted upon. But America seemed exactly a land of actualities and of no poetic or
picturesque connotations; hence, the removal of romance,
not only from actuality, but from America itself, and the

choice of a more congenial (i.e., European) setting for it—
Italy, in the specific case. But I present the full quotation
both to show Hawthorne as a close forerunner of Henry
James and to stress his later view that romance needed a
geographical dislocation away from America as well:

> Italy, as the site of his Romance, was chiefly valuable to
> him as affording a sort of poetic or fairy precinct, where ac-
> tualities would not be so terribly insisted upon as they are,
> and must needs be, in America. No author, without a trial,
> can conceive of the difficulty of writing a romance about a
> country where there is no shadow, no antiquity, no mystery,
> no picturesque and gloomy wrong, nor anything but a com-
> monplace prosperity, in broad and simple daylight, as is hap-
> pily the case with my dear native land. It will be very long, I
> trust, before romance-writers may find congenial and easily
> handled themes, either in the annals of our stalwart republic,
> or in any characteristic and probable events of our individual
> lives. Romance and poetry, ivy, lichens, and wall-flowers, need
> ruin to make them grow.[12]

This late conclusion seems to me rather disappointing and
to hearken back to the earliest considerations about the unsuitability of American materials for the purposes of romance. Yet Hawthorne's views of romance remain of great
importance, particularly on two accounts: the central role
he assigned to the freedom and latitude of romance; and
the connections he posited for it with a symbolical mode of
writing or rendering, on the one side, and with the psychological exploration of the human heart, on the other. These
two aspects or polarities were united in his well-known and
meaningful expression, "allegories of the heart," which he
formulated more as a pointer than as a theory. An analysis
of them does not fall within my intent, and they have often
been discussed.[13] I may simply recall here the predilection
Hawthorne expressed for Edmund Spenser, John Milton,
and John Bunyan in his "The Hall of Fantasy," his half-
mocking editor's introduction to "Rappaccini's Daughter,"

where he wrote of his "inveterate love of allegory," and Hilda's view as expressed in *The Marble Faun* that the highest merit of art is suggestiveness. There is, however, a third aspect worth discussing here, which establishes Hawthorne's crucial importance in a definition of American romance.

Just as he was shy, remote, and retiring in his expressed theories, he proved daring and almost revolutionary when he dealt with questions of art or fiction *within* his romances or stories, as themes or topics of problematic, sometimes dramatic purport. At various points in these embodied, rather than merely theoretical, formulations he presented art and romance writing not only as an exalting, totalizing experience but as a kind of "rival creation" as regards our life and our world. He was fully aware of the hubris and tragic consequences of trying to correct and improve nature ("The Birthmark"); yet he more than toyed with the idea that the artist had to do precisely that. In "The Great Stone Face" we read: "Thus the world assumed another and a better aspect from the hour that the poet blessed it with his happy eyes. The Creator had bestowed him, as the last best touch to his own handiwork. Creation was not finished till the poet came to interpret, and so to complete it." In "The Artist of the Beautiful" he wrote of the aspiration to produce "a beauty that should attain to the ideal which Nature has proposed to herself in all her creatures, but has never taken pains to realize"; finally, in *The Marble Faun,* Miriam's studio is likened to the poet's haunted imagination "where there are glimpses, sketches, and half-developed hints of beings and objects grander and more beautiful than we can anywhere find in reality."[14] Most of Hawthorne's artists think it necessary to put themselves at odds with nature: their ideal, though more often than not frustrated, baffled, or condemned, is found in that almost frightening enunciation: *"beings and objects grander and more beautiful than we can anywhere find in reality"* (my italics). This, regardless of its negative connotations or tragic bafflements in so many of his tales, seems to remain Hawthorne's most startling contribution to a definition of American romance, all the more important in that it was echoed almost verbatim and developed to its furthest conclusions by his great contemporary, Herman Melville.

III

Melville's main theoretical concerns seem to have been with the definition and expression of truth. As his conception of truth changed, so did his view of fiction, gradually leading him to a radical adherence to the idea of romantic and "rival creation." In his early works, based on his living experiences, he declared "his anxious desire to speak the unvarnished truth" (Preface to *Typee,* 1846) and his observance of a "strict adherence to facts" (Preface to *Omoo,* 1847: "Nothing but an earnest desire for truth and good has led [the author] to touch upon this subject at all"). In both cases he claimed that he was giving his readers a literal or factual truth, an account of what had actually happened, without inventions or pretensions to philosophical research. Since he was not believed, and his stories were considered fantastic, he decided to modify his attitude. In a letter of 1848 to his English publisher John Murray he maintained that he had changed his plans for a new book of adventure (*Mardi*) and that he would now write "a Romance of Polynesian adventure." Tired of being taken for a writer of invented stories, he would show the world what a true fantastic story of his could be. The half-resentful, half-humorous idea is repeated in his short Preface to *Mardi:* "Not long ago, having published two narratives of voyages in the Pacific, which, in many quarters, were received with incredulity, the thought occurred to me of writing a romance of Polynesian adventure, and publishing it as such: to see whether, the fiction might not, possibly, be received for a verity." In the letter he had defined the romance as poetic and allowing for the free play of invention, but growing out of a kernel, or at least developing from a beginning, of *facts*. In *Mardi* he has some of his characters discuss at length the conditions or the implications of fiction, and in such a way as to reveal his growing awareness of the potentialities of romance.[15]

In one of these discussions Yoomy, the poet, maintains that while historians deal in "mangled realities" the "poets are the true historians"; the exaggerations and distortions of poets are in a way closer to essential reality than mere facts are; and Babbalanja, the philosopher, steps in with the bold assertion "that what are vulgarly called fictions are as much realities as the gross mattress of Dididi, the digger of trenches; for things visible are but the conceits of the eye; things imaginative, conceits of the fancy. If duped by one, we are equally duped by the other." Melville began here to conceive of truth as an elusive and baffling entity, something that can only be perceived (and hardly reproduced) through a glass darkly: hence his growing concern with symbolic modes of literary presentation, of which both *Mardi* (and, later on, *White Jacket*) offer ample evidence. But the real shift in his conception was determined by his reading of Shakespeare and his acquaintance with Hawthorne's work: his famous essay "Hawthorne and His Mosses" (1850) marks and exemplifies this shift. In Shakespeare and Hawthorne—his American counterpart—Melville witnessed "those short, quick probings at the very axis of reality"—a fearless concern and indeed obsession with the "vital truth" that were the mark of the true artist and fiction writer, compared with a mere adherence or fidelity to actual life. In that impassioned salutation of the new bard and writer of America—and declaration of literary independence, if there was ever one—Melville wrote not only of the "depth of tenderness" and sympathy with all forms of being necessary to the writer but also of his need to face the "awful truth," of his "power of blackness," of his mastery of the "great Art of Telling the Truth,—even though it be covertly and by snatches."

The "power of blackness" was not only in the deep-rooted

awareness of sin but also in the sense of tragedy and in the courage to say "NO! in thunder," of which, in a letter to Hawthorne, Melville wrote as constituting the real greatness of the writer.[16] Recognizing the elusive or illusory nature of truth, and at the same time searching for it; saying no! in thunder to certainties and complacencies, and yet proceeding with probings and questionings: these were for Melville the tests of the great writer. Hence, his mature theory of fiction is to be defined by, and measured against, his deep affinity with Hawthorne. But Melville went further, in both his view and practice of symbolism; in his conception of the romance as offering a higher, more intense picture of reality; and in the emphasis he placed on the utmost freedom and openness of narrative forms.

His view and practice of symbolism has been amply studied and discussed; various statements could be culled from *Moby Dick* or *Pierre,* two books that embody explicit definitions of their symbolic nature and carry theoretical aperçus of their practice. "Some certain significance lurks in all things, else all things are little worth," Melville states in chapter 99 of *Moby Dick,* and in chapter 36 Ahab makes his impassioned avowal: "All visible objects, man, are but as pasteboard masks. But in each event—in the living act, the undoubted deed—there, some unknown but still reasoning thing puts forth the mouldings of its features from behind the reasoning mask". These quotes must suffice. In *Pierre,* the young hero must painfully perceive that "books in the world are but the mutilated shadowings-forth of invisible and eternally unembodied images in the soul." It is perhaps in the "Agatha letter," however, that Melville's conception of the symbolic procedure is best expressed. Writing to Hawthorne in 1852 to offer him for possible fictional use the story of a forsaken New England woman, Melville stressed that he had "a skeleton of actual reality to build about with fulness & veins and beauty" and proceeded to indicate in the most revealing way how the details were or could be "instinct with significance." The way in which in

the "Agatha letter" he set up the scene of the story for Hawthorne—the cliffs, the pasture, the lighthouse; the open sea;
the shadow of a sheep; Agatha looking forlornly over the
open space of the sea like an innocent lamb confronting
brooding evil—is a perfect lesson in the construction of a
symbolic structure and a symbolic tension.[17]

The second and third aspects of Melville's later view—his
conception of romance as offering a higher picture of reality, and his preference for open forms—require greater
treatment. Never mimetic (except in the early books), Melville's concept of fiction stressed the advantages of organic
form and of those "probings at the very axis of reality" that
were typical of romance. He used the organic metaphor—
of the narrative growing like a plant or a tree because of its
inner drive and inherent form—in the crucial essay, "Hawthorne and His Mosses"; in *Mardi;* explicitly in *Moby Dick*
("Out of the trunk the branches grow; out of them, the twigs.
So in productive subjects, grow the chapters"); and in *Pierre,*
where the hero muses on the inadequacy of "fixed principles" for fiction and is even too prone to follow the pattern
and the dictates of life rather than art. More than the organic metaphor, however, it is the view of fiction writing as
free from a too severe fidelity to real life, and as expressive
of a kind of heightened reality, that qualifies Melville's conception of romance writing. In chapter 33 of *Confidence Man*
(1857), answering the hypothetical charge "How unreal all
this is!" he first showed surprise at the readers' acquiescence
to a mimetic reproduction of the routine of daily life, and
then he proceeded to put forth his crucial idea that in fiction we must have more reality than life itself can offer:

> Strange, that in a work of amusement, this severe fidelity
> to real life should be exacted by anyone, who, by taking up
> such a work, sufficiently shows that he is not unwilling to
> drop real life, and turn, for a time, to something different.
> Yes, it is, indeed, strange that anyone should clamor for the
> thing he is weary of; that anyone, who, for any cause, finds

real life dull, should yet demand of him who is to divert his attention from it, that he should be true to that dullness.

There is another class, and with this class we side, who sit down to a work of amusement tolerantly as they sit at a play, and with much the same expectations and feelings. They look that fancy shall evoke scenes different from those of the same old crowd round the custom-house counter, and same old dishes on the boarding-house table, with characters unlike those of the same old acquaintances they meet in the same old way every day in the same old street. And as, in real life, the properties will not allow people to act out themselves with that unreserve permitted to the stage; so. in books of fiction, they look not only for more entertainment, but, at bottom, even for more reality, than real life itself can show.

If writer and reader are bound to and by nature, yet they want "nature unfettered, exhilarated, in effect transformed. . . . It is with fiction as with religion: it should present another world, and yet one to which we feel the tie." Such statements look forward to James's definition of romance in his 1907 Preface to *The American,* but above all they emphasize Melville's idea of fiction as "rival creation": fiction not only inhabits, it creates, another world, a different world from everyday life, where a dislocation from actuality has taken place, people "dress as nobody exactly dresses, talk as nobody exactly talks, and act as nobody exactly acts." Though we feel the tie with this world, its features, aspects, and colors have been "transformed": unfettered and exhilarated nature is freed from too close a resemblance to life, too strict an adherence to surface realism or, again, superficial truth. The "other" world is the world of romance where—as Melville noted in chapter 14 of *The Confidence Man* —inconsistency of character can be not only accepted but can be seen to reflect reality in a truer way.

A consistent character is a rara avis in life itself, hardly conducive to "some play of invention"; it may appear, above all, as a reduction or a limitation of the full range of humanity that the writer must confront or reveal. Nature is seen as producing greater inconsistency of character than any writer does (the flying squirrel; the duck-billed beaver of Australia); and indeed nature is seen as a storehouse of surprising and baffling creatures. Fiction, therefore, not only would do wrong not to reflect that wealth of strange forms; it must positively accept the challenge of the unknown and the unforeseen, the partly understood or the simply glimpsed even in the creation of character. Can we really expect, Melville asked, "to run and read character in those mere phantoms which flit along the page, like shadows along the wall?" A familiar doubt was here expressed as to the possibility of knowing man and of capturing truth; but Melville went deeper and stressed the idea that inconsistency or elusiveness of character could be the only answer to a true attempt at sounding the depths of human nature on the part of the writer.

"That fiction, where every character can, by reason of its consistency, be comprehended at a glance," he wrote, "either exhibits but sections of character, making them appear for whole, or else is very untrue to reality." If it was then claimed that writers should "represent human nature not in obscurity, but transparency, which, indeed, is the practice with most novelists," Melville's view was perfectly in keeping with his idea of the elusive character of truth, as well as with the need to fathom and explore it in all its complexities: "if these waters of human nature can be so readily seen through, it may be either that they are very pure or very shallow." For Melville, neither was the writer's true concern: he who says of human nature what is said of divine nature, "that it is past finding out, thereby evinces a better appreciation of it" than he who "leaves it to be inferred that he clearly knows all about it." The "tangled web" of life and of human character was to be fearlessly and, if need be agonizingly, explored. In a later chapter of *The Confidence Man* he even suggested that there is a godlike quality in the writer's task.[18]

When declaring himself against "the revelation of human nature on fixed principles," Melville was all for expressing

its "grand points"—its elusive, even contradictory features—
according to that freedom and latitude of approach that he
considered the distinguishing mark of the romance writer.
His concern here was clearly with the possible variations of
character presentation and with the postulated depths of
character analysis—a realm to which, as for Hawthorne, romance writing was to be particularly devoted. That both
possibilities appeared baffling and problematic was nothing
but a confirmation of the difficult though inescapable task
confronting the artist. Finally—and here we reach the third,
conclusive point—Melville came more and more to realize
explicitly what had been implicit in his narratives: that only
loose structures and open forms were suitable for fiction,
that the rigidity of the novel form had to be broken from
the inside and transcended.

In book VII, chapter 8, of *Pierre* he had already written
of his hero having "conned his novel-lessons" and of the
novels' "false, inverted attempts at systematizing eternally
unsystemizable elements; their audacious, intermeddling
potency, in trying to unravel, and spread out, and classify,
the more thin than gossamer threads which make up the
complex web of life." He wrote of Pierre that he

> saw that human life . . . partakes of the unravelable inscru-
> tableness of God. By infallible presentiment he saw, that not
> always doth life's beginning gloom conclude in gladness; that
> wedding bells peal not ever in the last scene of life's fifth act;
> that while the countless tribes of common novels laboriously
> spin veils of mystery, only to complacently clear them up at
> last; and while the countless tribe of common dramas do but
> repeat the same; yet the profounder emanations of the hu-
> man mind, intended to illustrate all that can be humanly
> known of human life; these never unravel their own intrica-
> cies, and have no proper endings; but in imperfect, unan-
> ticipated, and disappointing sequels (as mutilated stumps),
> hurry to abrupt intermergings with the eternal tides of time
> and fate.

At the beginning of chapter 28 of *Billy Budd*—his swan song and posthumous narrative—Melville was to reiterate the point in an even clearer way: "The symmetry of form attainable in pure fiction cannot so readily be achieved in a narration essentially having less to do with fable than with fact. Truth uncompromisingly told will always have its ragged edges; hence the conclusion of such a narration is apt to be less finished than an architectural finial."[19] Symmetry, proportion, close structures are alien to fiction based on facts; even more so, when "truth is uncompromisingly told"—as, for instance, in the greatest attempts at romance writing—fiction must be left with ragged edges, it cannot be properly "finished." Melville, then, was not only for romance and organic form as such; he was for open, unfettered, ever changing narratives, not to be fenced in or restricted by architectural laws but able to move freely from one genre to another.

Melville's final theoretical statements, therefore, betray how far a conception of American romance had moved in the direction of open forms, suspended structures, loose endings (a charge that was commonly brought against an upcoming younger author, Henry James, in the 1880s). They also reveal the profound motivation of Melville's fictional practice, of his untiring attempts to break loose from and go beyond the strict novel form. He had availed himself, in turn, of the travelogue, the allegorical fable, the reportage, and the disguised autobiography; of the epic form and the case history; of the essay-novel, the "anatomy" (in Northrop Frye's sense), and of the analogue with the classical tragedy. He kept looking beyond a nineteenth-century conception of the novel, even of romance. As F. O. Matthiessen reminds us, in 1869 he had marked this passage in Matthew Arnold's *Essays in Criticism:* "In prose, the character of the vehicle for the composer's thoughts is not determined beforehand; every composer has to make his own vehicle."[20] He did exactly that in his lifelong struggle with fiction; he pointed to and envisaged something that went beyond a theory of American romance to which he had so greatly contributed.

NOTES

1. See Harold H. Watts, "Lytton's Theories of Prose Fiction," *PMLA* 50 (1935): 274–89. Both essays appeared in the *Monthly Chronicle*.

2. Edward Bulwer-Lytton, Dedicatory Epistle to *The Last of the Barons* (London: Bradbury and Evans, 1843), pp. v–xiv (pp. v and xii for quotes); *Caxtoniana: A Series of Essays on Life, Literature and Manners* (Edinburgh and London: Blackwood, 1863), vol. II, pp. 131–69 (pp. 133–34, 151–52, 153 for quotes).

3. Lytton, *Caxtoniana*, pp. 163–64.

4. See John C. Stubbs, *The Pursuit of Form: A Study of Hawthorne and the Romance* (Urbana: The University of Illinois Press, 1970), p. 3 and passim. According to Lyle Wright, *American Fiction, 1774–1850* (San Marino: Huntington Library, 1948), twenty-two romances are recorded before 1840, forty between 1840 and 1845, seventy-one between 1846 and 1850.

5. *Our Old Home*, in *The Works of Nathaniel Hawthorne* (Boston and New York: Houghton Mifflin, Riverside Edition, 1882), vol. VII, pp. 165–66 (hereafter referred to as *Works*).

6. F. O. Matthiessen, *American Renaissance: Art and Experience in the Age of Emerson and Whitman* (New York: Oxford University Press, 1941), pp. 253–64; also Charles H. Foster, "Hawthorne's Literary Theory," *PMLA* 57 (1942): 241–54 and Roy Harvey Pearce, "Hawthorne and the Twilight of Romance," *Yale Review* 37 (1948): 487–506. For Hawthorne's quotation, see *Works*, V, pp. 54–55.

7. Hawthorne, *Works*, I, pp. 16–19; II, pp. 41, 108.

8. Hawthorne, *Works*, V, pp. 54–56. The twilight quality of early colonial America for the purposes of historical romance had been stressed in John Lothrop Motley's *Merry Mount* (1849): "The crepuscular period that immediately preceded the rise of Massachusetts Colony, possesses more of the element of romance than any other subsequent epoch. After the arrival of Winthrop with the charter, the history of the province is as clear as day-light; but during the few previous years there are several characters flitting like phantoms through the chronicle of the time." The importance of the Salem witchcraft trials for fictional purposes had been proposed by Henry William Herbert in the Preface to his Ruth Valley trilogy: "This, the only *American* romance of the author, is truly a historical romance; many of the persons being genuine historical characters,

and the facts generally and the spirit of the age carefully preserved. The period is one of the most interesting of the early times of North American history, being that of the subsistence of the terrible excitement of the Salem witchcraft, the tyrannous government of Sir Edmund Andros, and the first organized and successful resistance to the authority of the crown" (1844–45). See also Stubbs, *The Pursuit of Form*, pp. 40–41.

9. Hawthorne, *Works*, III, pp. 13–16. Hawthorne had commented on the blend of the marvelous and the natural in romance in a review of J. G. Whittier's *The Supernaturalism of New England*, in *The Literary World* I (April 1847): 247.

10. Hawthorne, *Works*, III, p. 386. In "The Prophetic Pictures" Hawthorne had written that "the artist—the true artist—must look beneath the exterior. It is his gift . . . to see the inmost soul" (*Works*, I, p. 202).

11. Hawthorne, *Works*, V, pp. 322–23.

12. Hawthorne, *Works*, VI, p. 15. Hawthorne made it clear, even in the text of the book, that he would not "meddle with history"—except "that the very dust of Rome is historic" and inevitably settles on the page— and that his setting and his figures would be as purely picturesque and as ethereally disembodied as possible (p. 124). His late disillusionment with American romance and his turning to Italy for a setting is studied by Pearce and related to Melville's contemporary unease about the romance ("Hawthorne and the Twilight of Romance").

13. See Matthiessen, *American Renaissance*, and Foster, "Hawthorne's Literary Theory." For what follows, see Hawthorne, *Works*, II, pp. 196–211 (where we read of "spiritualizing the grossness of this actual life, and prefiguring to ourselves a state in which the ideal will be all in all"), and II, p. 107; VI, p. 431; *Our Old Home:* "Facts . . . are covered with a stony excrescence of prose resembling the crust of a beautiful sea-shell, and they never show their most delicate and divinest colors until we shall have dissolved away their grossest actualities by steeping them long in a powerful menstrum of thought" (quoted in Foster, p. 250); and his *American, French and Italian* and *English Notebooks, Works*, VII–X.

14. Hawthorne, *Works*, III, pp. 432–33; II, p. 524; VI, p. 57. For a discussion of the idea of "rival creation" in the novel see Albert Camus, *The Rebel* (Harmondsworth: Penguin Books, 1971), chap. 4, and below.

15. Quotes are from *The Writings of Herman Melville* (Evanston and Chicago: The Northwestern-Newberry Edition, 1968–), I, p. xix; II, p. xiv; III, p. xvii (and pp. 280–84, chap. 93, for what follows); *The Letters of Herman Melville*, ed. M. R. Davies and W. H. Gilman (New Haven: Yale University Press, 1960), pp. 69–71 (hereafter referred to as *Letters*). See also Perry Miller, "The Romance and the Novel," in *Nature's Nation* (Cambridge: Harvard University Press, Belknap Press, 1967), pp. 241–78.

16. For ease of reference, see "Hawthorne and His Mosses," in *Moby-Dick* (New York: Norton Critical Edition, 1967), pp. 535–55; *Letters*, pp. 123–33, 141–44, 153–63.

17. *Letters*, pp. 154–57; for his symbolism, see Matthiessen, *American Renaissance*, chapter VII, 1 and chapters IX–XII; Charles Feidelson Jr., *Symbolism and American Literature* (Chicago: The University of Chicago Press, 1951); Allen Hayman, "The Real and the Original: Herman Melville's Theory of Prose Fiction," *Modern Fiction Studies*, 8 (1962): 211–32. See also Nathalie Wright, "Form as Function in Melville," *PMLA* 67 (1952): 330–40 for what follows.

18. In chapter 44 Melville stresses the superiority of the "original" over the odd, novel or singular characters. Their creator is like a lawgiver or the founder of a new religion; while they could have "something prevailing local or of the age" in them, a truly original character was a revolving light "raying away from itself all round it—everything is lit by it, everything starts up to it." This is also true of Hamlet, Don Quixote, or Milton's Satan. This type of character becomes a principle of fictional growth and definition: there can be but one to a book. See *The Confidence Man: His Masquerade* (New York: Norton Critical Edition, 1971), pp. 157–58, 58–59, 204–5.

19. For previous quotes see *The Writings of Herman Melville*, VII, p. 141; *Billy Budd, Sailor (An Inside Narrative)*, ed. Harrison Hayford and Merton M. Sealts, Jr. (Chicago: The University of Chicago Press, 1962), p. 128.

20. Matthiessen, *American Renaissance*, p. 409.

THE SHORT STORY AND THE GREAT AMERICAN NOVEL

I

A CONSIDERATION of the first half of the nineteenth century would be incomplete without at least a passing reference to Edgar Allan Poe's attack on the novel—both on account of his stature as a critic (he was certainly the greatest literary theorist of the period) and because his conception of the short story as the foremost form of fiction proves of particular importance in America and is to be found in many of its leading writers. There was very little theorizing on the nature, form, and value of the short story in eighteenth-century England while the great debate on the novel was gathering momentum, whereas in America almost at the very beginning ideas were vented on its great merits, pleasing characteristics, and utmost difficulty. "The Art of Story-Telling" was debated in *The American Magazine and Historical Chronicle* in 1744; Washington Irving made it soon very clear, in a letter of 1824, that he had preferred "adopting a mode of sketches & short tales rather than long works" in order to take a line of writing peculiar to himself, "rather than fall into the manner or school of any other writer." Nicety of execution and constant activity of thought were required by the genre, which was more difficult and exacting than a long narrative, where the mere interest in the scheme and characters carried the reader forward. In the tale, "The author must be continually piquant," while touches of pathos and humor can be properly valued; effects of style can be pursued; and even the moral, in an age of storytelling and storyreading fond of being taught by apologue (as Irving warned at the beginning of *Tales of a Traveller,* 1824), could be hidden from sight and disguised "as much as possible by sweets and spices" rather than carried on the surface. John Neal toyed with, and Hawthorne was to express, similar ideas; even in an anonymous 1825 review, tales and short stories were seen to require "greater vivacity of narration, and more point and polish of style . . . the highest and most delicate finish." Needing construction of plot as well as invention, their chief difference from the novel lay "in execution" and intellectual effort: hence a recommendation to young American writers to try the art.[1] Theirs was eminently an aesthetic challenge in a period of loose novel forms. This must have appealed to Poe, whose position, however, was stronger, more cogent, and more influential.

We need not expatiate on Poe's importance for the then revolutionary formulation of an aesthetics that repudiated didacticism and asserted the autonomy of artistic endeavor. He was a forerunner on the path that would lead to a theory of "art for art's sake" and of pure poetry. He, too, expressed a preference for suggestiveness and indirectness, for symbolic (or, in his case, merely allusive) values. It is well known that his theory hinged on the principle of *unity of effect* and of the *wholeness,* or unity of design, of the work of art—two crucial points that led him to vindicate more than once the superiority of the short over the long poem and, by analogy, of the short story or tale over the full-length novel.

Poe's aesthetic betrays, of course, deeper roots and wider ramifications, more complex implications and far-reaching anticipations. Poe was influenced by Coleridge and for the perfection of the artistic whole postulated an interplay between, or combining of, reason and imagination, poetic sentiment and constructive faculties, which led to the symbiosis expressed by the almost paradoxical and contradictory terms "poetic intellect" and "analytic imagination" (a combination that is at the very basis of his major works).[2] A fundamental aspect of Poe's aesthetic theory was the stress he placed on the psychological impact of the work of art on the reader—on the problem, as we would term it now, of the reader's response. For that impact to be effective, and for that response to be complete, Poe theorized the need for brevity and unity of design—two prerequisites, indeed two "musts"—in order to assure and to achieve unity of effect. Hence, as indicated, a long poem appeared to Poe to be impossible, a contradiction in terms, or the mere aggregation and precarious sequence of autonomously poetic moments. The same was true of the "long" novel in relation to the short story or tale:

> The tale proper, in our opinion, affords unquestionably the fairest field for the exercise of the loftiest talent, which can be afforded by the wide domains of mere prose. Were we bidden to say how the highest genius could be most advantageously employed for the best display of its own powers, we should answer, without hesitation—in the composition of a rhymed poem, not to exceed in length what might be perused in an hour. Within this limit alone can the highest order of true poetry exist. We need only here say, upon this topic, that, in almost all classes of composition, the unity of effect or impression is a point of the greatest importance. It is clear, moreover, that this unity cannot be thoroughly preserved in productions whose perusal cannot be completed at one sitting. . . .

Were we called upon, however, to designate that class of composition which, next to such a poem as we have suggested, should best fulfill the demands of high genius—should offer it the most advantageous field of exertion—we should unhesitatingly speak of the prose tale, as Mr. Hawthorne has here exemplified it. We allude to the short prose narrative, requiring from a half-hour to one or two hours in its perusal. The ordinary novel is objectionable, from its length, for reasons already stated in substance. As it cannot be read at one sitting, it deprives itself, of course, of the immense force derivable from *totality*.

A similar idea was expressed in *Marginalia* (no. 214): "The novel certainly requires what is denominated a sustained effort—but this is a matter of mere perseverance . . . [unity of effect] is indispensable in the 'brief article,' and not so in the common novel. The latter, if admired at all, is admired for its detached passages, without reference to the work as a whole—or without reference to any general design—which, if it even exists in some measure, will be found to have occupied but little of the writer's attention, and cannot, from the length of the narrative, be taken in at one view, by the reader." As with the delineation of the poet's working in "The Philosophy of Composition," in writing about the prose tale Poe emphasized that the chief aim of the writer, unity of effect, was to be attained through careful construction: "the skilful literary artist . . . has not fashioned his thoughts to accommodate his incidents; but having conceived, with deliberate care, a certain unique or single *effect* to be wrought out, he then invents such incidents—he then combines such events as may best aid him in establishing this preconceived effect." Or, as he put in *Marginalia* (no. 35): "In the tale proper—where there is no place for the development of character or for great profusion and variety of incident— mere *construction* is, of course, far more imperative than in the novel." Poe's conception seems to develop and work in a closed circle: if every word which is written must tend "to the one pre-established design," it is because unity of design is a condition of the unity of effect. One mirrors itself on the other, shirking all those "interferences" and "rumours" that beset novels. In the surprising modernity of some of his statements, given his premises Poe was led to place unusual emphasis on the constructive and combinatory aspect of storytelling and writing (or *écriture,* as we might call it in this context). This aspect made the short story superior even to the poem, if not for the expression of absolute beauty, at least for that of the passions and human feelings:

> We have said that the tale has a point of superiority even over the poem. In fact, while the *rhythm* of this latter is an essential aid in the development of the poet's highest idea— the idea of the Beautiful—the artificialities of this rhythm are an inseparable bar to the development of all points of thought or expression which have their basis in *Truth.* But Truth is often, and in very great degree, the aim of the tale. Some of the finest tales are tales of ratiocination. . . . Beauty can be better treated in the poem. Not so with terror, or passion, or horror, or a multitude of such other points. And here it will be seen how full of prejudice are the usual animadversions against those *tales of effect,* many fine examples of which were found in the earlier numbers of Blackwood.

Poe was very interested in the *mechanics* of fictional development that gave "a plot its indispensable air of consequence, or causation," and that led with almost mathematical rigor to the denouement. But he distinguished the *plot* from the sensational or merely mechanical *intrigue* ("a mere succession of incidents"): plot was for him the soul of the action, that in which "no one of its component parts shall be susceptible of *removal* without *detriment* to the whole." A tale was for him a perfect mechanical device but, at the same time—antithetically—it had to have an instantaneous, breathtaking impact on the reader; a self-contained unity, it was also the vehicle for a preordained effect (hence Poe's own achievement in both the tale of ratiocination and the Gothic tale). Without pausing over the implications of this paradoxical duality or combination of aims and views, we can note for our purposes that Poe was understandably opposed to the historical romance, whose interweaving of fact and fiction he considered hazardous ("we shall often discover in Fiction the essential spirit and vitality of Historic Truth," he wrote), though he was not averse to remoteness of setting.

Indifferent to the question of American materials, Poe launched another attack that is relevant in our context—an attack against allegorism, which he saw as compromising the flow of narration and threatening unity of effect. "In defence of allegory . . . there is scarcely one respectable word to be said," he wrote apropos of Hawthorne. "Its best appeals are made to the fancy. . . . The fallacy of the idea that allegory, in any of its moods, can be made to enforce a truth . . . could be promptly demonstrated. The thing is clear, that if allegory ever establishes a fact, it is by dint of overturning a fiction." Poe recognized that "where the suggested meaning runs through the obvious one in a very profound under-current so as never to interfere with the upper one without our own volition, so as never to show itself unless called to the surface, there only, for the proper uses of fictitious narrative, is it available at all."[3] But if his opposition to allegory went against the current of the times, this was perfectly in keeping with his rejection of didacticism and his exaltation of the autonomy of art. In either case, it would be a mistake to underestimate the historical as well as the general importance of Poe's aesthetic and critical views. Yet, his theory of the superiority of the short story over the novel appears as a startling as well as a significant countercurrent in a period when all efforts were directed toward extolling the boundless possibilities, the "latitude," and the "great form" of the novel. Poe was all for *in*tensity versus *ex*tension, for *in*tention versus looseness; what may be termed his centripetal bias would be of use later in the battle for an *artistic* form of novel.

We may note in passing that almost half a century later,

after the great divide of the Civil War, a similar predilection for the short story as against the novel was expressed by Mark Twain. Devoid of any theoretical bias, and indeed averse to methods and systems, Twain posed no questions of compositional unity or effectiveness: the short story form seemed a natural consequence of the oral origins of story-telling. That origin determined the loose, spontaneous, immediate character of the short story: far from being "constructed" as in Poe, for Twain the tale was to have the fortuitous pace and casual ease of oral storytelling. The novel, rather than the tale, required construction and architecture: Twain's favorite genre, the humorous story, though often finishing "with a nub, point, snapper," was "rambling and disjointed"; it "may wander around as much as it pleases, and arrive nowhere in particular."[4] It was a typically American manner. Although we shall return to Twain in due course, it is relevant to remark here that two of the most representative prose writers of the first and second half of the nineteenth century were both opposed, in the name of the short story, and for quite different reasons, to the novel form.

Also by way of anticipation, it is worth noticing that in the 1880s Julian Hawthorne, Nathaniel's son and biographer, was to expound a view of the short story as answering the peculiar needs of the conditions of American life. In his discussion of "The American Element in Fiction" (1884), Julian Hawthorne said a conclusive word on the old question of American materials. The national character of subject matter and setting—witness the examples of Homer and Shakespeare, Milton or George Eliot—was hardly a matter of definition for other literatures: "That must be a very shallow literature which depends for its national flavor and character upon its topography and its dialect." The real question was of point of view: "what is an American novel except a novel treating of persons, places, and ideas from an American point of view?" Hence a large spectrum of subjects and settings was at its disposal, including the "inter-

national theme" of its contrast with Europe. America was
no mere geographical condition but was, rather, the prefiguration of a new humanity. Yet there were difficulties besetting its fictional rendering, in both novels and romances.
Hence, for Julian Hawthorne, who discussed his father's
theories at length, the peculiar aptness of the short story for
America:

> American life has been, as yet, nothing but a series of epi-
> sodes, of experiments. There has been no such thing as a
> fixed and settled condition of society, no subject to change
> itself, and therefore affording a foundation and contrast to
> minor or individual vicissitudes. We cannot write American-
> grown novels, because a novel is not an episode, nor an ag-
> gregation of episodes; we cannot write romances in the Haw-
> thorne sense, because, as yet, we do not seem to be clever
> enough. Several courses are, however, open to us and we are
> pursuing them all. First, we are writing "short stories," ac-
> counts of episodes needing no historical perspective, and not
> caring for any; but so far as one may judge, we write the best
> short stories in the world. Secondly, we may spin out our
> short stories into long-short stories, just as we may imagine a
> baby six feet high; it takes up more room, but is just as much
> a baby as one of twelve inches. Thirdly, we may graft our
> flower of romance on a European stem.[5]

These emphases would be justified by the circumstances
of the theoretical and critical debate as one begins to move
toward the end of the century. Julian Hawthorne's advocacy
of the short story form, however, can also be seen as a conclusive word on a much-abused and drawn-out question
spanning the two halves of the century: the big question of
the "Great American Novel."

II

For most of the century (and beyond), the idea of the
Great American Novel was an obsession with writers and

critics. It looms large in the background, it often comes to the forefront, it seldom disappears from sight. It would be easy to provide extensive documentation, but only at the risk of being repetitive and inconclusive. More than a theory it is an idea, and more than an idea it becomes an obsession, a repeated claim and a constant reference. It may reflect a historical or innate tendency to bigness: when it will eventually make its appearance, the American Novel will be not only Great but final, the last word, a crowning and a culmination, the ne plus ultra. It will be big and conclusive, unbeatable and unsurpassable—the biggest of them all. All the dangers of an uncontrolled romantic *Streben* and all the implications and distortions of the sheer force of will are at work here; and it still sounds like contemporary history. For one Poe, who wanted it restricted to the self-sufficient and self-contained measure of the short story, there are dozens and dozens claiming that the novel must embrace and engulf all, contain multitudes, span the continent, encompass every aspect of the nation and express every shade of its soul, reveal its phantasmagoria and shed light on its secret sides, exalt its aspirations and ideas, ways of life and modes of thought. If the New World is by definition big and varied, multiform and all-encompassing, so must be the novel: hence an added motivation or urge to turn it into a saga and an epic, a poem and a romance.

In spite or because of all the vociferous statements, it cannot become a proper theory and is thus better approached as an obsession, running through almost every enunciation, peeping between the lines, a jack-in-the-box springing up at almost every turn. Never a fully developed argument or deeply rooted conviction, it is rather a mood, a presupposition, a mania. This is why it would be tedious and hardly rewarding to dwell on too many examples. But it would be unforgivable to neglect its presence, its conditioning power, its pervasive influence. Cooper and Simms had something of the kind in mind when they embarked on their fictional sagas; Hawthorne may never have expressed the idea, but

how else can one account for Melville's view of his fellow
writer and for the very scope and strain of *Moby Dick?* And
after finishing that book, didn't he write "Leviathan is not
the biggest fish;—I've heard of Krakens"? These are examples on a high level, and they must suffice here as indication
of the pre–Civil War tendency.

The very climate of transcendentalism was conducive to
such hopes. As in poetry, so in fiction, the ideas of Margaret
Fuller and Orestes Brownson, the impassioned admonitions
of Ralph Waldo Emerson ("We have listened too long to the
courtly Muses of Europe"), led to a buoyant kind of self-
reliance and to a striving for big things even in the field of
fiction.[6] The same attitude was found in members and sym-
pathizers of the "Young America" movement (from Corne-
lius Mathews to Evert Duyckinck in New York).

A crucial development seems to follow in the aftermath
of the war, however, and to steer the discussion away from
the trodden path. A marked tendency seems to appear for
what may be termed stocktaking: writers and critics assess
at length the state and condition of the American novel,
and in so doing they tend more and more to discuss it in
reference to, and in comparison with, its European counterparts. These assessments become more and more open discussions on the novel and on novel writing in general; they
introduce new filters, patterns, and models for a proper definition of fiction, and in so doing they bring about a remarkable change. Previously the discussion had been mainly
on views, conceptions, and theories of the American novel;
now it focused on the novel in general, and was to lead to
independently American theories of fiction as an art. Before the war the general tendency (as we have seen) was
toward fulfillment in the romance; now the basic tendency
was toward realism.

A transitional attitude can be exemplified by John William De Forest, author of *Miss Ravenel's Conversion from
Secession to Loyalty* and an acknowledged protorealist. In an
essay of 1868 he took careful stock of existing American

novelists and of the common claim for the Great American Novel in a rather defensive way: no real "G.A.N." had yet appeared, though it could be around the corner. "The nearest approach to the desired phenomenon is 'Uncle Tom's Cabin,' " he went on to say, because of the "national breadth to the picture, truthful outlining of character, natural feeling, and plenty of strong feeling." This view may be startling—or perhaps significant—in that that controversial novel portrayed and gave expression to "another" America, the America of Negroes and their dark conscience, of their resentment and search for freedom (just as Melville, rather than Cooper, had expressed the true motif of the Indian and the savage). Other attempts seemed to De Forest to fall short of the mark—including Hawthorne's revered achievements in the realm of romance—as expressing subjective aspects of humanity without real links with the nation. There were no *Newsomes,* no *Misérables,* no *Little Dorrit,* yet, in America. Are we listening to the usual complaint? Hardly, in that the set of references or terms of comparison have significantly changed. Regardless of contemporary judgment, when referring (as he did) to Thackeray and Honoré de Balzac, to Dickens, Anthony Trollope, and Alessandro Manzoni as models, De Forest adhered to a tentative, implicit, but clearly new conception of realism—the realism of observed surfaces and of reflected contemporary life. If the danger of sectionalism was inherent in America, given its historical and geographical conditions ("we are a nation of provinces"), yet the road of realism seemed by then the only suitable way to the "G.A.N."

This is confirmed by Thomas Sergeant Perry's position a few years later. A close friend of young Henry James, Perry discussed and disclaimed the "G.A.N." as a false aim; if it was ever to arrive on the scene, it would do so not ostentatiously but almost surreptitiously, disguised and masked, as it were. "By insisting above all things on the novel being American," he wrote, "we mistake the means for the end"— which may be taken as an epitaph for a concern with its

Americanness. Truth to human nature and formal accuracy were of greater importance: "in the true novel the scene, the incidents, are subordinated to the sufferings, actions and qualities of the characters. They are for the time living beings." Perry then proceeded to discuss, half-mockingly, the society novel, and to raise the usual point of the unsuitability of the American scene for such a novel because of its lack of a recognizable social system, distinct characters, a proper atmosphere. Because of "the very unformity of our social life," he wrote, "one would say that the natural tendency of the American novelist would be towards romance." Yet his lengthy stocktaking and assessment of contemporary writers, in whom a proper reflection of contemporary manners was hard to find, led him to some interesting remarks on the relation between character and plot (both indispensable to the success of the story, and both unamenable to a priori rules). Above all, he separated the question of the novel from that of its materials; he maintained that "the great novel is yet unwritten," yet he wanted the story to "rise above its geographical boundaries." On those premises, Perry ended his essay with a plea for poetic truth and idealization. The reader demands "beings true, not to fashion, but to those higher laws and passions that alone are real." In contrast,

> The real novelist, he who is to write the "great American novel," must be a poet; he must look at life, not as the statistician, not as the census-taker, nor yet as the newspaper reporter, but with an eye that sees, through temporary disguises, the animating principles, good or bad, that direct human existence; these he must set before us, to be sure, under probable conditions, but yet without mistaking the conditions for the principles. He must idealize. The idealizing novelist will be the real novelist. All truth does not lie in facts.[7]

This idea seems to turn the clock back thirty years and to betray an unexpected suspicion of realism. We shall find such a suspicion creeping up even in avowed supporters and theorists of realism. In Perry, it smacks of anticlimax, but it should not obscure his sober view of a Great American Novel, where both its greatness and its Americanness are subordinated to its being a novel, rather than a romance, in what begins to appear as the current postbellum view.

NOTES

1. *Short-Story-Theorien (1573–1973)*, ed. Alfred Weber and Walter F. Greiner (Kronberg: Athenäum Verlag, 1977), pp. 24–31 (and p. 42 for William Gilmore Simms's view in 1866).

2. Edd Winfield Parks, *Edgar Allan Poe as Literary Critic* (Athens: The University of Georgia Press, 1964).

3. For ease of reference see *Literary Criticism of Edgar Allan Poe,* ed. Robert L. Hough (Lincoln: University of Nebraska Press, 1965), pp. 134–37 ("Hawthorne's *Twice-Told Tales,*" 1842); p. 20 ("The Philosophy of Composition," 1846); p. 18 ("On Relevant and Irrelevant Plots," 1845); pp. 145–48 ("Tale Writing: Nathaniel Hawthorne," 1847). For *Marginalia,* see *The Complete Works* (Boston: Colonial Press, 1884), vol. V, pp. 209 and 335–36.

4. "How to Tell a Story" (1845), in *A Storied Land: Theories of American Literature,* ed. Richard Ruland (New York: Dutton, 1976), pp. 128–29. Poe, too, had written "How to Write a Blackwood Article": the difference in the title (how to *tell* versus how to *write*) is crucial.

5. In Ruland, ed., *A Storied Land,* pp. 108–20 (p. 120 for quote).

6. For ease of reference, *The Native Muse,* ed. Richard Ruland (New York: Dutton, 1976), pp. 340–44, 352–56, 398–408, and passim.

7. Ruland, ed., *A Storied Land,* pp. 24–32 and 32–40.

PART II

4.
THE DEBATE OVER REALISM
IN
THE 1870s AND 1880s

I

THE FIRST THEORISTS and supporters of fictional realism in England had been George Henry Lewes and George Eliot; Anthony Trollope had trivialized its scope and import. A common tendency was to reconcile (or compromise) realism with other literary forms and concerns (with "sensationalism"; with idealism and romance; and finally, with *écriture artiste* and art for art's sake).[1] To accept the principle of realism, but to limit its consequences and applications, was part of the so-called Victorian compromise.

In G. H. Lewes, realism stemmed from a philosophical basis. As a believer in positivism, he considered only the natural world a possible subject of investigation; art was a product of social circumstances, which it could modify in turn. A student of Goethe, Lewes saw the novel as a serious

art form: it was the "representation of human life by means
of a story." He wrote that "only *that* literature is effective
. . . which has *reality for its basis* . . . and effective in proportion to the depth and breadth of that basis." Lewes expounded such views in various essays published in the *Westminster Review* in the 1850s, culminating in the 1858
discussion of "Realism in Art: Recent German Fiction": "Art
is a Representation of Reality," which must be limited only
by the nature of its medium; Reality is Truth, "and no departure from truth is permissible"; the antithesis of Realism
was not Idealism but *Falsism*. Accuracy of presentation was
of paramount importance, especially in depicting forms of
ordinary life, where idealizing or "beautifying" could be only
a falsification of nature: "Either give us true peasants, or
leave them untouched." In Lewes's conception of realism—
and this would be true of George Eliot or the Goncourt
brothers as well—the serious treatment of the lower classes,
till then excluded from the novel, was essential. Equally important was the connection to be established between characters and milieu: "a story is the result of character acting
upon circumstance, and of circumstance acting upon character." Owing to his scientific interests, Lewes also insisted
on psychological realism (which he called "dramatic ventril-
oquism"), and he vindicated the realm of inner life for the
novel—a realm to which it had often been denied access.
Objective representation was thus to be combined with a
"strong power of subjective representation. . . . We do not
simply mean . . . the psychological intuition of the artist,
but the power also of connecting external appearances with
internal effects."[2] He found his ideal not so much in Jane
Austen, with her precise and intense objectivity, but rather
in Goethe, George Sand, Balzac and, naturally, George Eliot,
with their increasingly mature psychological realism.

George Eliot's conception of realism was also developed
along partly dependent, partly parallel lines in the pages of
the *Westminster Review* in the 1850s. First, in the wake of
Wordsworth, she insisted that "art's greatest benefit to men

is to widen their sympathies"; then she stressed the need for a faithful representation of life: "our social novels profess to represent the people as they are, and the unreality of their representation is a great evil." All truth and beauty, she wrote, "are to be attained by a humble and faithful study of nature, and not by substituting vague forms bred by imagination on the mists of feeling, in place of definite, substantial reality." In another essay she maintained: "Art is the nearest thing to life. . . . Falsification here is far more pernicious." She wrote explicitly of the novel as the "natural history of social classes," of its social and political implications, of the need of a psychological characterization that went beyond Dickens's superficial attempts. The very idea of the moral purpose of fiction was, as it were, reversed: only by being true to life and by representing reality faithfully could fiction be endowed with a moral aim. In chapter 17 of *Adam Bede* she openly refused to "beautify" her characters and to "improve" the facts, claiming that all her efforts should be "to avoid any such arbitrary picture"; most of all she valued the "rare, precious quality of truthfulness" evident in Dutch paintings, their sense of homely existence. The novel thus aspired, not to *la belle nature* or to the *beau idéal*, but to provide a quiet and humble picture of ordinary life.[3]

Realism was thus defined, on the one hand, by the choice of subject matter—the life of common people—and, on the other, by its faithfulness of representation, that is, by the novelist's ethical and aesthetic attitude. A consequence was the tendency to dramatic representation: to *paint*, not to *write about*, as George Eliot put it. Therefore, her insistence on the superiority of character over plot was due to the fact that characters had to move autonomously and to express the theme of the novel by objective behavior and dialogue, not through commentary. Lewes had dwelt on similar points, and Eliot would later take them up again in her *Leaves from a Note-Book* (1872–78), where she faced more technical and functional aspects of fiction writing (questions of poetics more than of theory), such as the order of telling, indirect ways of arriving at knowledge, the exercise of a veracious imagination in historical picturing, the value of originality, and so on. In both writers the Victorian compromise led to an upholding of the role of good feelings, a kind of moderate idealism, an attenuation of tones and contrasts, and an obvious reticence in some areas of life. Yet both recognized the potentialities of psychological realism and of the interplay between individuals and social contexts, the role of ideas and intellectual awareness in the novel—which was indeed one of their greatest contributions to its development.

Realism was for them both the mark of a total engagement in life and, the application of a high literary conscience. For Anthony Trollope, instead, realism was humble and drab, a deliberate refusal of mystery and romance: "I have attempted to confine myself absolutely to the commonest details of commonplace life among ordinary people allowing myself no incident that would be even remarkable in everyday life. I have shorn my fiction of romance," he wrote to George Eliot herself in 1863 (similar views were expressed in chapter 15 of *Barchester Towers,* 1857). He is well known—or notorious—for his idea of the shoemaker novelist, turning out an article of mere utility, writing a given number of pages a day, and of the novel as a chunk of the world under glass, a total "make-believe." In an 1870 lecture (which became chapter 12 of his *Autobiography,* and was then reworked under the title of "Novel Reading"), Trollope not only insisted on the novel as "a picture of common life" at the minimum level of literary elaboration, inferior to poetry, and centered on a love story, but discussed the prevalence of character over plot and set forth the clearest expression of the Victorian concept of literary characters as "living people." Without any intervening filter, life and fiction tended to coincide and to mingle: "art" was no more than a glass partition. Hence, Trollope could admit the coexistence of realism and "sensationalism," be prone to moralism, and contribute to a vulgarization of the problematic aspects of realism.[4]

Others, like Charles Reade, believed in a novel based on facts, thus making it an effective instrument of social protest and denunciation. Reade, however, still believed that "fiction is the art of weaving fact with invention"; and in his well-known definition in the Preface to *Hard Cash* (1863), he wrote of a "matter-of-fact Romance." This documentary realism could accept a degree of "sensationalism" because such was the pattern of life, whereas for Charles Kingsley, although the novel was a vehicle for social discussion and reform, it could not be limited to a transcript of facts. In his later years, Dickens too was interested in the objective quality of dramatic presentation; but his view of realism was qualified by a strong sentimental and romantic bias ("I have purposely dwelt upon the romantic side of familiar things," he wrote in his Preface to *Bleak House*) and relied heavily on chance, coincidence, and surprise. If his Preface to *Oliver Twist* (1841) may be read as a protomanifesto of populist realism (the sordid lives of underworld characters would be dealt with as an antidote to romance; nothing would be changed or "beautified"), in the years of the battle for realism Dickens seems to have retreated into the safe portrayal of domestic life (witness his statements in *Household Words* and *All the Year Round*). Even Thackeray, who declared himself for truthfulness and frankness and invented the novel "without a hero"—that is, the novel as a panoramic view of society, as a privileged mirror of contemporary manners— did not believe in fictional illusion and was skeptical about the possibility of representing man in his totality. Fiction writing was for him a benign way of conversing with his readers rather than of creating a meaningful, autonomous world.[5]

No sooner was it launched than realism came under attack by writers like Edgar Bulwer-Lytton or by critics like David Masson, who saw the novel as the prose counterpart of the epic, and therefore dealing with ideal beings. One of the most interesting midcentury studies of fiction, *The Gay Science* (1866) by Ernest Sweetland Dallas, rightly postulated that the main theme of the novel was the contrast between the individual and society, but was fully aware of the negative conditioning of the growing female reading public. By the early 1880s there was a surge of opposition against realism and its so-called banality: Marie Louise de la Ramée (better known as Ouida) and Robert Louis Stevenson voiced the need for romantic richness; Arthur Tilley attacked the "new school of fiction" for its analytic excesses. Émile Zola had brought scientific awareness to realism and both individual and social pathology into the novel—hence new debates and even stronger diffidence in England. These were later developments, however. The theoretical debate that stirred postbellum America had mainly to do with the ideas of realism propounded by, or identified with, George Eliot. She provided a good starting point, a common set of references, and a tolerably safe frame of discussion for most practitioners, critics, and reviewers. But novelists too found it convenient to start with and from her; this was the case with James and, at least partly, with William Dean Howells. Both James and Howells developed her indications, and in their long critical and theoretical careers of militancy, reaching well into the twentieth century, became aware of other forms and other frontiers of realism. In the 1870s and the early 1880s, however, the debate was still rather tentative in America. It was mainly a question of clearing the ground; of reestablishing certain values of the novel of contemporary life against the overpowering claims of romance; of reintroducing a concern for the depiction of common people and events, of manners and local customs. It was a battle against great odds, which had peculiar developments and took on particular colors in America.

II

The debate over realism (which can be interpreted as one of the first great battles fought by a literary avant garde) was given a great deal of attention in the pages of the *Atlantic Monthly*. For our purposes, we propose to focus on a transitional figure, George Parsons Lathrop, who in 1874 contributed two long and significant essays to this magazine.[6] Both started as discussions of the state and scope of the novel, and can therefore be referred back to those stocktakings and assessments that were dealt with at the end of Part I. Yet, when Lathrop wrote that the novel encompassed "the great circle of the horizon," he had something different in mind than the Great American Novel and entertained a more revolutionary idea: the novel had ceased being an outcast or subordinate genre and had become its own master, indeed a master genre. In these two long historical and theoretical reviews of its condition and status, the novel gradually emerged as the peculiar form of modernity. It seemed, at first, limited to dealing with the surface of life, to rescuing ephemeral appearances from nothingness. But in establishing its long pedigree, from the Greeks to the nineteenth-century prose writers (whom he discussed in great detail and with a wealth of references), Lathrop strengthened, as nobody else had done before, the contemporary and artistic role of the novel.

In the first essay, "Growth of the Novel," Lathrop began with a complaint about the sorry state of contemporary criticism of the novel, and about the existing impression "that anybody, without having subjected himself to artistic discipline, can write a novel." He pleaded for "skilled judgement" to be applied in such matters and for a "thoughtful endeavor" to determine some of the principles governing prose fiction. First was the necessary awareness of its pedigree ("the novel comes to us with the mark of a long and laborious culture upon it"). Lathrop started with the Greeks, went through the Renaissance writers (Boccaccio, Rabelais, Cervantes) and the eighteenth-century practitioners (notably Henry Fielding) down to Scott, Dickens, Thackeray, and George Eliot: each of the prominent writers was seen to make a particular contribution and add something to a tendency "toward the increase of a dramatic spirit and dramatic methods in novel-writing." This long tradition led to a kind of impersonality and "inofficiousness" of the creative writer, which was just another name for the then tentative notion of realism:

> The standpoint of entire impartiality, by taking nature out of the hands of the *man,* so to speak, and putting it under the calm, indicative finger of the *novelist,* necessitates a constantly renewed study of surrounding life, and study of the most sincere and sympathetic kind.

Lathrop had the advantage and the merit of referring, not only to English, but to European writers and critics. He thus saw that "the excess of subjectivity in the average, contemporary novel" was traceable to Jean Jacques Rousseau and Goethe, though the latter also endowed it with objective and systematic power, with a sense of architecture and "crowning structure." In Goethe "the mental discoveries are so wholly the subject of attention" that the novel moved drastically away from the "surface appearances" of its infancy. By enlisting the aid and studying the example of the great German writer, Lathrop saw the novel as oscillating between a marked degree of subjectivity, on the one hand, and what he called "the scientific motive," on the other ("our fiction-writers become minute and sectional investigators. They are in search of specimens"). Both poles seemed present in the contemporary novel but as such were insufficient to ensure its greatness. A combination of the two was needed to move from "familiar narratives" to "finished studies," and to approach the ideal state of the novel—organic form:

> "a totality of forms, sounds, and incidents, in short elements and details, so closely united among themselves by inward dependencies, that their organization constitutes a living thing, surpassing in the imaginary world the profound harmony of the actual world."

This was one of the earliest and strongest claims, in America, for such a "unifying and creative view" of the novel. Such was Lathrop's awareness of its aesthetic dignity that he perceived the futility of mechanical morality. The moral purpose was to be reached by indirect means; it was inherent in the proper perception of our common human nature. The novelist had better "renounce the purpose of actually reforming anybody. . . . Let him look well to his art." His main obligation was understanding of life and impartiality of outlook; insight into human passions and a view of the tragic plight "of his mimic humanity." Thus, not only was the proper sphere of the novel human drama, but it also had to approach the highest form of artistic endeavor—tragedy. Lathrop concluded: "For something like a century, we have been feeling earnestly after real life. The era of conscientious and artistic novel-writing has been fairly and fully inaugurated." It remained for the new masters to expand further and to ennoble this "vital and speaking form which we call the novel."[7]

In the subsequent essay, "The Novel and Its Future," the novel was hailed as the privileged vehicle of communication that in modern times had taken the place of poetry. "At the head of all literary forms for present popularity and power. . . . the novel is still the more subtle, penetrative and universal agent for the transmission of thought. . . . an organism of a higher type than the lyric;" it is "portable drama" that "embraces a wide range of subjects not fitted for the salient treatment of the playwright. It is, further, specially adapted for the various and complex inner life of the modern world." Quoting from the fifth book of Goethe's *Wilhelm Meister,* and disagreeing with some of the points made by Goethe, Lathrop saw the modern novel as exhibiting not only *sentiments* and *events* but also (as in drama) *characters* and *deeds.* It did not "go slowly forward" but moved with the same speed and compression as the drama. Goethe had stressed the hero's passivity in the novel; Lathrop saw here

> a special superiority of the novel over the drama, in that it is
> thus fitted to exhibit the hero as the recipient of impressions
> only,—concentrating in him the phantasmagoric elaboration

of all surrounding life through his individual senses and perceptions; while, at any moment, his position may be reversed, so that *his* views of things shall no longer predominate, a purely dramatic development being accorded to all alike. In this way a double order of effects lies open to the novelist.

Lathrop could thus discuss the crucial relation between subjectivity (including the form of autobiography) and objectivity, narrating "I" and narrated "I"; the technical advantages provided by the novelist's prerogative of description; and so forth. Precisely because he held such a high opinion of the novel, he rejected its "conventional" and melodramatic forms ("By dropping into the stage-manner . . . the writer of a novel not only fails to draw nearer to life than before, but . . . separates himself from it by a double remove"). Instead, he favored the presence in the novel of "views" (in the sense of Balzac's *opinions arrêtées*), of psychological insights, of a picture of manners. Lathrop's discussion was based on a close analysis of the major contemporary novelists, and even if his observations and conclusions are sometimes questionable, the distinctions he drew were of notable importance. He clearly distinguished theatricality from dramatic form, realism of intent (impartiality) from romantic concessions, novels of manners from depictions of "good manners," intrigue from organic plot, rhetoric and sensationalism from stylistic control, commentary from action. Style included for him "not only phraseology, but the character of an author's observation, likewise." A distinct point of view, "from which to contemplate the revolving world," was the mark of a good novelist:

> Pausing at some standpoint of ideal perception, they let the variety of life pass under their eyes, and translate its meanings into the new language of their new genius. Hence comes it that large poetic genius is at once radical and conservative: it can look into the roots of things, but it also highly appreciates the value of calm, unchanging heights, upon which to build securely and live happily.

Lathrop developed significant analyses of, and contrasts between, Lytton and Trollope, Dickens and Wilkie Collins, Victor Hugo and Thackeray, Thackeray and Hawthorne. Such analyses led him to confront the question of idealism and realism (Hawthorne had blended spiritual idealism with descriptive realism) and to postulate their respective values in a historically meaningful way. The import of realism was not merely in supplying "visual distinctness" but also in exploring psychological functions and motivations:

> As the painter will study anatomy, in order to have a better structural idea of the human form, so the novelist will investigate the functions of all those complicated impulses, emotions, and impressions which we experience from hour to hour, from day to day, and by which our actions and characters are continually controlled, modified, or explained. With his investigation of psychological phenomena, or insight into the mysteries of spiritual being, he must unite the study of all that accompany these in the individual; as corporeality, with that curious net-work of appearances, habits, opinions, in which each human person is enveloped.

Ivan Turgenev was the case in point, a more artistic writer than Dickens or Balzac (who was "often too matter-of-fact," neglecting the "more elastic motions of the mind"). This emphasis on psychological investigation and artistic elaboration as correctives of "crude" realism would soon become a fairly common position in America. Lathrop's idea clearly verged on a conception of "higher realism":

> Realism sets itself at work to consider characters and events which are apparently the most ordinary and uninteresting, in order to extract from these their full value and true meaning. It would apprehend in all particulars the connection between the familiar and the extraordinary, and the seen and unseen of human nature. Beneath the deceptive cloak of outwardly uneventful days, it detects and endeavors to trace the outlines of the spirits that are hidden there; to measure the

changes in their growth, to watch the symptoms of moral decay or regeneration, to fathom their histories of passionate or intellectual problems.

"Realism reveals," Lathrop argued; "it shows everything to be rife with significance." It "calls upon imagination to exercise its highest function, which is the conception of things in their true relation"; it is not "plan-drawing," no mere copy or report of life, but "the painting of a picture." Realism, here, is seen explicitly in pre-Jamesian terms. What makes Lathrop a transitional figure in this context, however, is his eventual preference for Hawthorne over George Eliot, for the writer who expresses "a subtler truth" over and above "the appearances of realness in and for itself." He was right in denouncing the dryness and limitations of Trollope's brand of "literalism," but he was still bound to a traditional view of the superiority of idealistic, and hence romantic fiction. Hawthorne, with his "resonant undertone of poetic revery," was valued higher than Eliot and Balzac, whose "modern instances," though instructive, betrayed a loss of art and a loss of ease: "I think we are ready for something less medicinal than these magic potions—these bitter brews from sad experience, and deep, undeluded thought—with which the novelists, in these latter and greater days of their dynasty, have come to treat us."

Thus, Lathrop concluded his essay with a eulogy on the Norwegian writer Bjőrnstjerne Bjőrnson and with the idea that "Christ's thought . . . has assuredly taken root in the novel." Pity and charity for the poor, the common, and the unfortunate were to be its mark. Lathrop wrote prophetically that the "great circle of the horizon may draw its ring around whatever spot shall be chosen as the groundwork of a fiction, and the exact zenith hang above the heads of its personages." Yet, although he undoubtedly cleared the way that led to contemporary realism, he stopped short of a full acceptance of it: "we must have more than any photograph can give us; with the accuracy of that, should be combined

the aesthetic completeness of a picture and a poem in one,—
and always of a picture and a poem."[8]

The process of reversing the trend, of stressing the "picture" over the poetic side, reached its completion only in
the 1880s, with Henry James, William Dean Howells, and
their "school." Another reversal was then taking place: the
novel and its theoretical implications were discussed with less
and less emphasis on the question of the American materials. Full-fledged American theories of the novel developed
independently of, and substituted for, theories of the *American* novel.

III

Surprisingly enough, Lafcadio Hearn was among the first
to recognize the value of realism in the novel. The contemporary vogue of the novel was counterbalanced, according
to Hearn, by the near exhaustion of all possible imaginative
ideas and plots. "New worlds must be discovered, perhaps,
to create new ideas for fiction writers," he maintained in an
essay of 1879; hence "[m]odern fiction, whether poetry, or
prose, is obliged to seek realism for novelty's sake." Realism
rendered the novel valuable beyond the mere artistic construction or the gratification of the imagination—"its portrayal of actual life," its "picture of society," made it su-
premely instructive. "The more perfect the novel of today
the more truthful must it be as a reflection of actual life,"
he continued, with explicit references to Zola and Eliot. He
was, however, for what he termed "conservative" and aesthetic realism rather than for its harsher forms: "Art is not
the minute imitation of nature, but the power to render the
agreeable impressions created by nature." By 1882 this future extoller of Orientalism and magic fables registered the
death of romance and "idealism of types and characters,"
the end of "high moral purposes" and of love stories. The
novel, therefore, "discarding the imaginative," manifested

"a steady tendency to a revival of first principles—the description of things as they are, rather as we would wish them to be. This is realism." Although quoting James and the "analysis of motives and sentiments to be made by careful and impartial observation," Hearn declared himself in favor of a kind of social narrative that eschewed European worldliness, the Bostonian milieu, and the "international theme" and that would seek "for the beautiful and the picturesque in the lower strata of society as well as the upper," in the "agricultural home life" as well as in the drawing room. "For strong and characteristic color and sentiment" the novel wanted what was found "in the workshops and factories, among the toilers on river and rail . . . in mining districts and frontier towns, in the suburbs of vast industrial centers . . . among men who, without culture, have made themselves representative of an enormous financial force."[9]

As is often the case in such instances, Hearn ran the risk of identifying realism with regionalism and local color. His references here were to George Washington Cable and Bret Harte, and the question of Americanness was thus brought back by stealth into the picture: the society or drawing room novel was seen as basically European, whereas sectionalism and localism would provide a distinct realistic flavor. Such equivocal formulations of the scope and aim of fictional realism became more and more common in American theories, leading to critical views that, toward the end of the century, systematically identified (or confused) realism with regionalism and Americanism. But there is no denying the early value of Hearn's view of realism as a step beyond romance, and of his recognition that this modern form was more difficult to realize aesthetically than the former one (witness the sophistication reached by the school of James and Howells).

"Fiction is the handmaid of Truth," declared Albion W. Tourgée in the Preface to his novel *Hot Ploughshares* (1882), declaring along with Hearn that "imagination is almost always the forerunner of fact." Indeed, history gave only "the outlines of the world's life," the actions of rulers and leaders: "Of the motives that inspire the rank and file" it took little notice. Biography both supplemented and obscured history, both "by showing the relation of great events to a particular individual" and "by magnifying his causative relation to them." Contrary to Thomas Carlyle, Tourgée held that fiction labored under no such disadvantages: "It fills out the outlines History gives, and colors and completes its pictures. . . . It vivifies the past of which History only furnishes the record."[10] Realism, in other words, was the answer or the recipe for historical fiction as well.

Tourgée's view, it must be added, was a quite popular one: a sophisticated view of the "scientific" origin and nature of the novel was unexpectedly proposed by the delicate and musical southern poet Sidney Lanier. While his theory may appear idiosyncratic, it does show the level of maturity that the discussion of fiction had reached; it is worth examining here as part of the general debate then in course. In 1881 Lanier had devoted a series of twelve public lectures (posthumously collected in book form) to *The English Novel,* which he saw as a direct development of Greek drama passed on through Elizabethan drama. In this long, often confused, and inconclusive study, there are open attacks against the "animal voice" of realism and Zola's "absurd and infernal misconception" of the novel as an "experiment" to be conducted along scientific lines. But Lanier also expressed a keen interest in the possible connections between fiction and science, and between fiction and poetry, and he considered the novel a great meeting ground for reconciling them: "The great modern novelist is at once scientific and poetic; and here, it seems to us, in the novel, we have the meeting, the reconciliation, the kiss, of science and poetry."[11]

Lanier's starting point is quite interesting: the "very remarkable and suggestive fact" that modern science, modern music, and the modern novel all arose at the same time, in the seventeenth century. Isaac Newton, Johann Sebastian

Bach, and Samuel Richardson stood for that meaningful coincidence of origin which Lanier linked to the rise of the
principle of personality (today we might prefer the term
"individualism"). This was expounded in Lecture I; in Lecture VII he fully developed this important concept. The
growth of the principle of personality toward the unknown
gave rise to music; its growth toward nature gave rise to the
physical sciences; and its growth toward the social sphere of
other men gave rise to the novel. Lanier provided a diagram of these three new processes or relations based on the
rise of the concept of personality, which is as follows:

Unknown (Music)
↑
Personality ──→ Fellow-Man (The Novel)
↓
Nature (Physical Science)

The concept of brotherhood and sympathy, therefore, is
inherent in the novel, as is the idea of a "common level" (a
move neither upward nor downward). These observations
on the novel were crucial but seem to have had little relevance for the debate on realism. Not surprisingly, however,
the culmination of Lanier's study (and theory) of the novel
was none other than George Eliot, to whom the last six lectures were mainly devoted. Eliot was a good case for testing
a theory of sympathy and the three relations sketched in the
accompanying diagram—referring to that which is above,
beneath, or on a level with man. But she was also the pro-
pounder and the living example of a realistic conception of
the novel. Hence, in his impassioned appraisal of this great
English novelist (whose equal he would have liked to see in
America), Lanier was led to view the novel, not only as
stemming from the principle of personality, but as developing into a free and elastic form, particularly suited to reflect complexities of relations, to reveal the true nature of
man, and to explore the unsounded secrets of his mind and

heart. Through his reading of Eliot, Lanier came to recognize the unbounded potentialities of the novel, its superiority over the drama, the "wholly supernatural power" that is necessarily involved in revealing the "most secret workings of the mind and heart."[12] By establishing a theoretical rather than a historical pedigree for the novel through the rise of individuality, Lanier—in spite of his dislike for "animal realism" and his aversion to contemporary excesses—contributed both to a recognition of the new status of the novel and to an awareness of its artistic value. Realism was kept in the background, but it was incidentally confirmed by his full appreciation of George Eliot.

Through such discussions, the novel began to be considered as an authentically artistic form. While the very idea of the "novel as art" was used to counteract the strain or the vogue of realism, realism itself was regarded as a necessary premise for a true art of fiction. If the former view was exemplified by Charles Dudley Warner in the early 1880s, the latter, as we shall see, was developed at greater length by Henry James.

Charles Dudley Warner began his 1885 essay on "Modern Fiction" with the idea that "one of the worst characteristics of modern fiction is its so-called truth to nature." If fiction was an art, like painting or sculpture, it required "an idealization of nature"; neither a photograph of a natural object nor the plaster cast of a man's face was art. Though dependent on nature, art was a "separate creation." It was "selection and idealization, with a view to impressing the mind with human, or even higher than human, sentiments and ideas." Thus, the novel was condemned, rather than praised, for its photographic fidelity; the "creation" of the novel—a term Warner insisted upon—was to be a "synthetic process," which would enable it to impart "ideal qualities" to human actions. Warner used Heinrich Heine's view of the prosaic nature of the English novelists and their bourgeois novels (with the exception of Scott) and emphasized that "the essential of fiction is not diversity of social life, but artistic treatment of whatever is depicted. The novel . . . must idealize the nature it touches into art." If nothing was vulgar to the poet, or uninteresting to the artist, the vulgar, sordid, and ignoble were unbearable in the novel, unless creative genius fused "the raw material in its alembic." "The failure," he insisted, "is not that vulgar themes are treated, but that the treatment is vulgar; not that common life is treated, but that the treatment is common; not that care is taken with details, but that no selection is made, and everything is photographed regardless of its artistic value." Warner was particularly heated in his disapproval of the *domestic* novel, but his open attack on realism also included the contemporary tendency to psychological analysis. "A delight in representing the worst phases of social life; an extreme analysis of persons and motives; the sacrifice of action to psychological study; the substitution of studies of character for anything like a story; a notion that it is not artistic, and that it is untrue to nature, to bring any novel to a definite consummation, and especially to end it happily"—all were considered negative aspects of realism.

A moral undertone, as well as a consideration for art, ran through Warner's conception. For him, too, the present age was preeminently the age of the novel, whose office was to hold the mirror up to nature; yet a middle view of life (including "poetic justice") had to be upheld and some degree of entertainment maintained. He declared himself against the "narrowness of vision and of treatment" evident in recent fiction—against *superficial* realism that tended to deal "with lives rather than with life," which was conditioned and debased by the mass market, ready to please the demands of the reading public, and devoid of a true artistic motivation. Even American materials, in spite of their alleged poverty and uniformity, could be raised above those shallows and made to serve (if only in a sectional and regional way).[13]

Such ideas were reinforced in a later essay, "The Novel and the Common School," where it is clear that Warner's criticism of the realistic trend was mainly an account of its vulgarization ("The making of novels has become a process of manufacture") and of its stooping to popular taste, to the demands of circulating libraries and juvenile audiences. Yet, it is equally evident that he opposed realism simply because he had a high opinion of the novel and believed in its creative aspects, its artistic possibilities, its power of selection as well as of organic synthesis. Most of these aspects were explored and given expression, in those very years, by Henry James. James, however, came to his lofty conception of the artistic nature of the novel through a recognition, and not a disclaimer, of its realistic charge. But some of Warner's points are related to, and can be understood only in terms of, a crucial and well-publicized controversy of the early 1880s over the so-called analytic school. The insistence on, and the predominance of, psychological studies of character at the expense of action, story, and plot was seen as still another debatable aspect or consequence of realism. The controversy began with Howells and James, raged on both sides of the Atlantic, and colored the debates on the novel for quite a number of years. Here we will be concerned with it neither as a literary episode nor in all its ramifications, but inasmuch as it was part of the *querelle* over realism and qualified it in an unexpected and quite unusual way.

IV

In an essay entitled "Henry James, Jr.," published in the *Century Magazine* in 1882, Howells had taken stock of the career and achievement of his compatriot, whose *The Portrait of a Lady* had appeared the previous year as the culmination of his early phase. Howells praised James's "artistic impartiality" (a word often associated with the practice of realism); his interest in the character, rather than the fate, of his people ("when he has fully developed his characters he leaves them to what destiny the reader pleases"); and his "analytic tendency." "No other novelist, except George Eliot,"

Howells wrote, "has dealt so largely in analysis of motive, has so fully explained and commented upon the springs of action in the persons of the drama, both before and after the facts." Fiction had become a finer art than in the past, owing to the influence that French fiction was exerting on narrative form (the realism of Alphonse Daudet, specifically, rather than that of Zola); consequently, James was identified with an "analytic school," largely American, derived mainly from Hawthorne and George Eliot, in which character analysis predominated over plot, psychological motives were the center of interest, and instead of a rounded story one had loose endings, open solutions, suspended conclusions. "Will the reader be content to accept a novel which is an analytic study rather than a story, which is apt to leave him arbiter of the destiny of the author's creations? Will he find his account in the unflagging interest of their development?" Howells wondered. It was, of course, a rhetorical question. Character painting instead of storytelling was a new form of fiction, as all stories had been told long ago: "now we want merely to know what the novelist thinks about persons and situations."

Since it was thought that James gratified this desire and exemplified this new artistic mode better than the old school of Dickens and Thackeray ("These great men are of the past—they and their methods and their interests"), Howells's view was deeply resented in England. An essay in the London *Quarterly Review* in January 1883 ("American Novels") took up the point almost immediately and blasted the "new school of fiction, based upon the principle that the best novelist is he who has no story to tell." Both Howells and James were severely taken to task on that account; the answer to Howells's question was an emphatic no. A month later, in the London *National Review*, Arthur Tilley took up the challenge in an essay entitled "The New School of Fiction" and offered several qualified answers. The plot had to be "rounded" and the story properly concluded by the writer in order to satisfy "our natural craving for completion"; the narrative had to move forward; analysis of character was more acceptable in George Eliot, because of her ethical interest, than in Howells or James (who, being "artistic," ought to create rather than describe character). Yet Tilley developed a third point to which Howells only incidentally alluded in his discussion—the study of nature "in its wonted aspects"—and he gave it such a twist as to make of the analytic school a further vulgarization of realism. In his essay Tilley drew a surprising parallel that was to gain more and more ground in the 1880s. Not only did the analysis of motives and psychological states stem from realism; it also became the equivalent, in the regions of the soul, of an extreme version of French naturalism: "May it not be said that while George Eliot elevates the commonplace, the new school vulgarises it? And if so, is this true realism? Is it not rather the sin of Zola—the sin, to borrow Goethe's distinction, of being naturalistic rather than natural?"[14]

According to Tilley, both James and Howells worked "within the region of art"; they would, therefore, have little sympathy with the method of Zola. On the one hand, "elaborate analysis" could hardly be supported by commonplace character; on the other, overanalytic studies of inner states and motives, the subtleties of psychological investigations, and the searchings into the secret recesses of the soul appeared to be the result of a cold, detached, scientific mentality—the same that operated in Zola's "scientific" naturalism—or of an intellectual attitude. The "morbid introspection" of American novelists, the painful search for psychological motivations in Meredith and James, seemed a danger equivalent to naturalism. In both cases there was insufficient respect for the sanctity and the privacy of the human person. Thus, a few years later, James's revelation of character in *The Bostonians* would appear as "a violation of every conceivable rule of literary good breeding." "The mistake is a result of that obsequious deference which Literature has in these days shown to triumphant Science; an instance of that obliteration of all reserve which the new lawgiver demands and she abhors." The analogy was to be made even clearer in 1888 by the influential English critic George Saintsbury in an essay entitled "The Present State of the Novel": [15]

> The analyst . . . is in this worse off than the naturalist pure and simple, that instead of mistaking a partial for a universal method, he takes for a complete method what is not strictly a method at all. The faithful copying of an actual scene or action sometimes results in something that is at least an integral part of a story. The elaborate dissection of motives and characters can only result in something that stops short of being even part of a story—that is only preliminary to part of a story.

We seem to go back here to the very origin of the controversy—Howells's emphasis on the nonstory novel. Analysis was rejected as a violation of the privacy of conscience (the equivalent of the naturalist's violation of prudery, decorum, and social or sexual taboos) and as a renunciation of the task of telling a story. The Americans and the French were thus joint causes and examples of the degeneration of the novel. In both instances, however, psychological analysis was seen as basically connected with, or belonging to, realistic treatment. What in George Eliot had been a strengthening and a confirmation of the realistic impulse and role of the novel was now regarded as a weakness and a danger. But the connection was there and was to last even when the controversy over the analytic school had petered out. It shows in Charles Dudley Warner's attack on realism, to which we now return by way of a temporary conclusion.

Warner rejected the "analytic method" because, according to him, it destroyed illusion. "We want to think that the characters in a story are real persons," he wrote in a typically midcentury way. Of course, this was not possible if the author insisted on breaking them to pieces and showing "their interior structure, and the machinery by which they are moved." Such a method was inferior to the dramatic, where the characters show what they are by what they do. It was artificial and mechanical; while it was a possible advance in intellectual terms, it had to be combined with action and plot. "The highest fiction," Warner wrote, "is that which embodies both." He wanted the novel to have a story and a proper end. If life was "full of incompletion, of broken destinies, of failures, of romances that begin but do not end," it was also full of endings and completions. Warner favored the happy ending, even in terms of escapism and consolation, "to lighten the burdens of life by taking us for a time out of our humdrum and perhaps sordid conditions." He rejected Howells's claims for the analytic school on the basis of his own view of the idealizing, nonrealistic function of the novel. Yet, when he protested "against the notion that the novel of the future is to be, or should be, merely a study of, or an essay or a series of analytic essays on, certain phases of social life,"[16] it becomes clear that "analysis" for him pertained to the psychological as well as to the social side of the novel. His rejection of analysis was thus motivated both by its failure to be true to life (insofar as it destroyed illusion) and by the too realistic quality of its possible dissection, its "scientific" bias.

Warner wanted "a more ideal, that is to say, a more artistic, view": art was for him opposed to realism. It took someone like Henry James, who formed his views and began to expound his theory of fiction in the 1870s and 1880s, to establish and emphasize the connection between realism and the art of fiction; between objectivity of presentation and psychological analysis; between plot and character, reality and imagination, the *données* of experience and personal impressions, social illustration and point of view, life and art, story and structure. Because of the wealth of problems faced and solutions offered, because of its range and depth of references, James's is the first full-fledged theory of fiction worthy of this name.

NOTES

1. For relevant texts see *Documents of Modern Literary Realism,* ed. George J. Becker (Princeton: Princeton University Press, 1963, 1964); *Realismus Theorien in England, 1692–1912,* ed. Walter F. Greiner and Fritz Kemmler (Tübingen: Niemeyer, 1970). The term "realism" had been used for the first time in the *Westminster Review* in 1853. In France *réalisme* had been applied to painting in 1830, to literature in 1846, and to the novel in 1851; see Richard Stang, *The Theory of the Novel in England, 1850–1870* (London: Routledge & Kegan Paul, 1959).

2. *Literary Criticism of George Henry Lewes,* ed. Alice R. Kaminsky (Lincoln: University of Nebraska Press, 1964), in particular pp. 87–90; Alice R. Kaminsky, "George Eliot, George Henry Lewes, and the Novel," *PMLA* 70 (1955): 997–1013. All this went against the prevailing early Victorian view of the novel, which was often denied artistic value and access to the inner life. For Carlyle (see Carlisle Moore, "Thomas Carlyle and Fiction: 1822–34," offprint from *Nineteenth Century Studies* [Princeton, 1940], pp. 131–77) the novel was one of the simplest forms, inferior to both biography and history; fiction was a trivialization of history. For John Stuart Mill (in *What Is Poetry?,* 1833), poetry could represent feelings and the human soul, but the novel was restricted to the external circumstances and events of life; it was a preliminary stage to poetry. For Thomas Hill Green, in *An Estimate of the Value of Fiction in Modern Times,* as late as 1862 the novel could give only the outer, not the inner, aspects of things. For De Quincey (in his study of *Oliver Goldsmith,* 1848), the novel was an ephemeral production, bound to rapid decay, and appealed to the lower part of human sensibility. Both Dickens and Thackeray, as is well known, saw themselves more as entertainers than as literary artists.

3. Floyd Weldon Casey, "George Eliot's Theory of Fiction," *West Virginia University Bulletin,* 9 (1953): 20–32; Alice R. Kaminsky, "George Eliot, George Henry Lewes, and the Novel"; James D. Rust, "The Art of Fiction in George Eliot's Reviews," *Review of English Studies,* n.s., 7 (1956): 164–72; Stang, *The Theory of the Novel in England;* Kenneth Graham, *English Criticism of the Novel, 1865–1900* (Oxford: Clarendon Press, 1965), chapter 2. While for most of her contemporaries plot was almost always identified with intrigue, George Eliot was much more aware of the relevance of form, including "organic form" (Darrel Mansell Jr., "George Eliot's Conception of 'Form,' " *Studies in English Literature,* 5 [1965]: 651–62).

4. See "On English Prose Fiction as a Rational Amusement," *Four Lectures,* ed. Morris L. Parrish (London: Constable, 1938), pp. 94–124; *An Autobiography* (Oxford: Oxford University Press: 1980); Walter M. Kendrick, *The Novel Machine: The Theory and Fiction of Anthony Trollope* (Baltimore: The Johns Hopkins Press, 1980). A kind of doctrinaire realism,

which also blurs the distinction between life and art, and saw the novel as a mere transcript of reality, with no imaginative or artistic reworking, was proposed by Fitzjames Stephen in "The Relation of Novels to Life" in *Cambridge Essays* (London: John W. Parker and Son, 1855), pp. 148–92.

5. For Charles Reade, see also his Preface to *An Autobiography of a Thief* (1858) and to *A Simpleton* (1873); for Charles Kingsley, see *Nineteenth Century British Novelists on the Novel,* ed. George L. Barnett (New York: Appleton-Century-Crofts, 1968), pp. 170–71; Monroe Engel, "Dickens on Art," *Modern Philology,* 53 (1955): 25–38; Phillip Enzinger, "Thackeray, Critic of Literature," *North Dakota Quarterly Journal,* 20 (1930–31), pp. 318–33; 21 (1931–32), pp. 52–65, 145–60 in particular.

6. G. P. Lathrop, "Growth of the Novel," *Atlantic Monthly,* 33 (June, 1874): 684–97 and "The Novel and Its Future," *Atlantic Monthly,* 34 (September, 1874): 313–24. See Helen Macmahon, *Criticism of Fiction: A Study of Trends in the "Atlantic Monthly"* (New York: Bookman Associates, 1952).

7. Quotes are from the *Atlantic Monthly,* 33 (June, 1874): 692, 695, 697.

8. Quotes are from the *Atlantic Monthly,* 34 (September, 1874): 314, 318, 321, 323–24. It would be tempting to consider Lafcadio Hearn's and Sidney Lanier's theories in this connection. The former saw the novel as the peculiar form of the age, as instinct with a pedagogical as well as an artistic function; hence his early preference for "conservative," rather than avant-garde realism. The latter viewed the novel as the blending and reconciliation of science with poetry. See below, Section IV.

9. Lafcadio Hearn, "The Value of Novels" (1879), "Realistic Fiction" (1882), and "Novelists and Novels" (1882), all reprinted in his *Essays on American Literature,* ed. Sanki Ichikawa (Tokyo: The Hokuseido Press, 1929), pp. 21–22, 100–107; also in *A Storied Land,* ed. Richard Ruland (New York: Dutton, 1976), pp. 69–71.

10. Albion W. Tourgée, *Hot Ploughshares* (Upper Saddle River, N.J.: Literature House, 1970); pages of Preface are not numbered.

11. *The English Novel and Other Essays or Literature,* ed. Clarence Gohdes and Kenneth Malone (Baltimore: The Johns Hopkins Press, Centennial Edition, 1945), vol. IV, p. 61. See also pp. 159–60, where the scientific and the poetic imagination must "come together and incorporate themselves," not simply work side by side: the union must not be mechanical, but chemical, producing something better than either.

12. For quotes see ibid., pp. 9–10, 129–31, 221, and passim.

13. Charles Dudley Warner, "Modern Fiction" (1885) and "The Novel and the Common School" (1890), reprinted in his *Complete Writings* (Hartford, Conn.: American Publishing Co., 1904), vol. XV, pp. 151–75, 256–75. A number of parallels could be drawn with Julian Hawthorne's

view, expressed in 1884 in his "The American Element in Fiction" for which see Ruland, ed., *A Storied Land*, pp. 108–20.

14. *Discovery of a Genius: W. D. Howells and Henry James*, ed. Albert Mordell (New York: Twayne, 1961), pp. 112–22 (pp. 120–22 in particular); Charles Dudley Warner, "American Novels," *Quarterly Review*, 155 (January, 1883): 201–29 (pp. 203–4, 208–9, 213–14, 216–17 in particular); Arthur Tilley, "The New School of Fiction," *National Review*, 1 (March, 1883): 257–68. The two novels most often referred to and used as examples were James's *The Portrait of a Lady* and Howells's *A Modern Instance*.

15. See Julia Wedgwood, review of *The Bostonians* in the *Contemporary Review*, 1 (1886): 300–301; George Saintsbury, "The Present State of the Novel: II," *Fortnightly Review*, n.s., 43 (1888): 116–18. See also Kenneth Graham, *English Criticism of the Novel, 1865–1900* (Oxford: Clarendon Press, 1965), pp. 102–4, where Maxwell Gray (i.e., Mary Gleed Tuttiett) is quoted as stating in 1894 that "human character is to this Paganism as the rapidly decomposing corpse under the knife and the microscope."

16. See Warner, "Modern Fiction," pp. 159–61 (and pp. 174–75 for what follows).

5.
HENRY JAMES AND THE ART OF FICTION

I

HENRY JAMES'S first crucial formulations of his theory of fiction related to the age-old problem of employing American materials and to the debate over realism. These two aspects are implicitly, even dialectically, linked in his early views; one might even say that they are two sides of one question. Although he moved beyond both in his mature theoretical considerations, they do constitute the real starting point of a lifelong, many-faceted, and constantly revised theory of fiction.

In several well-known passages of his early, important, and revealing study of *Hawthorne* (1879), James added his own voice to the already lengthy litany of complaints over the paucity and unsuitability of strictly American subjects and summed up the drama of the contemporary American novelist. "The flower of art blooms only where the soil is deep . . . it takes a great deal of history to produce a little literature . . . it needs a complex social machinery to set a writer in motion," he wrote, and continued: [1]

> one might enumerate the items of high civilisation, as it exists in other countries, which are absent from the texture of American life, until it should become a wonder to know what was left. No State, in the European sense of the word, and indeed barely a specific national name. No sovereign, no court, no personal loyalty, no aristocracy, no church, no clergy, no army, no diplomatic service, no country gentlemen, no palaces, no castles, nor manors, nor old country-houses, nor parsonages, nor thatched cottages, nor ivied ruins; no cathedrals, nor abbeys, nor little Norman churches; no great Universities nor public schools—no Oxford, nor Eton, nor Harrow; no literature, no novels, no museums, no pictures, no political society, no sporting class—no Epsom nor Ascot! Some such list as that might be drawn up of the absent things in American life.

These absences were to lead James to choose the expatriate life in England, where the social and historical "signs" needed by the novelist were not only present but visible, and to devise the "international theme" (i.e., the social and moral contrasting of American and European characters and *moeurs*) that characterizes so much of his fiction. Some forty years earlier these same absences had caused Hawthorne to opt for the rarefied atmosphere of romance and to fall into what James, together with Poe, considered the trap of superficial symbolism and allegory. "A want of reality and an abuse of the fanciful element" was the price Hawthorne had to pay for America's lack of history and custom, of manners and types. In spite of his sense of the local terrain and his historical imagination, Hawthorne *had* to choose romance rather than realism. "I have alluded to the absence in Hawthorne of that quality of realism which is now so much in fashion," James wrote at the beginning of his study, immediately evoking, by way of implicit contrast, the spirit of Balzac and his descendants—Gustave Flaubert and Zola. Now, a reliance on purely ideal or idyllic conditions, on pastoral and ingenuous modes, might be possible and acceptable in pre–Civil War America but not in the postbellum period, which had "introduced into the national consciousness a certain sense of proportion and relation, of the world being a more complicated place than it had hitherto seemed." The tree of knowledge had been eaten from, the prelapsarian spell broken: one had now to face reality.[2]

Accordingly, the postbellum novelist would be characterized by his sense of, and concern with, contemporary reality and the social milieu, manners and visible signs, recognizable places and people. In spite of James's admiration for his great compatriot, in his study of Hawthorne he dealt with a negative (or surpassed) form of fiction, and this study must be read in connection with those collected in *French Poets and Novelists* (1878), where a positive view was expounded—a view that, in the wake of his French contemporaries, stressed commitment to contemporary reality, the value of illustrative and descriptive realism, the novel of manners and social awareness. James's early theory of fiction leaned heavily toward French realism. There he found a strong interest both in the actual and in aesthetic form, a strong sense of reality expressed in artistic terms.

His readings of Théophile Gautier and Balzac, Flaubert, and Turgenev reveal this growing acknowledgment of realism and of its connections with the art of fiction. Its main traits were the pictorial "setting" of life, the "illustration" of every phase of life and manners, the "grasp of actual facts," of "the machinery of government, of police, of the arts, the professions, the trades" (all the things absent in Hawthorne's romances). Balzac, who "created a complete social system," attempted to "faire concurrence à l'état civil"—to vie with the census officers and the historian. The idea of "another world" was totally alien to Balzac, so engrossed was he in the world of the senses, in the palpable world of palaces and clothes; so mighty was his passion for *things*. "This overmastering sense of the present world was of course a superb foundation for the work of a realistic romancer," James stated, harping on his "huge, all-compassing, all-desiring, all-devouring love of reality"; on the authority that the real had for his imagination; on his sense of background and the *mise en scène;* on his sense of place and people. For Balzac, power was more important than charm (a word James often uses when writing about Hawthorne); the best quality to be found in a novelist, we read, is "that tender appreciation of actuality which makes even the application of a simple coat of rose-colour seem an act of violence."

The novelist, therefore, is a "social chronicler." The novel deals with man caught in the machinery of money and social institutions; it reflects or creates a whole system. It dramatically faces contemporary life and the moral nature of man by relying on the visual evidence. This "realistic, descriptive novel" begins, as in Flaubert, from the outside because "the real is the most satisfactory thing in the world, and if we once fairly advance in this direction nothing shall frighten us back." It works *sur le vif,* as in Turgenev. If the novel is "to represent the pictorial side of life," it must be complete and "a very serious matter." It will "render" things as painters render them. Distinctness, attentive observation, a general and impartial view of the great spectacle of human life, variety and completeness of references—all are traits of the "searching realist" in Turgenev and Flaubert. Moreover, in both these writers, a "susceptibility to the sensuous impressions of life" and a strong sense of form combine to make of the realistic mode the gateway to the art of fiction.

"We value most the 'realists' who have an ideal of delicacy," James wrote toward the end of his essay on the Russian writer, with whom, for more reasons than one, he must have felt in greater sympathy.[3] We may take this last sentence as a prefiguration of James's own development: at this stage he saw realism and the novel of manners as a necessary antidote to the exploded mode of romance. The chief aim of the novel, as he would soon repeat, was to represent life. This idea became the cornerstone of his next, openly theoretical and influential essay significantly called "The Art of Fiction," where the connections so far implicit or lightly sketched were brought to the foreground.

II

"The Art of Fiction" (1884) is James's clearest plea on behalf of the artistic nature and status of the novel—a far from "undisputed" notion until then. James took his cue from a lecture delivered in April 1884 in London by the English critic Walter Besant, entitled "The Art of Fiction" and immediately printed in pamphlet form. Incidentally, Besant took sides against the analytic school and stressed the value of the story as such. His main purpose, however, was to vindicate the artistic dignity of fiction. Fiction, Besant argued, was not a mechanical, but a *fine* art. It was on the same plane as painting and sculpture, music and poetry. Its field of application was vast and its possibilities endless; it was both a theater and a school for customs, converting as it does abstract ideas into living models. One of the oldest and "most religious" arts, it favored participation, human sympathy, and reverence for man. Dealing with the whole of mankind, it created popular consensus and acted as a moral guide.

The first part of the essay was an impassioned plea for the new status of fiction. Besant went on to emphasize that the novel was "governed and directed by general laws" and faced most of its contemporary problems. He advocated an underlying idealism while at the same time recognizing the need for natural realism. He wanted the "story" but accepted psychological analysis; selection (which he put on the plane of genius) and dramatic rendering were of the utmost importance. Besant considered personal experience and observation prerequisites for any novelist of standing; only in passing did he touch upon technical matters, what he called simply "beauty of execution." He also stressed that the modern novel almost always began "with a conscious moral purpose." A Victorian bias was clearly at work here, and it is undeniable that Besant's essay is often jumbled, confused, and naive. Yet, through the very force of its title and its main proposition, it had a liberating effect, as is evidenced by the lively controversy it stirred up.[4] Andrew Lang and Henry James took him up immediately on the main point; shortly afterward, Robert Louis Stevenson voiced his "humble remonstrance" against some of the essay's implications.

Being "what the French call *discutable,*" the novel, according to James, had come of age; no longer *naïf* and to be swallowed as such, "it must take itself seriously." "Fiction is one of the *fine* arts," he repeated with Besant; "it is at once as free and as serious a branch of literature as any other." But James would not yet propose a theory of his own, for he recognized the novelist's need of a far-ranging freedom of choice and discussion. "The only obligation to which in advance we may hold a novel . . . is that of being interesting," he wrote. The innumerable ways of fiction were "not to be marked out or fenced in by prescription"; the novelist found "no limit to his possible experiments, efforts, discoveries, successes." This did not prevent James from making some crucial observations, however, not only about the artistic, but also about the "illustrative" and realistic aspects of fiction.

The novel decidedly had nothing to do with "make believe": indeed, this admission of Trollope's seemed to James "a betrayal of a sacred office" and "a terrible crime." "The only reason for the existence of a novel is that it does attempt to represent life"; or, as James had put it in the original version of the essay, "that it *does* compete with life."[5] There is a complete analogy here—allowing for the different types of vehicle—between the art of the novelist and that of the painter: "as the picture is reality, so the novel is history." Like the historian, the novelist is occupied in "looking for the truth," in representing and illustrating "the

past, the actions of man." Here lay the reason for the art of
the novel: not only in its freedom from superimposed morality or the "happy ending," from a priori rules and conditions, but in "the importance of exactness—of truth of detail." James acknowledged that "the air of reality (solidity of
specification) seems to me to be the supreme virtue of a
novel—the merit on which all its other merits . . . help-
lessly and submissively depend." This was "the beginning
and the end of the art of the novelist. . . . It is here in very
truth that he competes with life" (an echo of Balzac's "faire
concurrence à l'état civil"?). Or, if the novelist competed with
his brother the painter, it was "in *his* attempts to render the
look of things, the look that conveys the meaning, to catch
the color, the relief, the expression, the surface, the substance of the human spectacle."

These were commonplace ways of describing the realistic
mode. For his painting analogy, James had in mind Titian
and Tintoretto. Stressing the "illustrative" task of the novel,
or referring, toward the end of his essay, to Zola as the
novelist "to whose solid and serious work no explorer of the
capacity of the novel can allude without respect," James
made it clear that at this stage the novel should have a realistic range and scope. "Art is essentially selection," he
wrote, "but it is a selection whose main care is to be typical,
to be inclusive . . . the province of art is all life, all feeling,
all observation, all vision."

Here we move into another area of definition. When stating that the novel had to be "as complete as possible," James
opposed Besant's idea of a "conscious moral purpose" as
well as Victorian *pruderie,* the implicit blackmailing of the
"young reader": "the essence of moral energy," as he put it,
"is to survey the whole field." As the Goncourt brothers and
Zola had advocated, this meant that the writer should also
deal with the lower as well as with the upper or middle
classes (witness Flaubert's *Un coeur simple*). It also meant
flying in the face of Mrs. Grundy: the great issue of the
sexes could no longer be ignored.[6] Thus, the novel as a pic-

ture of social life, as an illustration of life in its entirety, which it achieves through completeness of reference and specification, was both a realistic and an artistic product. The two aspects—indeed the two main threads of James's argument and belief—were brought together in the final part of the essay, where he enjoined the young novelist to "try to be as complete as possible—to make as perfect a work." In the middle sections of the essay James faced more specific but not less significant questions.

"Art derives a considerable part of its beneficial exercise from flying in the face of presumptions"; still, checks and balances were desirable, if not necessary, and James qualified his implicit or explicit adherence to realism in a way that would lead to important developments. Besant had stated that the novel must be "the result of personal experience and observation" and had disclaimed the role of invention. James, conversely, emphasized "the power to guess the unseen from the seen, to trace the implications of things, to judge the whole piece by the pattern." The writer's imagination and sensibility were a part of, and superior to, direct experience. "Experience is never limited, and it is never complete," he wrote, adding that "it is an immense sensibility, a kind of huge spider-web of the finest silken threads suspended in the chamber of consciousness, and catching every air-borne particle in its tissue." James found that "the measure of reality is very difficult to fix," and in a novel it is "a reality so colored by the author's vision" that it can hardly be offered as a model. "If experience consists of impressions, it may be said that impressions *are* experience": all emphasis is here shifted from the object to the subject, from reality to the viewer, from life to the artist. Hence James's crucial and far-reaching specification: "A novel is in its broadest definition a personal, a direct impression of life," whose value was "greater or less according to the intensity of the impression." Not only did this proposition open the way to the poetics of literary impressionism; it also colored and qualified James's later conception of the novel. Here, too, he shifted the value from the object to the writer's vision. The artist must be granted not only his subject, his idea, and his *donnée* but his individual point of view. This personal view, as it were, took the place of objectivity and impersonality (two basic tenets of realism as it was then understood).

Life could be imagined, or seen and presented in a personal way by someone "on whom nothing is lost"; in like manner, the form was not preordained but was "to be appreciated after the fact." The novel was a kind of living organism, catching "the strange, irregular rhythm of life," following its movement and offering it to us *without* rearrangement. James could thus radically do away with some of the most abused questions of the contemporary debate. There was little meaning in the opposition of description and dialogue, incident and description, for there was no description that was not intentionally narrative, no dialogue that was not intentionally descriptive. Furthermore, there was little point in the distinction between the novel of character and the novel of incident, or between novel and romance (the French, fortunately, had only one term, *roman*). "What is character but the determination of incident? What is incident but the illustration of character?" James asked. Novel and romance were equally qualified by their standard of execution.[7] Sound observations. With one in particular James dealt with obvious relish—that of the "story," which touched him directly because of his supposed identification with the analytic school. James denied the existence of a school that urged that the novel be all treatment and no subject, and he rightly pointed out that the "story" always represented the *donnée*. "The story and the novel, the idea and the form, are the needle and thread," he wrote: How could one recommend the use of one without the other? As for "adventure," all sorts of things could be reckoned an adventure in the novel, which led James to the following insight: "A psychological reason is, to my imagination, an object adorably pictorial. . . . There are few things more exciting to me, in short, than a psychological reason, and yet, I protest, the novel seems to me the most magnificent form of art."

This was his answer to the controversy over the use of psychology in the novel: psychological realism was as important as the outward illustration of life. The real questions concerning the novel remained questions of execution, of artistic rendering, in the sense that the execution of a work of art was part of its very essence. In "The Art of Fiction," however, James balanced his view of the novel (as he would hardly do later on) between the realistic impulse and the personal impression, life and art, outer and inner reality. This final point would soon receive a great deal of attention; James was to be more and more drawn to seeing the field of reflection as the novel's proper domain, with the soul and mind of man becoming its exalting stage. In this sense, according to James's concluding remarks in the 1884 essay, not only was the novel aesthetically independent of a moral purpose, but it relied on "the very obvious truth that the deepest quality of a work of art will always be the quality of the mind of the producer. . . . No good novel will ever proceed from a superficial mind."[8]

In the late 1880s and 1890s James's theory labored over, and focused on, the above points and underlined in particular the view of the novel as a "great form" and at the same time as a personal impression of life, more and more qualified by the assumption of a specific, and often limited, point of view. Part of the impulse behind this development was Robert Louis Stevenson's essay "A Humble Remonstrance," which also added in 1884 to the "art of fiction" debate. Stevenson accepted the point about the artistic quality of fiction but went on to extend its realm and definition to all "fictitious" literature and emphasized its poetic nature. Hence, fiction (or narrative, as he preferred to call it) did not and could not "compete with life"; it fled the direct challenge and pursued instead "an independent and creative aim." Realism was a means, not an end. "The novel

which is a work of art exists not by its resemblances to life
. . . but by its immeasurable difference from life," Stevenson wrote; "It substitutes a certain artificial series of impressions" for the welter of impressions that life presents; it is
more like "a proposition of geometry" than like nature. "So
far as it imitates at all, it imitates not life, but speech; not
the facts of human destiny, but the emphasis and the
suppressions with which the human actor tells of them,"
Stevenson maintained with surprising modernity. Art, he
insisted, makes us turn away or half shut our eyes "against
the dazzle and confusion of reality" and gets us to "regard
instead a certain figmentary abstraction."[9]

For Stevenson, in short, art "composed" but was independent of, and antithetical to, reality. Whereas life was a welter
and a dazzle, art tried to arrest the flow of impressions, to
project them in a subjective and passional way. In its highest
form narrative led to abstraction; not to exactitude but to
"significant simplicity" (today, we would say to "open forms").
With these propositions Stevenson anticipated Joseph Conrad's concept of fiction (as expressed, for instance, in his
1897 Preface to *The Nigger of the "Narcissus"*) and the development of James's own theory. His essay might, indeed, have
contributed to it.

III

"Do something from your own point of view," James wrote
in his 1888 letter to the Deerfield Summer School. He continued: "Any point of view is interesting that is a direct
impression of life. You each have an impression colored by
your individual conditions; make that into a picture, a picture framed by your own personal wisdom." The field was
open for free study; life was infinitely vast and various; it
was to be considered not only directly and closely but within
the frame provided by the observer. So far James had emphasized the "picture" of life. Now most of the stress went

to a consideration of the "frame," which was gradually identified with the inner life of the observer and the limited point of view. Reality was what was lived or relived within a character's consciousness, experienced in his (more often, her) mind and soul, seen through his eyes, colored and qualified by his vision, filtered by his sensibility. Narrated reality was to be more and more equated with that reflected field of life. At the same time, it was to be increasingly presented by a character involved in the action, to be "foreshortened" and personalized by that particular, circumscribed (and often unreliable) point of view.

In his extremely interesting essay "Guy de Maupassant" (1888), James saw action in the novel as the illustration of motives, and motives as constituting drama. The best picture of life was not necessarily viewed and presented from the outside. In fact, the reverse was more likely to be true. In discussing Guy de Maupassant's influential Preface to *Pierre et Jean,* James wholeheartedly accepted the French writer's view that "something fine" had to be made according to the writer's temperament, and he stressed that "if a picture, a tale, or a novel be a direct impression of life (and that surely constitutes its interest and value), the impression will vary according to the plate that takes it, the particular structure and mixture of the recipient." "Any form of the novel is simply a vision of the world from the standpoint of a person constituted after a certain fashion." James's extensive quotation from Maupassant dwelt on the idea that our view of the world is strictly personal, and adapts itself to our organs and senses. Maupassant had written:

"How childish, moreover, to believe in reality, since we each carry our own in our thought and in our organs. Our eyes, our ears, our sense of smell, of taste, differing from one person to another, create as many truths as there are men upon earth. And our minds, taking instruction from these organs, so diversely impressed, understand, analyze, judge, as if each of us belonged to a different race. Each one of us, therefore, forms for himself an illusion of the world, which is the illusion poetic, or sentimental, or joyous, or melancholy, or unclean, or dismal, according to his nature. And the writer has no other mission than to reproduce faithfully this illusion, with all the contrivances of art that he has learned and has at his command."

"It is of secondary importance that our impression should be called, or not called, an illusion," James commented. The real point was that "the value of the artist resides in the clearness with which he gives forth that impression." All the emphasis was put on the subjective side, on the viewer's, the artist's side. Halfway through the essay, James took up Maupassant's idea that the analytic fashion of telling a story was "much less profitable than the simple epic manner which 'avoids with care all complicated explanations, all dissertations upon motives.' " For him, psychology could not, and should not, be hidden "as it is hidden in reality under the facts of existence." James maintained that "it is as difficult to describe an action without glancing at its motive . . . as it is to describe a motive without glancing at its practical consequence." If psychology was hidden, the question then came up, "From whom is it hidden?" All depended upon the observer and the nature of his observations. Reference to motives was of the essence of fiction; the task of conveying "the impression of something that is not one's self," no matter how difficult, was the constant concern of the novelist. In James's opinion, it was a limitation to eschew analysis, to skip "that reflective part which governs conduct and produces character." In short, it was a false attempt at impersonality. In this respect, he was clearly moving away from a strict adherence to that tenet: for him, fictional impersonality was too imbued with the personality of the author in subtle and "invisible" ways. The answer he gave to the question was the same that Flaubert had given: "The artist must be present in his work like God in Creation, invisible and almighty, everywhere felt but nowhere seen."[10] But there is no doubt that at this stage James put the accent more on the reflective than on the illustrative aspect of fiction, that he was tempted more by its subjective than by its objective side.

This choice was to lead him in the 1890s to his conception of the "limited point of view." The author was thus transposed tactically into one of his characters, while the point of view was internalized through a specific agent in the story. The growth of James's conception of the limited point of view (or "intelligent observer") can be traced through his Notebook entries of the 1890s. Too much has been said, however, of its subjective bias and potential ambiguities. As I have tried to show elsewhere,[11] James's discovery and theory of the limited point of view went hand in hand with his discovery and celebration of the "scenic method"; the combination of the two principles answered once again the need to reconcile subjective vision and objectivity of presentation in the novel. I shall touch only briefly on this issue because it pertains more to a poetics than to a theory of the novel, that is, more to technical ways and means to write a particular kind of fiction than to a general conception of its nature and aims. Furthermore, it has been dealt with often and extensively. Yet, it is highly significant, for James as well as for the end-of-the-century fiction, that the analogy for the novel was now sought no longer in the "picture," in sweeping, illustrative frescoes, but in the compression, tightness, and objectivity of the drama. The drama provided the example of an "economy of clear summarization," of a "clear order and expressed sequence," of a "mastery of fundamental statement," of the "sacred mystery of structure." Narrative action was to be based on a carefully worked out sequence of dramatic scenes—not of melodramatic *coups de théâtre* as in the nineteenth-century masterpieces, but of "little masses and periods in the scenic light," of "dialogue which is always action"—that is, of intense and compressed moments of dramatic presentation. This "scenic method," as James was to point out later on in the Prefaces, results in a kind of "guarded objectivity" that came, in turn, from "the imposed absence of that 'going behind,' to compass explanations and amplifications" that was so typical of the analytic school and of any attempt at psychological investigation. The emphasis was on "the presented occasion," which was to "tell all of its story itself." For a while James even seemed to renounce his ideal of compositional richness.

This concept of the scenic method was immediately qualified, however, by the device of the intelligent observer, the narrator who is involved in the action and presents it to the reader from his limited point of view. According to this principle, developed simultaneously with the idea of the scenic method, the narrator is in a position to present the relevant facts as they objectively happen, as on a stage, and at the same time to invest them with a personal perspective and angle of vision. Of course, this perspective is necessarily "foreshortened," but it is also oblique, ambiguous, and possibly biased. Thus, the self-sufficiency of the dramatic scene is made to depend on the narrator's personal point of view. In turn, his mind and consciousness are presented dramatically. The subjective side and the "going behind," which had been at first excluded from the guarded objectivity of the scene, reenter that very scene under the guise of the narrator, through his limited, wondering, often worried interpretations. This would compel the author to a careful, laborious juxtaposition and montage of scenes and moments, aperçus and sights, and force him painstakingly to readjust his views and interpretations without end. On the other hand, the principle of the limited point of view combined with the scenic form would also provide the novelist with unexpected opportunities, not only for dramatic compression, but for psychological investigation as well. Since much has been written about the implications of the use of the limited point of view in fiction, we need not go into it here. But it is true, as one critic remarked,[12] that owing to that device James—and the novelist in general—could pass from "the dramatization of events to the dramatization of states of mind and soul, the conditions of what is happening below the surface of the dialogue and the action." If the novel was no longer picture but drama, it could still cultivate, indeed enlarge, that particular realm of psychological inquiry and application even *below* the surface. Not only did James give us a glimpse of the impending psychoanalytic turn of the novel; the analytic school reasserted its rights and its presence *within* a conception of the novel as the objective presentation of events. Intelligent observers and narrators, at first introduced into the novel to ensure neatness and terseness of presentation, soon claimed the central position and pride of place. They tended to change, almost at once, from a technical device into a main narrative concern.

All this would lead to a form of fictional mannerism and ambiguity, but it was of the greatest importance if the novel were to grow out of its nineteenth-century habits into twentieth-century patterns. It is difficult to disengage here points of theory from points of poetics. One or two, however, can be identified. The question of narrative rhythm became of paramount importance: in this kind of novel narrative rhythm was provided by the significant juxtaposition and montage of moments, episodes and scenes that the narrator presented and projected subjectively but that he also isolated and objectified as dramatic evidence. Epistemological and even philosophical implications gradually came to the surface; the limitation of point of view implied a doubt concerning the novelist's way of apprehending and re-creating reality. Ambiguity of presentation and interpretation betrayed perhaps a growing doubt about the very possibility of the novelist's apprehending and re-recreating reality. These were, however, more properly twentieth-century developments. At this stage James still conceived of the novel as a window (indeed, an infinite number of windows) on the world. For him it was still a form and a viewpoint that selected, limited, and circumscribed the presentation of reality; still the novelist's—or the narrator's—view acted as the intervening frame, window, and point of perspective; still scenic, dramatic (and very often architectural) construction was of the essence of the novel's method.

IV

Contrary to some of the implications so far described, two related concepts seem to mark James's view of the novel as he approached the end of the century. The idea that the novel "competes with life" acquired new impetus. "Imagined reality" seemed more and more to gain the upper hand over "represented" reality. Actual life seemed not so much unamenable to artistic creation as antithetical to it; the novelist's adherence to real life could indeed jeopardize artistic creation. According to this stance, the novel evolves not from actuality but from the moral conscience of the writer. It creates its own autonomous, independent, self-sufficient world, where its links with actual life can, indeed ought to, be severed. In Fëdor Dostoevski's view, the novel aims at a kind of "rival creation." It is no longer an "incremental creation" (to use the medieval term of St. Augustine); it does not even hold the mirror up to nature (as the Renaissance would have it). Instead, it *creates* its own world and its own reality, which is in a sense opposed to, and different from, life on earth.[13]

Historically, this shift in the conception of art can be traced back to the Italian and English theorists of the late Renaissance (Scaligero, Fracastoro, and Sir Philip Sidney) who began to write of poets as those who "make things either better than Nature bringeth forth, or, quite new, forms such as never were in Nature." The artist, in other words, moves from *effingere* to *creare*. This idea was most important for the romantic writers, and it began to form part of the nineteenth-century view of the novel. As Albert Camus maintains in his *L'homme revolté* (1951), the genre of the novel is a typical form of dissident literature and has always expressed the spirit of revolt. It succeeds in creating an imaginary world by correcting the existing one. "Le roman fab-

rique du destin sur mesure . . . il concurrence la creation":
it was a wide-ranging expansion of Balzac's dictum.

James was more than tempted by this view; he contributed to it. As pointed out elsewhere,[14] the "central intelligence" in a novel controls, indeed creates, the very substance and form of the narrative. The limited point of view,
by circumscribing the angle of vision, intensifies its subjectivity and makes it the only standard of judgment. The novel
itself is a creation of the narrator rather than a reflection of
life. The self-contained world (the form) of the novel chal-
lenges and defies outward reality. It is neither a duplicate
nor an imitation of life but an alternative to it. This idea is
at the core of James's short story "The Real Thing" (1892),
where he dramatized the artist's innate preference for the
represented subject over the real one, "the perverse and
cruel law in virtue of which the real thing could be so much
less precious than the unreal"—or, (as he was later to repeat) "that odd law which somehow always makes the minimum of valid suggestion serve the man of imagination better than the maximum." Writing of Gustave Flaubert in
1902, he would say that "expression is creation . . . it *makes*
the reality, and only in the degree in which it *is*, exquisitely,
expression." In a well-known letter to H. G. Wells, he would
sum up this view with passionate intensity: "it is art that
makes life, makes interest, makes importance."[15]

James wrote this at a very late date, in 1915, as part of a
heated and controversial appeal for the supremacy of art
over life. In 1897, however, in a passage of his "London
Notes," he gave what is perhaps his best definition of the
novel as "rival creation." Seeking private diversion, he tells
us, he looked for "the great anodyne of art . . . a supreme
opportunity to test the spell of the magician, for one felt
one was saved if a fictive world would open." After having
read a number of novels, James proceeded to express their,
and the novelists', value in terms that are closely reminis-
cent of the late Renaissance theorists:

The great thing to say for them is surely that at any given moment they offer us another world, another consciousness, an experience that, as effective as the dentist's ether, muffles the ache of the actual and, by helping us to an interval, tides us over and makes us face, in the return to the inevitable, a combination that may at least have changed. What we get of course, in proportion as the picture lives, is simply another actual—the actual of other people; and I no more than anyone else pretend to say *why* that should be a relief, a relief as great, I mean, as it practically proves.

In spite of some concession to the concept of art as "relief," the definition could not be clearer: novels and novelists give us "another world," "another actual."[16] If pursued to its extreme consequences, this position would ultimately be untenable. At this stage of James's theoretical progress, however, it represented the clearest claim for the boundless possibilities of the novel as a vehicle for capturing, reproducing, organizing, and *creating* reality in fictional terms. Not only is the field of the novel immense, but its potentialities are endless. This was James's—and perhaps the period's—greatest claim for the *creative* nature of fiction, for the absoluteness and wholeness of its quality—when its supposed ability to capture and organize experience was already beginning to be questioned.

James's position contributed both to a supreme exaltation of the novel and to the eventual dissolution from within of its form, function, and role. By favoring the "center of interest," the drama of conscience, and the "subjective adventure" of his narrators, for whom the acquisition of consciousness becomes identified with and absorbs the unfolding of the action, James inserted in the novel the principle of subjectivity, with its corollaries: the ambiguity of vision and presentation, the baffling nature of narrated facts, the interpretative and constructive role forced on the reader. If the "fine consciousness" becomes the mirror of the subject and the field of reflection breaks up reality into a myriad of images and impressions, then the hope of reordering it into a fictional whole is inevitably upset as well. If, in this regard, "relations never stop," the novel is bound to become kaleidoscopic and phantasmagoric: Virginia Woolf, if not James Joyce, would be the heralds of this transformation and usher in the new form. (As this development can be traced in James's Prefaces to the New York Edition of his novels and tales, which are outside the chronological and conceptual limits of this study, I will deal with this matter briefly in the Appendix to Part II.)

Toward the end of the century James seemed mainly concerned with the question of form; with the *unity* of form and substance, expression and idea; and, above all, with artistic execution. Writing on "Turgenev and Tolstoy" in 1897, he extolled in the former the unity "of material and form— of their being inevitable faces of the same medal," and he rejected the clumsy assumption that subject and style could be different and separable things. In Flaubert, "the form is in *itself* as interesting, as active, as much of the essence of the subject as the idea." Gabriele D'Annunzio was praised for his complete and admirable fusion of matter and manner. In Shakespeare, the phrase "*is* the object and the sense, in as close a compression as that of body and soul, so that any consideration of them as distinct . . . becomes a gross stupidity." As James was later to repeat in his Preface to *The Awkward Age,* "the grave distinction between substance and form in a really wrought work of art signally breaks down." [17] James, of course, had disapproved of "art for art's sake"; now he was championing the novel as a work of art, the product of painstaking but perfect execution, which required the closest attention and endless toil. This was his most radical commitment as a theorist, and his most valuable legacy to our century.

V

The intrinsic "dissolution" of the novel was, of course, implicit rather than explicit in James's theoretical writings. His latest formulations, at the turn of the century, make it quite clear that the novel needs reality (and freedom) as much as it needs artistic awareness and form.[18] His essay on "The Future of the Novel" of 1899 reads like a variation (over an interval of years) on his earlier "The Art of Fiction." According to it, the novel ("the prolonged prose fable") has asserted itself as the genre of the age: as a matter of fact, the danger lies with its inarticulate, absorbent, immense public. Public libraries as well as female and young readers constitute both a lure and a threat, for they have given rise to a literature of consumption and commercialism. Yet the novel can survive and even thrive, owing to its pliancy and adaptability, to its artistic form. As James wrote: "The novel is of all pictures the most comprehensive and the most elastic. It will stretch anywhere—it will take in absolutely anything . . . for its subject, magnificently, it has the whole human consciousness." It satisfies the desire for vicarious experience and knowledge. This "high prosperity of fiction" has marched in step with "the vulgarization of literature in general"; one could witness "monstrous multiplications." James was prophetic in describing the advent of mass-produced novels, including the equivocal role played by the mass media. Yet, as he wrote:

> The more we consider it the more we feel that the prose picture can never be at the end of its tether until it loses the sense of what it can do. It can do simply everything, and that is its strength and its life. Its plasticity, its elasticity are infinite; there is no color, no extension it may not take from the nature of its subject or the temper of its craftsman. It has the extraordinary advantage—a piece of luck scarcely credible— that, while capable of giving an impression of the highest perfection and the rarest finish, it moves in a luxurious independence of rules and restrictions.

The novel must hold our attention, in James's opinion, and not make its appeal on false pretenses. It can perish only by being superficial or timid. These ideas had already been expressed in "The Art of Fiction." Here James went even further in seeing the future of fiction as "intimately bound up with the future of the society that produces and consumes it." The only form of the novel to be "unhesitatingly pronounced wrong" was that incapable of its freedom: freedom of subject, attitude, and form was the answer, given the fact that "the novel is at any moment the most immediate and, as it were, admirably *treacherous* picture of actual manners." This picture was to include "an immense omission in our fiction," the treatment "of the great relation between men and women, the constant world-renewal" (a lovely circumlocution for "sex"), the "revolution taking place in the position and outlook of women," but also other areas of interest:

> There are too many sources of interest neglected—whole categories of manners, whole corpuscular classes and provinces, museums of character and condition, unvisited; while it is on the other hand mistakenly taken for granted that safety lies in all the loose and thin material that keeps reappearing in forms at once ready-made and sadly the worse for wear.

Here the next important question arose: the novel was by now an old, self-conscious form. The achievement of artistic self-consciousness was not to be jeopardized by questions of mass consumption and commercialism. The novel was to develop into an ever changing form: there was "no real health" for an art that did not move "a step in advance of its farthest follower." This was, in a nutshell, the emerging idea of the avant-garde. Moreover, it was still true that "so long as life retains its power of projecting itself upon his imagination, [man] will find the novel work off the impression better than anything he knows."

James concluded that "anything better for the purpose has assuredly yet to be discovered." As to the menace of vulgarization, it must be combated on the one hand by observation and perception and, on the other, by art and taste. If one got "too little of the firsthand impression, the effort to penetrate—that effort for which the French have the admirable expression to *fouiller*—and still less, if possible, of any science of composition, any architecture, distribution, proportion," it was a sign "that the novelist, not . . . the novel, has dropped." James's final words were, again, an impassioned, clinching claim for the artistic status and quality of fiction: [19]

> So long as there is a subject to be treated, so long will it depend wholly on the treatment to rekindle the fire. Only the ministrant must really approach the altar; for if the novel *is* the treatment, it is the treatment that is essentially what I have called the anodyne.

These lines may serve as an apt conclusion for James's long commitment to define the nature and import of the novel in the nineteenth century. In the new century, on returning to Flaubert and Balzac (particularly the latter, on three separate occasions), he reemphasized the importance of a close adherence to the facts of life, the aspects of reality, the call of the actual—the effort at *representation* on the part of the novel. In the Prefaces he laid out a poetics of fiction that is a plea for discrimination and conscious artistic application, an almost systematic attempt to define its various aspects and problems, and assumed the absolute, creative value of the novelist's endeavor. In his final essay, "The New Novel," he expanded the view and the contention that while life is all saturation and confusion, fiction is all discrimination and selection, that it reorders and organizes experience, imposes a meaningful form on the turmoil and welter of reality.[20]

NOTES

1. For ease of reference, see *Theory of Fiction: Henry James,* ed. James E. Miller, Jr. (Lincoln: University of Nebraska Press, 1972), pp. 48–50. This was taken almost verbatim from an early Notebook entry: see *The Notebooks of Henry James,* ed. F. O. Matthiessen and Kenneth B. Murdock (New York: Oxford University Press, 1947), p. 14.

2. *Hawthorne,* ed. Tony Tanner (New York: Macmillan, 1967), pp. 54–56, 111–13, 24, 135.

3. *French Poets and Novelists,* ed. Leon Edel (New York: Grosset & Dunlap, 1964), pp. 47, 78–80, 86–92, 116, 148, 185, 197–202, 206, 210, 216–19, 250. See also his early *Notes and Reviews,* ed. Pierre de Chaignon La Rose, 1921; and *Views and Reviews,* ed. Le Roy Phillips, 1908 (both books reprints [Freeport, N.Y.: Books for Libraries Press, 1968]). As early as 1864 James recommended "the famous 'realistic system'" and advised the novelist to "cultivate a delicate perception of the actual" (*Notes and Reviews,* pp. 23, 32).

4. See Mark Spilka, "Henry James and Walter Besant: 'The Art of Fiction' Controversy," *Novel,* 6 (1973): 101–19; John Goode, "The Art of Fiction: Walter Besant and Henry James," in *Tradition and Tolerance in Nineteenth-Century Fiction,* ed. David B. Howard et al. (London: Routledge and Kegan Paul, 1966), pp. 243–81.

5. "The Art of Fiction," originally appeared in *Longman's Magazine* (September, 1884); reprinted, with revisions, in *Partial Portraits* (1888), ed. Leon Edel (Ann Arbor: Michigan University Press, 1970), pp. 375–408; it can also be found in Miller, ed., *Theory of Fiction,* pp. 28–44. The magazine version is available in *Henry James and Robert Louis Stevenson: A Record of Friendship and Criticism,* ed. Janet Adam Smith (London: Hart-Davis, 1948), pp. 53–84, along with Stevenson's "A Humble Remonstrance." I have drawn on some of the ideas already developed in my *Henry James and the Experimental Novel* (Charlottesville: University Press of Virginia, 1978), pp. 11–19. See also *L'art de la fiction: Henry James,* ed. Paul Zéraffa (Paris: Klincksieck, 1978). In his 1883 essay "Alphonse Daudet" James had written that "the main object of the novel is to represent life," while "the *effect* of a novel . . . is to entertain" (*Partial Portraits,* p. 227).

6. For the links with French realism and naturalism see Lyall H. Powers, *Henry James and the Naturalist Movement* (East Lansing: The Michigan State University Press, 1971); Philip Grover, *Henry James and the French Novel* (London: Elek Books, 1973); Franca Bernabei, *La teoria del romanzo americano e la lezione francese (1865–1900)* (Brescia: Paideia, 1981). For James's interest in the lower classes as subject matter, see his essay "Guy

de Maupassant" (1888), where he wrote about the French treatment of them with relish and approval (Edel, ed., *Partial Portraits*, pp. 283–84).

7. In his early essay "The Poetry of George Eliot" (1868), James defined the romance in opposition to the novel in fairly traditional but also original terms: "Whether the term may be defined I know not; but we may say of it, comparing it with the novel, that it carries much farther that compromise with reality which is the basis of all imaginative writing. In the romance this principle of compromise pervades the superstructure as well as the basis. The most that we exact is that the fable be consistent with itself." (La Rose, ed., *Views and Reviews*, p. 123). In the 1907 Preface to *The American*, James gave a well-known definition of the romance as the cutting of the cable that ties the balloon of experience to earth (Miller, ed., *Theory of Fiction*, pp. 108–9).

8. In the 1908 Preface to *The Portrait of a Lady*, James wrote of "the perfect dependence of the 'moral' sense of a work of art on the amount of felt life concerned in producing it." See Miller, ed., *Theory of Fiction*, p. 313.

9. "A Humble Remonstrance" appeared in *Longman's Magazine* (December 1884); reprinted in Smith, ed., *Henry James and Robert Louis Stevenson*, pp. 86–100. Stevenson discussed three types of novel—that of adventure, of character, and the dramatic (i.e., of passion, coming very close to romance).

10. See "Guy de Maupassant" in Edel, ed., *Partial Portraits*, pp. 246–47, 256–59, 285; also in Miller, ed., *Theory of Fiction*, pp. 64–65, 176–78 (the reference to Flaubert was in his "Gustave Flaubert" [1893]); his letter of 1888 to Deerfield Summer School can be found in Henry James, *The Future of the Novel, Essays on the Art of Fiction*, ed. Leon Edel (New York: Vintage Books, 1956), pp. 28–29.

11. See my *Henry James and the Experimental Novel*, chap. 2, pp. 47–76, for a full treatment of the question; Matthiessen, ed., *The Notebooks*, pp. 208, 258, 263; and passim; Henry James, *The Art of the Novel*, ed. R. P. Blackmur (New York: Scribner's, 1934), pp. 109, 110–11.

12. Michael Egan, *Henry James: The Ibsen Years* (London: Vision Press, 1972), p. 32.

13. See my *Henry James and the Experimental Novel*, pp. 94–104, for further details (pp. 96–98 for the following quotes).

14. Ibid., pp. 99, 93.

15. See *The Complete Tales of Henry James*, ed. Leon Edel (Philadelphia: Lippincott, 1962–64), vol. VIII, p. 258; James, *The Art of the Novel*, p. 161; Henry James, *Notes on Novelists* (New York: Scribner's, 1914), p. 100; *Henry James and H. G. Wells*, ed. Leon Edel and Gordon N. Ray (London: Hart-Davis, 1958), p. 267; see also Miller, ed., *Theory of Fiction*, pp. 89–91, and Appendix to Part II, below.

16. Henry James, "London Notes" (July, 1897), reprinted in his *Notes on Novelists*, p. 436. As Albert Camus put it, "The art of the novel can reconstruct creation itself, in the form that it is imposed on us and in the form in which we reject it" (*The Rebel*, trans. Anthony Bower [Harmondsworth: Penguin Books, 1971], p. 232).

17. Miller, ed., *Theory of Fiction*, pp. 280–81 ("Turgenev and Tolstoy," 1897); pp. 259–60 ("Gustave Flaubert," 1902); pp. 283–84 (Gabriele D'Annunzio," 1904; "The Tempest," 1907); James, *The Art of the Novel*, pp. 115–16.

18. One may note in passing that his "American Letters" (which appeared in 1898 in *Literature*), constitutes a revaluation of American themes and American writers—from Hawthorne to Whitman, from Garland to Owen Wister. He discussed the "Western imagination," localism, and representative, hardly exploited types such as the businessman, which the American novel was to confront: "The romance of fact, indeed, has touched him in a way that quite puts to shame the romance of fiction." The businessman was *"the* magnificent theme *en disponibilité"* (Miller, ed., *Theory of Fiction*, pp. 53–55).

19. Henry James, "The Future of the Novel," in Miller, ed., *Theory of Fiction*, pp. 338, 339–41, 343–44. Studies of James's criticism and theories abound: among others, see Percy Lubbock, *The Craft of Fiction* (London: Jonathan Cape, 1921); Morris Roberts, *Henry James's Criticism* [1929] (New York: Octagon Books, 1970); René Wellek, "Henry James's Literary Theory and Criticism," *American Literature*, 30 (1958): 293–321 and his *A History of Modern Criticism* (New Haven: Yale University Press, 1965), vol. IV, pp. 213–37.

20. For further documentation, see Appendix to Part II, below.

6.
GENTEEL REALISM AND REGIONALISM

———•◦•———

I

THE NEW STATUS of fiction, ennobled in both theory and practice by Henry James, was recognized by the popular press and by university treatises and handbooks. Examples are numerous, but one representative case must suffice. In his *The Philosophy of Fiction in Literature* (1890), Daniel Greenleaf Thompson gave a thorough if uninspired account of the question.[1] By "fiction" he meant the prose story or novel, which provided "communication of thought" and "a record of experience . . . of what one has inferred or imagined." Slightly removed from reality and therefore artificial, fiction was all the same dependent on truth; it had to conform to natural conditions and aim at consistency and unity. According to Thompson, the novel must give aesthetic pleasure while imparting information and influencing conduct—hence Thompson's close analysis not only of the aesthetic, but also the scientific and moral dimensions, of fiction. Its scientific value had to do with the knowledge of history and society it was expected to transmit through the novelist's analyses and descriptions: "The novel, then, has a very decided and marked psychological, ethological, and sociological utility."

The novel's moral value had to do not so much with improving character as with indicating "the true relations of cause and effect in human life." Its fundamental value, however, was aesthetic. Fiction was "a product of the constructive powers of the human intellect," and as such it had a synthetic function: "it unites a manifold of particulars into a whole whose parts have an organic connection" (thus the need for unity, not so much for a "purpose" as for a plan or a central idea). It was not simply a reproductive, but a creative, art, the product of selection as well as introspection. This quality transmitted "the sense of life" and its powers: it was apprehended through the senses but led to a contemplative, quiescent (not striving) pleasure—as Joyce was to maintain in his *Portrait of the Artist as a Young Man*. Fiction worked through and by means of language, in selective, associative processes, "by which a totality of impression is formed." Furthermore, it dealt with real or possible *relations* between human beings and between the individual and society. Finally, it offered hypotheses and suppositions, drew inferences, and embodied a kind of "transfigured realism."[2]

This last view was Thompson's answer to Zola's idea of the novel as a scientific "experiment," which was discussed in a chapter entitled "Realism and Idealism." "Neither an individual character nor the *'milieu'* can be successfully depicted without minute anatomical dissection," Thompson granted; yet, if documentation was needed, "introspective analysis must go along with extrinsic observation." Zola put the accent on the observer and the experimenter, who instituted "a series of events in accordance with the laws of cause and effect discovered" in order to illustrate some general fact and modify existing conditions. For Thompson, however, the role of the imagination could not be ignored or minimized. Realism required "both reproduction and crea-tion." This is why Maupassant's conception of the "realists of talent" who "ought rather to call themselves *Illusionists*" was more acceptable. The reduction of art to science led to knowledge rather than to aesthetic pleasure. In short, the scientific method in fiction was a contradiction in terms: the personal as well as the artistic dimensions were of far greater importance. Naturalism, and even realism, "only endows us with a method to be used under the guidance of ideals formed by the synthetic and selective activities of the mind," Thompson concluded,[3] thereby codifying and consolidating a great part of the contemporary discussion on the art, rather than the science, of fiction. The following premise, in fact, summed up the contemporary attitude toward fic-tion: "The only true theory of the novel is that which places the artistic foremost. But the truly great artist is he who has the noblest and best ideals." Thompson's contribution lay in his detailed discussion and recognition of the artistic condi-tions and elements of fiction even under the pressure of the scientific tendencies of the age. But acceptance of the pre-vailing "exhibition of social life" did not imply the rejection of what Thomas De Quincey had called the "literature of power"—a literature that made "its appeal to universal hu-man experience":

> If we represent experience, accuracy and exactness are nec-essary, but a skill in combination and construction is just as important as correct copying of nature. . . . The result is a whole which is true to nature in its details, but in which those details have been gathered, put together, and connected in an organic relation by a creative power.[4]

Naturalism was a limitation, in other words. So was too great a concern with morality in the novel. In this Thomp-son shared James's opinion that the French novelists en-joyed greater freedom than their American counterparts. He did, of course, have qualms about "Gallic freedom" in the depiction of sexual passion but was strongly attracted by it on aesthetic grounds. The scarcity of great American novelists was, he suggested, probably due to their timidity, to their willingness to be blackmailed by the "Young Person." "The healthy growth of a literature depends upon its freedom for expression," he wrote in Jamesian fashion, and went on to quote to that effect from "The Art of Fiction." Thompson even ventured to maintain that the knowledge of evil had advantages equal to the knowledge of good. In spite of his claims for its fundamental aesthetic value, his view of fiction paid its tribute to Mrs. Grundy in accepting the restraints of genteel or reticent realism. Still, he recognized the novel's exalted aims, its ability to gather information and to document and understand contemporary life in its hidden workings. His program for fiction brought together what had been expressed on the subject by the best minds of the age—from James to Stevenson, from Besant to Flaubert and Maupassant, from Hippolyte Taine to Zola, from Jules Lemaître to Ferdinand Brunetière to Paul Bourget.[5]

Thompson's was a sound consolidation of years of debate on the novel at a crucial point in its development and opened the way to a series of similar handbooks. Ten years later, at the turn of the century, for example, Bliss Perry gathered his lectures at Princeton University into a volume entitled *A Study of Prose Fiction*, which recognized a relative lack of interest in aesthetic questions in Anglo-Saxon countries. He considered fiction, "the great modern art," to be inferior to poetry but of more universal appeal and having qualities that distinguished it from other literary kinds. Its field was human life itself; it kept knowledge and feelings in their due relation while exhibiting character in action. Furthermore, it was the democratic art of the real (not of romance), aiming as it did at the "divine average," but could investigate mental phenomena and enter man's soul to discover the marvelous. Fully aware of the scientific bias of the age, which he discussed at length (including, of course, Zola),

Perry saw the "compensation" value of fiction and in particular of the psychological novel. He also saw their role as "criticism of life": the application of Matthew Arnold's definition to the novel implied a full recognition of its artistic nature as well. A glance at his—and Thompson's—chapter titles and sections immediately indicates the handbook quality of their approach.[6] They both got down to the specific questions of writing fiction, but with rather sketchy surveys of contemporary trends attached. Still, it is highly significant that through these books the debate on the novel reached a middlebrow audience, taking for granted and spreading a view of its artistic nature that was not wholly unquestioned, in James's phrase, some twenty years before.

In his final chapters Perry noted the growth in America of the short story form and underlined the Americans' excellence in limited fields; hence the difficulty in producing the Great American Novel and the tendency to create sectional fiction. He also stressed the fundamental morality and optimism of the American novel, while his definition of the current trend, realism, was rather guarded.[7] Both aspects reflected the developments of American theories of fiction in the last decade of the century toward genteel realism and regionalism.

II

The most articulate theory of realism in its genteel, "reticent," and sometimes limited sense was provided by William Dean Howells, the Dean of American Letters, a friend, adviser, and supporter of both Henry James and Mark Twain. Howells had begun his battle for realism quite early in his career, as editor of the *Atlantic Monthly,* spurred on by his firsthand knowledge of the Italian dramatist Carlo Goldoni as much as by his familiarity with contemporary French novelists. From the very first, he advocated "truth and sanity in fiction" and looked at life "without literary glasses." A sworn enemy, along with Mark Twain, of romantic fiction, he wanted novelists to portray men and women as they really were, to depict the average and the commonplace, to be ruled and inspired by common sense.

His clearest and most effective observations appeared in his column "Editor's Study" in *Harper's Magazine* in the late 1880s; these were then rather casually collected in his book *Criticism and Fiction* (1891). But his early essays also contain interesting views, as does his fiction where his ideas are sometimes openly discussed. (In his masterpiece, *The Rise of Silas Lapham,* for example, he extolled the commonplace as "that light, impalpable, aërial essence" that the novelist had to get into his books.) He had written about the Norwegian novelist Bjórson's portrayal "of humble but decent folk" and his "naturalness"; about Turgenev and Tolstoy (two of his acknowledged masters); about the Italian novelist Giovanni Verga—praising their mastery of the real, their direct sense of life (though for Bjórson and Turgenev he was significantly aware that theirs was a realism of the spiritual type, as opposed to the sensual type of the French). In his controversial essay "Henry James, Jr.," which had launched in 1882 the *querelle* over the Dickens and Thackeray novel and the new analytic school in America that took its inspiration from Hawthorne and George Eliot, Howells defended that type of novel that studied "human nature more in its wonted aspects," finding its "ethical and dramatic examples in the operation of lighter but not really less vital motives." As he wrote, "The moving accident is certainly not its trade; and it prefers to avoid all manner of dire catastrophe." It was, of course, the realism of Daudet rather than of Zola,[8] but even the emphasis Howells placed on analysis and on the comparative lack of incident was part of a theory of realism that he fully articulated in his "Editor's Study" series.

There are two contrasting opinions on the value of the original magazine series versus their version in book form. This is due to the hasty scissors-and-paste job that characterizes the latter, thus supposedly compromising the clarity and the context of Howells's formulations.[9] I shall refer mainly to the book (with occasional glimpses at the magazine versions) because *Criticism and Fiction* has the advantage—and historical value—of bringing together in a fairly coherent and unified way the ideas and observations that lay scattered in *Harper's Magazine,* where they ran the risk of appearing to be repetitive, casual, and uncontrolled. Furthermore, I think it is safe to assume that Howells included in the book what he considered to be the most important material.

Howells recognized that the scientific spirit of the age involved a rejection of idealism and romance, defended the commonplace as a source for fictional material, and called for naturalness in attitude and outline. "Truthful treatment of material," he held, had to take the place of the unreal, improbable, and purely fanciful treatments of romantic writers. In fact, adherence to the probable and the average was the best way of understanding things, the best way of fostering communion and sympathy among men. For Howells, the only romance was reality in its free and simple design. If common life was—or could be—dull, because of its lack of incident and drama, then it was the task of the novelist to mirror it as such. Howells's idea that the story was of relatively little importance was based on his desire to record life faithfully in its everday occurrences rather than in its impassioned and exceptional moments. In this sense he shared James's view that character was of greater importance than plot, that the novel should largely grow out of the natural unfolding of the character—as in Turgenev or James himself, for that matter. This implied a rejection of "sensationalism" (the type of novel developed in England by Wilkie Collins and his followers) as well as a rejection of intrigue as "unreal," that is, opposed to everyday life. (The "supreme form of fiction," he wrote in *My Literary Passions,* was *Don Quixote* with its free and simple design, "where event follows event without the faltering control of intrigue, but where all grows naturally out of character and conditions.")

At the same time, such a stance led to the avoidance of passion (and all that accompanied it), so that Howells was naturally led to advocate what he himself called "reticent realism."

The novel, of course, was not mere make-believe or simple entertainment: it had a function to perform, a seriousness to attain, a purpose to fulfill. Howells's positive theory of realism, in fact, led to an avowed moral conception of fiction according to which it was instrumental in bringing relief and fostering equality among men. Realism was particularly suited to democracy and thus to America in that it celebrated the common man and the basic goodness of the people. "Genteel" in attitude, it had to be circumscribed by the nature of the national experience it mirrored, where goodness and optimism were cardinal tenets of Americanism. "What is unpretentious and what is true is always beautiful and good," Howells wrote with disarming simplicity at the beginning of *Criticism and Fiction;* "Beauty is Truth, Truth Beauty," he quoted from John Keats; and, from Edmund Burke, the following: "an easy observation of the most common, sometimes of the meanest things, in nature will give the truest lights." The young writer must attempt "to report the phrase and carriage of every-day life," to tell "just how he has heard men talk and seen them look"; he must not follow models or celebrate heroic adventures. What the Spanish writer Armando Palacio Valdés called "effectism" had to be carefully avoided. This brought Howells back to "the divine Jane" (Jane Austen) and to a firm plea for the realistic quality of fiction:

> Realism is nothing more and nothing less than the truthful treatment of material, and Jane Austen was the first and the last of the English novelists to treat material with entire truthfulness. Because she did this, she remains the most artistic of the English novelists.

The line went from her to George Eliot to Trollope to Thomas Hardy. In chapter 18 Howells surveyed the risks involved in reading a novel—falsehood, wantonness, immorality, the vain posturings of the "gaudy hero and heroine," obsolete ideals and savage ethics—and came up with his well-known test for the validity of fiction:

> We must ask ourselves before we ask anything else, Is it
> true?—true to the motives, the impulses, the principles that
> shape the life of actual men and women? This truth, which
> necessarily includes the highest morality and the highest art-
> istry—this truth given, the book cannot be wicked and cannot
> be weak.

In Thomas Carlyle he found (and quoted) the formula that states that "the only genuine Romance (for grown persons), [is] Reality." Fiction must cease to lie about life: "let it portray men and women as they are . . . let it leave off painting dolls . . . let it speak the dialect, the language . . . of unaffected people," even in the face of the temptation of mere solace and entertainment; even in view of the fact that the historical romance, as practiced by Hawthorne, could offer worthy examples of a different type. What, indeed, distinguished the American from the English novel was the former's concern with character and naturalness of approach, as against "the love of the passionate and the heroic" of the latter. As Howells put it in one of his final pleas:

> If I were authorized to address any word directly to our
> novelists I should say, Do not trouble yourselves about stand-
> ards or ideals; but try to be faithful and natural: remember
> that there is no greatness, no beauty, which does not come
> from truth to your own knowledge of things.[10]

Yet, since the beginning, Howells declared (with George Eliot and Wordsworth as his sources) that realism seeks "to widen the bounds of sympathy," that it "pictures" rather than maps life: "Every true realist instinctively knows this . . . and feels himself bound to express or to indicate its meaning at the risk of overmoralizing. . . . He feels in every nerve the equality of things and the unity of men." This concept of the morality of fiction, and of realism in particular, was an essential thread in his theory. He quoted Valdés at length on the sadness and narrowness of French naturalism, writing that "the idea of the beautiful . . . is perforce moral." Disclaiming, against another Spanish novelist, Benito Pérez Galdós, the idea of art for art's sake, he held that the finest effects of the beautiful would be "ethical and not aesthetic." The novel could, after all, offer legitimate solace and relief to humankind; it could take the reader's mind off himself, make him forget life's cares and duties: "No sordid details of verity here, if you please," no sheer wretchedness and struggling. In fact, Howells ended his book with a plea for the didactic, as well as ethical, function of fiction:

> The art which in the mean time disdains the office of teacher is one of the last refuges of the aristocratic spirit which is disappearing from politics and society, and is now seeking to shelter itself in aesthetics. The pride of caste is becoming the pride of taste. . . . Democracy in literature is the reverse of all this. It wishes to know and tell the truth, confident that consolation and delight are there.

Here lie the springs of that "reticence" and those limitations that Howells imposed on realism. The field of the novel was not as open and as boundless as James had, at least theoretically, declared. Questions of taste, morality, and decorum restricted it. Howells was averse to the novel's "larger freedom" with the sexual passions, even with regard to the protection of the "young." In chapters 24 and 25, which were devoted entirely to the question, he motivated his espousal of "reticence" by arguing that passionate love was exceptional and therefore against the averageness of everyday life. The novel "was all the more faithfully representative of the tone of modern life in dealing with love that was chaste," he pointed out. "The guilty intrigue, the betrayal, the extreme flirtation even was the exceptional thing in life," and it would be "bad art to lug it in," he continued. There were many other passions one could write about, such as grief, avarice, pity, ambition, hate, envy, devotion, and friendship—"and all these have a greater part in the drama of life than the passion of love, and infinitely greater than the passion of guilty love." [11]

There was still another motive for reticence in the fact that the realistic novel was the characteristic genre of democracy and therefore especially suited to America. Now, not only was "the strength of the American novel in its optimistic faith" (as Howells put it in a rather notorious passage), but that faith was based on the favorable conditions of the American experience:

> it is one of the reflections suggested by Dostoievsky's novel, The Crime and the Punishment, that whoever struck a note so profoundly tragic in American fiction would do a false and mistaken thing . . . in a land where journeymen carpenters and plumbers strike for four dollars a day the sum of hunger and cold is comparatively small, and the wrong from class to class has been almost inappreciable, though all this is changing for the worse. Our novelists, therefore, concern themselves with the more smiling aspects of life, which are the more American, and seek the universal in the individual rather than the social interests. It is worth while, even at the risk of being called commonplace, to be true to our well-to-do actualities; the very passions themselves seem to be softened and modified by conditions which formerly at least could not be said to wrong any one, to cramp endeavor, or to cross lawful desire. [12]

Toward the end of the essay Howells seems to contradict this view by writing that "art, indeed, is beginning to find out that if it does not make friends with Need it must perish." This much John Ruskin understood all too well and, after him, William Morris. So, in his conclusion Howells emphasized, as we have seen, not only the optimistic but the didactic and humanitarian aspects of fiction as well. This emphasis was in turn due to one of the obvious implications of his theory of limited realism. If fiction could lighten the burden of the people, the writer was then obliged to consort and become one with the masses. As the typical genre of a democratic society, the realistic novel could become instrumental not only in widening the range of human sympathy but also in fostering equality. Hence, its didactic and moral purpose; hence Howells's Tolstoyan partisanship. Realism could instruct and enlighten the masses, and that seemed one of the main reasons for its being.[13]

III

One aspect that Howells developed at some length in his "Editor's Study" column and did not fully incorporate into *Criticism and Fiction* was the question of American literature and fiction. As the answer he gave bears directly on our next point of discussion—regionalism—I will discuss it at the end of this section. Toward the turn of the century, after Howells had given up his "Editor's Study" column and had become a "free-lance" writer, he devoted himself mainly to the cause of realism, both practically and critically, and to a series of literary reminiscences. The latter have more to do with his development as a writer and with the cultural trends of the period. As for his defense of realism, he became the outspoken champion of Hamlin Garland, Stephen Crane, Frank Norris, and James A. Herne, and he wrote of such foreign writers as Tolstoy and Henrik Ibsen with great fervor. Out of this battle a few (mainly corroborative) new touches were added to his theory of fiction. For example, he blasted Max Nordau's theory of "Degeneration" but heralded in Norris's *McTeague,* which was rather thoroughly imbued with that concept. Indeed, in 1902 Howells devoted a full-scale essay to this younger writer. Besides Garland's stories of the Middle West, which he valued for their grim and pitiless realism, he praised Crane's novels and sketches

of city life for their truthfulness and "fatal necessity"—a re-
cogniton of their naturalist bias. He also warmly reviewed
Abraham Cahan's *Yekl* and was ready to admit the use of
dialect in this type of fiction (another ingredient of regionalism).[14]

Through these writings Howells joined in the controversy
over naturalism that flared up in the 1890s, but kept on the
safe side in spite of his obvious interest in the new theories.
As he summed it up in an "Interview" in 1897, by combining truthfulness and conscience Tolstoy remained the best
realist of them all, since he put "honesty and kindness above
all heroism," never preached, and was always very clear
about the meaning of facts. In America, on the other hand,
it was Mark Twain, Harold Frederic, and Henry B. Fuller
who offered the best examples of social realism as defined
by the limits of Howells's taste. As foreshadowed by the last
pages of *Criticism and Fiction,* the latter's concept of realism
was based on an implicit meliorism, which, moreover, coincided nicely with the purposes of social usefulness. In this
context his interest in utopian fiction was quite logical; witness his 1898 essay on Edward Bellamy, as well as his own
significant contributions embodied in the Altrurian romances. One further point in this balanced view of the purposes, ways, and means of realism, of its possible themes
and implications, was Howells's recognition of the opportunity offered to American fiction by Thorstein Veblen's *Theory of the Leisure Class,* published in 1899. The rise of the
American magnate and his almost inevitable "intermarriage
with the European aristocracies, and residence abroad,"
seemed "the most dramatic social fact of our time." Both for
him and for James, here lay "the material of the great
American novel": the theme, in that it combined democracy
and the patrician class, was synthetic and comprehensive,
and allowed for a great deal of psychological and dramatic
play.[15]

Utopian explorations (by their very nature and genre
charged with ideological and melioristic current) and themes

based on the particular conditions of the leisure class confirmed Howells's preference for a genteel, rather than full-
fledged or proletarian, brand of realism—a bourgeois realism of decency and decorum that steered a safe middle
course. In his comprehensive essay "Novel-Writing and
Novel-Reading, An Impersonal Explanation" (which was
written in 1899 for a lecture tour, but published only in
1958), Howells developed a more general theory of the novel
that took into consideration the changing conditions of the
reading public and the age as a whole. Here boundaries and
limitations were to a considerable extent removed: "realism
excludes nothing that is true," he wrote. And again, the
"historical" type of narration, where the material is treated
as real history, was the great form of the novel, which was
in turn "the supreme literary form, the fine flower of the
human story."

Howells went on to reiterate his cherished concepts, according to which beauty means truth and truth beauty. Only
the false in art is ugly. But he went even further: "The truth
may be indecent, but it cannot be vicious, it can never corrupt or deprave." This should be said "in defense of the
grossest material honestly treated in modern novels," as
against the meretriciousness of those that preceded them.
(He had originally written "naturalistic novels" instead of
"modern novels" and "romantic novels" instead of "those
that preceded them.") His ideas could not have been made
clearer: "I make truth the prime test of a novel. If I do not
find that it is like life, then it does not exist for me as art; it
is ugly, it is ludicrous, it is impossible." Tolstoy's novels came
closest to this requirement, followed at some distance by the
usual list, which opened with Austen and George Eliot and
closed with Bjórson and Zola. On the other hand, Dickens
and Thackeray and Dumas and Juan Valera were untruth-
ful novelists, "working from an ideal of effect" as they did.
In Howells's opinion, the imagination could work "only with
the stuff of experience. It can absolutely create nothing; it
can only compose." The realist's categorical imperative was

the close and severe study of life; the reader would test the fictional results according to the degree of its truthfulness: "It will not avail that it has style, learning, thinking, feeling; it is no more beautiful without truth."

Howells defined the novel as "the sincere and conscientious endeavor to picture life just as it is, to deal with character as we witness it in living people, and to record the incidents that grow out of character"; and he distinguished it from romance, which dealt with life allegorically rather than representatively, employed types rather than characters, studied them in terms of the ideal rather than the real, and handled the passions broadly. The novel must also not be confused with the "romanticist novel," the novel that professed to portray actual life but that did so with an excess of drawing and coloring that were false to life (again, Dickens and Victor Hugo). The second and third types were on the wane. As for the novel, Howells went on to describe its moral and spiritual purposes. The novelist "had better not aim to please, and he had still better not aim to instruct; the pleasure and the instruction will follow from such measure of truth as the author has in him to such measure of truth as the reader has in him." If it is a work of art, the novel "promptly takes itself out of the order of polemics or of ethics, and primarily consents to be nothing if not aesthetical. . . . It shall do no good directly"—its mission is to the higher self of the reader; it must charm his mind and win his heart. It can teach "only by painting life truly."

To make sure that fidelity to life would not be carried too far, Howells introduced a further specification. He acknowledged the inescapable rift or hiatus existing between life and its reproduction, between reality and artistic rendering:

> After all, and when the artist has given his whole might to the realization of his ideal, he will have only an *effect* of life. I think the effect is like that in those cycloramas where up to a certain point there is real ground and real grass, and then carried indivisibly on to the canvas the best that the painter

can do to imitate real ground and real grass. We start in our novels with something we have known of life, that is, with life itself; and then we go on and imitate what we have known of life. If we are very skillful and very patient we can *hide the joint*. But the joint is always there, and on one side of it are real ground and real grass, and on the other are the painted images of ground and grass.[16]

Each novel had a law of its own, which it seemed to create for itself. Above all, "In fiction you cannot, if you would, strike twice in the same place." Still less, Howells went on, "can you twice treat the same theme. For the novelist there is no replica." In seeing the novel as a self-sufficient organism, Howells betrayed an almost twentieth-century awareness of its continual, unremitting, unrepeatable experimentation with subject and form. Every novel is a wholly new start; no rule, habit, or previous experience can determine its existence or ensure its success. The writer must live with it as an obsession, unable to free himself from thinking about it. And "history is never out of it . . . consciously or unconsciously it pervades his being." One senses here a premonition of the avant-garde, of the need to move ever forward: in his struggle with art the writer finds no repose. In short, fiction was for Howells "the chief intellectual stimulus of our time . . . the chief intellectual influence." He maintained that "scarcely any predicament, moral or psychological, has escaped its study"; once having dealt with the fable of princes, "now it includes all sorts and conditions of men . . . it compasses the whole of human nature." Moreover, Howells added, he was not sorry "to have had it go into the dark places of the soul, the filthy and squalid places of society, high and low, and shed there its great light. Let us know with its help what we are, and where we are. Let all the hidden things be brought into the sun, and let every day be the day of judgment. If the sermon cannot any longer serve this end, let the novel do it." This was one more reason why the report should be exact and the representation truthful. The novelist cannot transport life really into his story, any more than the cycloramist could carry the real ground and the real grass into his picture. But he will not rest till he has made his story as like life as he can, with the same mixed motives, the same voluntary and involuntary actions, the same unaccountable advances and perplexing pauses, the same moments of rapture, the same days and weeks of horrible dullness, the same conflict of the higher and lower purposes, the same vices and virtues, inspirations and propensities. He will not shun any aspect of life because its image will be stupid or gross, still less because its image will be incredibly noble and glorious. He will try to give that general resemblance which can come only from the most devoted fidelity to particulars.[17]

The representation of life in modern novels was distorted by the writer's urge to be startling and impressive. The novelist ought instead to "conceive the notion of letting the reader's imagination care for these things"; his own affair was "to arrange a correct perspective in which all things shall appear in their very proportion and relation." Thus, as for James, the whole of human life and human nature was open to the novel. Its author was a frame of vision, a window on the world, a provider of perspective, totally engrossed in his purpose. Fiction was the beginning and the end of his task. In more specific terms, Howells distinguished the autobiographical, the biographical, and the historical types of the novel. He considered the first to be "the most perfect literary form after the drama," since it was entirely within the writer's range of mastery even if it was limited to his inner experience and observation. The biographical novel must have a dominating central figure in order to be valid formally, while "the historical form is the great form." Howells was not referring here to the historical novel but to that kind of novel "whose material is treated as if it were real history." Here the writer can do anything—report and reconstruct as the historian does; enter the mind of his characters; give passages of dialogue; invent speeches, reveal their deepest thoughts, feelings, and desires; and move from the narrative to the dramatic form:

> He dwells in a world of his own creating, where he is a universal intelligence, comprehending and interpreting everything not indirectly or with any artistic conditions, but frankly and straightforwardly, without accounting in any way for his knowledge of the facts. The form involves a thousand contradictions, improbabilities. There is no point where it cannot be convicted of the most grotesque absurdity. The historian has got the facts from some one who witnessed them; but the novelist employing the historic form has no proof of them; he gives his word alone for them. . . .
>
> The historical form, though it involves every contradiction, every impossibility, is the only form which can fully represent any passage of life in its inner and outer entirety. It alone leaves nothing untouched, nothing unsearched. It is the primal form of fiction; it is epic.[18]

Howells insisted that this form was the least artistic, the least clever, "almost shapeless," and hardly amenable to symmetry—but for these very reasons was also closer to life. Yet one finds here a momentary disclaimer of his adherence to the principle of truthfulness: the novelist is his own master; fiction creates its own world. Howells seems to be carried away by a Jamesian recognition of the innumerable ways and endless possibilities of the novel, of its dignity and supreme *disponibilité*.

Most of Howells's references, here as elsewhere, were European. The question of *American* fiction hardly came up in this essay. Yet, he kept it in mind throughout most of his critical and theoretical work. His answer to James's list of the novelistic "properties" that were absent in America is well known: after setting these items aside, "we have the whole of human life remaining." In his letter of 1912, which he wrote on the occasion of Howells's seventy-fifth birthday, James himself recognized with a degree of half-concealed envy that Howells had succeeded, through his fiction, in giving a full picture of American life and manners. We have already pointed out Howells's late-nineteenth-century interest in the great social and fictional theme of the American magnate who expatriates to Europe, often to marry into the aristocracy. In *Criticism and Fiction,* however, he had taken up the question of the American novel in two crucial ways, which are worth considering here by way of conclusion.

In chapter 21 he accepted the view of the English essayist Eilian Hughes who noticed that whereas the English novel worked from within and then proceeded outward, the American novel worked from the outside and then proceeded inward. This was part of the quarrel over the analytic school, but Howells quoted and developed with approval the idea that American fiction possessed greater intellectual grip and greater penetration, less heroics and less concern with plot, a preference for the natural predicament, and a finer thread. Natural, investigative, discursive, refined in thought and spirit, the American novel reflected a different attitude from its English counterpart. Later, in an essay of 1901 on Mrs. Humphrey Ward's story "Eleanor," he maintained that while the English novel measured itself against society, the American measured itself against the psyche, not so much against the incidents of life, as against the "subliminal effects" of incidents. American novelists, who had to make "the most of the depth which seems to be their characteristic," were denied "English breadth." Howells argued that "to put it paradoxically, our life is too large for our art to be broad. In despair at the immense variety of the material offered it by American civilization, American fiction must specialize, and turning from the superabundance of character it must burrow far down in a soul or two." In this, contemporary realists were one with Hawthorne: "In their books, so faithful to the effects of our every-day life, the practical concerns of it are subordinated to the psychical." Psychological phenomena took the upper hand. The English were social, the Americans personal. (Here Howells came closer than he knew to James's views in his *Hawthorne* book.) "Their denser life, we will say, satisfies them with superficial contrasts, while in our thinner and more homogeneous society the contrasts that satisfy are subliminal"; this theory would justify English breadth versus American depth without mortifying either. Obvious geographical and historical differences were at play here. "Our personality is the consequence of our historic sparsity, and it survives beyond its time because the nature of our contiguity is still such as to fix a man's mind strongly upon himself," Howells repeated with de Tocqueville. (Changes would be brought about by the contemporary American's wish to travel and sojourn in foreign countries, notably Europe, and this would legitimize the "international theme" on representative as well as social grounds.)

Howells saw that America was a thinner but more homogeneous society. "For all aesthetic purposes the American people are not a nation, but a condition," he wrote in an 1891 "Editor's Study" column and he was tempted to see in this fact a spur to universality (rather than nationality) of approach and treatment.[19] Yet the opposite outcome was more natural, and as such it was often taken up by Howells: American conditions pointed rather to sectionalism and regionalism. Ontologically speaking, regionalism is a condition, and often a danger, of any radical realistic approach. If a writer had to write of what he knew and had experienced, more often than not he would have to rely on—and be bound by—his immediate surroundings, what he had experienced in depth rather than in geographical extension. If in realistic portraiture the use of imagination was barred and lifelikeness extolled, then all chances were rather restricted to one's soil and one's region, to one's particular geographical and social environment. This tendency to "narrowness" of scope was implicit—as a feature, I insist, as much as a danger—in most theories of realism and certainly in the practice of the realistic novel: from Giovanni Verga to Alphonse Daudet and Pierre Loti, from Flaubert to Galdós or Valdés. Howells recognized this fact in chapter 23 of

Criticism and Fiction: the "restricted range" could be found in England as in Italy, in France as in Norway, in Spain as in Russia (with the exceptions of Zola and Tolstoy).

This tendency was even stronger in America, owing to the enormous expanse of its geography and its deep regional differences. How else could one explain the growth of regional writers and their attempts to make one region known to another, one section familiar to another? Decentralization operated here as in other areas, "and the novelist is not superior to the universal rule against universality", he wrote, owning that "as I turn over novels coming from Philadelphia, from New Mexico, from Boston, from Tennessee, from rural New England, from New York, every local flavor of diction gives me courage and pleasure." Especially in his "Editor's Study" column and in his essay "Dialect in Literature" (1895), Howells often paused to discuss and welcome "regional" writers among whom one might mention James Russell Lowell, Poe, Cable, Thomas Nelson Page, Mary E. Wilkins, Sarah Orne Jewett, Artemus Ward, Petroleum V. Nasby, Joel Chandler Harris, Harriet Beecher Stowe, Bret Harte, Hamlin Garland, and Mark Twain, who helped to create what one might call the composed unity of American fiction. Howells wrote that "the writer who is able to acquaint us intimately with half a dozen people, or the conditions of a neighborhood or a class, has done something which cannot in any bad sense be called narrow; his breadth is vertical instead of lateral, that is all; and this depth is more desirable than horizontal expansion in a civilization like ours, where the differences are not of classes, but of types, and not of types either so much as of characters." Moreover, these writers were to write in the local idiom, "true American, with all the varying Tennessean, Philadelphian, Bostonian, and New York accents," without a loss of dignity or depth. Cases in point were the Venetian Carlo Goldoni and the Sicilian Verga, Hardy and possibly Dickens in England, Zola with his Parisian slang, and of course Mark Twain in America.

One final point that Howells touched upon was the growth and the spread of the short story in America. As he put it in chapter 21 of *Criticism and Fiction,* given the sparseness of the American scene, writers excelled "in small pieces with three or four figures, or in studies of rustic communities"; hence, as Julian Hawthorne had already noted, the American preference for the short story (including Thanksgiving and Christmas stories). Howells no more than flirted with Poe's idea that the novel itself was basically a grouping of tales: "A big book is necessarily a group of episodes more or less loosely connected by a thread of narrative." He refused to believe that the popularity of the short story was due to American hurry. Rather, it was due to the development of the American magazine, and to the growth of regionalism that was intrinsic to the new continent.[20]

IV

Just as he had praised Henry James, the use of the international theme, and the novel of manners for their realism, on various occasions Howells also praised Mark Twain for his adherence to life and his adoption of local dialects, for using "in extended writing the fashion we all use in thinking"—for flouting literary conventions altogether. East and West were both valid subject matter: Twain had naturalized the West in a profoundly serious, almost tragic way.

Twain, as we saw at the end of Part I, espoused the idea that the tale was a peculiarly American form because of its oral origins. He had few things to say from a theoretical point of view, but what he said was important. Storytelling was superior to fiction writing, which flourished only as storytelling; regionalism was not only a condition but an imperative of American writing; and, as a result, slang and dialect were the proper language to cultivate. These three points can be seen as corollaries of a realist approach; humor—a common ingredient in the writing of Twain and other regionalists—was narrative spice but not necessarily a condition. The frontier or western tradition of the tall tale, from which he drew original inspiration, could provide picturesque features, but what mattered was the writer's application. Naturally suspicious of theory, Twain was all for direct knowledge, observation, and a realistic approach. He had learned to be a writer on the Mississippi River and wrote that "experience is an author's most valuable asset." In a note written in 1888, he stressed the need for a factual basis in fiction:

> If you attempt to create a wholly imaginary incident, adventure or situation, you will go astray and the artificiality of the thing will be detectable, but if you found on a *fact* in your personal experience it is an acorn, a root, and every created adornment that grows out of it, and spreads its foliage and blossoms to the sun, will seem reality, not invention.

The idea of organic form, which was implicit here, became explicit in his *Autobiography*, where we read that "narrative should flow as flows the brook . . . always flowing . . . the law of *narrative* which has *no law*." In a letter to George Bainton dated 1891, Twain doubted that there was a conscious method of composition; the writer's training was unconscious or half conscious at most. The taste that guided one functioned automatically. Perhaps the search for the right word was a question of choice and composition; but in the realm of method Twain stressed what André Gide would have called "la part de Dieu," the hand of God that intervenes mysteriously in the writing process.[21]

Unconscious absorption was thus more important than conscious observation for the novelist because it took years to reach the proper level of saturation:

> How much of his competency is derived from conscious "observation"? The amount is so slight that it counts for next to nothing in equipment. Almost the whole capital of the nov-

elist is the slow accumulation of *un*conscious observation—absorption.

This is what Twain wrote in an essay that appeared in the *North American Review* in 1895, and behind this view lay Twain's preference for regionalism: "There is only one expert who is qualified to examine the souls and the life of a people and make a valuable report—the native novelist." This native writer needed a good twenty-five years of absorption in, rather than intentional observation of, manners, speech, character, and ways of life; but, Twain continued, "I should be astonished to see a foreigner get at the right meanings, catch the elusive shades of these subtle things. Even the native novelist becomes a foreigner, with a foreigner's limitations, when he steps from the State whose life is familiar to him into a State whose life he has not lived." Twain then gave the example of Bret Harte whose career waned as he went from California to the Atlantic, and he seemed unaware of the danger that such a restriction of the writer's scope and potentialities implied. Yet, the wider meanings are relevant here: the local novelist will not generalize about the nation but will concentrate on "narrow" realities. America in fiction will be the sum of those realities:

> To return to novel-building. Does the native novelist try to generalize the nation? No, he lays plainly before you the ways and speech and life of a few people grouped in a certain place—his own place—and that is one book. In time, he and his brethren will report to you the life and the people of the whole nation—the life of a group in a New England village; in a New York village; in a Texan village; in an Oregon village; in villages in fifty States and Territories; then the farm-life in fifty States and Territories; a hundred patches of life and groups of people in a dozen widely separated cities. And the Indians will be attended to; and the cowboys; and the gold and silver miners; and the negroes; and the Idiots and Congressmen; and the Irish, the Germans, the Italians, the Swedes, the French, the Chinamen, the Greasers; and the

Catholics, the Methodists, the Presbyterians, the Congrega-
tionalists, the Baptists, the Spiritualists, the Mormons, the
Shakers, the Quakers, the Jews, the Campbellites, the infi-
dels, the Christian Scientists, the Mind-Curists, the Faith-
Curists, the train-robbers, the White Caps, then [*sic*] Moon-
shiners. And when a thousand able novels have been written,
there you have the soul of the people, the life of the people,
the speech of the people; and not anywhere else can these be
had. And the shadings of character, manners, feelings, am-
bitions, will be infinite.

I have quoted this passage in full because the ideal of
regionalism is here expressed in all its purity and force, as
well as in some of its shortcomings. As for causes, another
was that "there isn't a single human characteristic that can
be safely labelled 'American.' " Twain went on to explain
that no single human detail, inside or outside, could "ra-
tionally be generalized as 'American.' " Peculiarities did not
exist as "American"; there was no "American temperament"
as such. Twain was skeptical of "generalized" human peculiarities even in other nations. ("Devotion to ice-water," he
found, with his typical humor, to be an American specialty.)
Only adherence to *local* features, aspects, and tempera-
ments would eventually contribute to the formation of an
American epic and express the American soul or temperament.[22] This included the use of local dialects (provided the
writer knew them well and managed to be consistent), an
"exceedingly difficult" task. Twain's note at the beginning
of *Huckleberry Finn* about the dialects he had used there—
"the Missouri negro dialect; the extremest form of the back-
woods Southwestern dialect; the ordinary 'Pike County dialect'; and four modified varieties of this last"—made it clear
that a great amount of literary skill was required: "The
shadings have not been done in a haphazard fashion, or by
guesswork; but painstakingly, and with the trustworthy
guidance and support of personal familiarity with these several forms of speech."
Slang and dialect, which many of Twain's contemporaries

used merely for purposes of local color or picturesqueness, were for Twain a mainstay of realism and expressiveness and were to achieve full literary dignity (in *Huckleberry Finn* they were used not simply to reflect an environment but to express the vision and the nature of Twain's "uncivilized" young protagonist). Regionalism (and humor) allowed for truthfulness and an adherence, not only to life, but also to authenticity. This is why Twain blasted romance and romantic notions. On one particular occasion, in his "Fenimore Cooper's Literary Offenses" of 1895, he came closest to formulating his poetics of the novel in terms of direct application. His "nineteen rules governing literary art in the domain of romantic fiction"—eighteen of which Cooper had violated in *The Deerslayer*—required that episodes and characters should serve a coherent purpose; that characters should be alive, clearly defined, relevant, and consistent in both speech and action; that personages confine themselves to possibilities and let miracles alone; that directness and precision of language, economy and tautness of form, and "a single and straightforward style" be achieved. It seems quite evident that Twain was mainly interested here, as elsewhere, in the construction and behavior of character and, understandably, less in questions of plot. Granting his polemical attitude, however, this was again proof of his reliance on realism—even if he himself, as novelist, was to produce a notorious example of genteel, limited, indeed repressed fictional works.

The importance of regionalism for American fiction, and its connection with local dialects, was underlined by Edward Eggleston in his 1892 Preface to *The Hoosier Schoolmaster*. He believed that his novel was the file leader in "the most significant movement in American literature in our generation," that is, the dialect novel. On the wave of the New England folk speech of James Russell Lowell, which had acquired the standing of a classic *lingua rustica*, new areas of speech and life were opened in the United States, at first in the direction of rude burlesque stories, then in that of serious fiction. Eggleston wrote:

> The taking up of life in this regional way has made our literature really national by the only process possible. The Federal nation has at length manifested a consciousness of the continental diversity of its forms of life. The "great American novel," for which prophetic critics yearned so fondly twenty years ago, is appearing in sections.

Eggleston felt that he was the first "to depict a life quite beyond New England influence" in its dialect and attitude. Bret Harte was credited—as usual—with foreshadowing "this movement toward a larger rendering of our life. But the romantic character of Mr. Harte's delightful stories and the absence of anything that can justly be called dialect in them mark them as rather forerunners than beginners of the prevailing school," Eggleston wrote. What he termed "provincial realism" was thus qualified by the presence of local dialect and by the absence of superficial comic intentions. His was rather a Biedermeier, Dutch school-of-painting sort of realism inspired by Taine ("It chanced that in 1871 Taine's lectures on 'Art in the Netherlands' . . . fell into my hands. . . . These discourses are little else than an elucidation of the thesis that the artist of originality will work courageously with the materials he finds in his environment.") Yet Eggleston's first motivation was linguistic—the use of dialect:

> Many years previous to the time of which I am now speaking, while I was yet a young man, I had projected a lecture on the Hoosier folk-speech, and had even printed during the war a little political skit in that dialect in a St. Paul paper. So far as I know, nothing else had ever been printed in the Hoosier. Under the spur of Taine's argument, I now proceeded to write a short story wholly in the dialect spoken in my childhood by rustics on the north side of the Ohio River.[23]

On at least two important occasions, the writer Hjalmar Hjorth Boyesen wrote about realism in America: the first to denounce the influence exercised by the young American girl, the "Iron Madonna who strangles in her fond embraces the American novelist" by making him write limited, genteel, and repressed fiction lacking all evidence of sex and politics; the second, in an essay of 1892 on "The Progressive Realism of American Fiction." After a survey of American novelists touching upon Cooper, Poe, Hawthorne, Stowe, Bret Harte, and Howells, Boyesen maintained that it was "because the American novel has chosen to abandon 'the spirit of romance,' which never was indigenous on this continent, and devoted itself to the serious task of studying and chronicling our own social conditions," that it now commanded so much attention. For him, Howells was the very epitome of realism—neither the "extreme wing which believes only that to be true which is disagreeable" nor "the minute insistence upon wearisome detail, which, ignoring the relation of artistic values, fancies that a mere agglomeration of incontestable facts constitutes a truthful picture." As he put it, and rather well at that: "Broadly speaking, a realist is a writer who adheres strictly to the logic of reality, as he sees it; who, aiming to portray the manners of his time, deals by preference with the normal rather than the exceptional phases of life, and, to use Henry James's felicitous phrase, arouses not the pleasure of surprise, but that of recognition." Yet the main point of Boyesen's argument, by his own admission, was that "nothing could testify with more force to the fact that we have outgrown romanticism than this almost unanimous desire, on the part of our authors, to chronicle the widely divergent phases of our American civilization. There are scarcely a dozen conspicuous states now which have not their own local novelist."[24]

If some saw regionalism as a triumph of American fiction, others considered it with a degree of mistrust and reservation, ridiculing the excesses of the local colorists. After noticing the lack of the so often invoked Great American Novel, an anonymous writer for the *Nation* lamented in 1892 that "meanwhile, American fiction has distinctly forsaken the expansive and the illimitable to run after the contracted and the limited. Instead of a national novel, we now have a rapidly accumulating series of regional novels—or, rather, so far has the subdividing and minimizing process gone, of local tales, neighborhood sketches, short stories confined to the author's back-yard." This writer suggested that "leaving the prairie and taking up with the pasture," American fiction was guilty of parochialism (just as in other quarters it was guilty of cosmopolitanism). For William B. Chisholm, writing in 1897 in *The Critic,* regionalism was in constant danger of being passé: like the international novel, dialect stories could not be a final type but only a stepping-stone to future developments. They "have pictured a state of life and manners which is rapidly disappearing," Chisholm wrote, and continued: "Even sectional *differentiae* have been so much modified that a novel of twenty or thirty years ago would hardly picture the average American of to-day."[25] The danger of sketchiness, fragmentation, of picturesqueness for its own sake and of unintentional caricature was indeed inherent in sectionalism and regionalism; so was the risk of sentimentality, of romanticizing small geographical areas (as one romanticized small virtues), which was, for instance, apparent in Bret Harte—the recognized leader of regionalism for most contemporaries, who did not, however, develop a theory of this genre. For Edward Noyes Wescott, in his Introduction to his novel *David Harum, A Story of American Life* (1899), regionalism was a result of the "hybridization" of American society based on its extraordinary mixing of races. The differences in human and racial types, together with the diversities of the environment ranging from the Everglades of Florida to Alaska, had resulted in "a gallery of brilliant *genre* pictures which to-day stand for the highest we have yet attained in the art of fiction." Wescott's list of regional novelists justified the claim that every section of the country had, or was in the process of getting, its own painter and historian—each of whom had carefully chosen for his field of study that part of the country "wherein he passed the early and formative years of his life."

That regionalism in the 1890s was the most frequent and widely spread answer to the need for truthfulness and realism in fiction was made evident by handbooks like Bliss Perry's *A Study of Prose Fiction* (which focused on regionalism as well as on realism) and by the role it played, as a starting point rather than as a point of arrival, in the works of Hamlin Garland and Frank Norris. Along with James, both of these writers contributed significantly to the theory of the novel toward the end of the nineteenth century. Their role, therefore, will be examined in the following chapters. A few preliminary remarks here will suffice.

For Garland (who rejected provincialism), regionalism and local color were inherent characteristics not only of the American experience but of fiction itself; they were its condition and support. "Local color in fiction is demonstrably the life of fiction," he wrote in *Crumbling Idols* (1894); "It is the native element, the differentiating element." Garland distinguished it from the study of the picturesque and italicized the following observation: *"Local color in a novel means that it has such quality of texture and back-ground that it could not have been written in any other place or by any one else than a native."* Devoting two chapters of his book to "Local Color in Art" and "The Local Novel," he made it clear that it was one of the central issues of the day and of fictional practice in general. "Localism," as he called it, was present in Chaucer as well as in contemporary European and American writers. Thus, the "local novel seems to be the heir-apparent to the kingdom of poesy," he wrote. Yet, it is "hopelessly contemporaneous," natural, and spontaneous; it "means national character" and "will redeem American literature" by allowing for the treatment of subjects until then excluded from fiction; the Negro, the southern rebel, urban life, the slums. The local novel will be colloquial and will use "the actual speech of the people of each locality" because "dialect is the life of a language." For Garland, local color was the great test of sincerity and of truthfulness of inspiration; it was the mark that narrative was rooted in reality. More than once (as we shall see), he insisted that the writer had to write out of his experience. Yet local color, according to his other tenet, ensured that the novelist would give his personal, individual view of the facts as well. Localism was a principle of individuality that checked universalizing tendencies: "It is the subtle coloring individuality gives which vitalizes landscape art," just as subtle differences in the interpretation of life vitalize literature.[26] As such, local color became part of Garland's theory of "veritism" and impressionism. It was also part of his drive to herald in the West (up to and including the Pacific coast) as the great, open field for fiction.

Regionalism served a similar purpose in Frank Norris's theory. It was a ground or a pretext for the Great American Novel, and a means through which the West could find a place in fiction—both as a natural, rural, geographical expansion, as the scene of new types of budding industrialism, and as a land of crucial human confrontations and developments.[27] In both writers there was more than an echo of the American frontier as it was reaching toward its final goal in the West (Norris devoted a chapter of his book on the theory of the novel to "The Frontier Gone at Last"). And it must be noted, in conclusion, that both Garland and Norris, after having stressed its importance, went beyond the concept of regionalism and local color as it was understood in the 1890s—that is, as a corollary or condition of realism. For Garland, it served the purposes of his concept of veritism, which was heavily colored by impressionistic epistemology. For Norris, it led to a new, and very personal vision and version of romance.

NOTES

1. The author was a New York lawyer, the author of such titles as "A System of Psychology" and "The Problem of Evil." An English equivalent

would be Ernest Sweetland Dallas's *The Gay Science* (London: Chapman and Hall, 1866), in particular chapters 16 and 17, where the prevalence of prose fiction in the contemporary age was studied in terms of growth of the reading public, the rise of individualism and the private man, the feminine influence, and so on.

2. Daniel Greenleaf Thompson, *The Philosophy of Fiction in Literature, An Essay* (New York: Longmans, Green and Co., 1890), pp. 3–4, 7–8, 10, 22, 25, 31, 35, 42, 44, 49, 58.

3. Ibid., pp. 51–52, 55–57, 59, 68–70, 82.

4. Ibid., pp. 202, 136–37, 148. It is interesting to note that Thompson referred to "popular" as well as to "high" treatments of the subjects: to G. L. Lathrop's essay (discussed in chapter 4) and to David Masson's *British Novelists and their Styles* (Cambridge, 1859; reprinted New York; Arno Press, 1973).

5. Thompson, *The Philosophy of Fiction in Literature*, pp. 172–73, 192, 200, 216–25.

6. Bliss Perry, *A Study of Prose Fiction* (Boston: Houghton Mifflin, 1902); besides quoting the more obvious critical texts on the novel, from Maupassant to Zola, Perry cited in an appendix at least half a dozen end-of-the-century handbooks on fiction (pp. 366–67 and passim).

7. Ibid., p. 229: *"Realistic fiction is that which does not shrink from the commonplace* (although art dreads the commonplace) *or from the unpleasant* (although the aim of art is to give pleasure) *in its effort to depict things as they are, life as it is"* (Perry's italics).

8. See William Dean Howells, *Representative Selections*, ed. Clara Marburg Kirk and Rudolf Kirk (New York: American Book Co., 1950), pp. cxxxiii ff.; *European and American Masters*, ed. Clara Marburg Kirk and Rudolf Kirk (New York: Collier, 1963), pp. 32–35, 49, 24–25, and passim.

9. See Everett Carter, *Howells and the Age of Realism* (Philadelphia: Lippincott, 1950), chap. 4 ("Critical Realism"), sec. 5 ("The Invalidation of *Criticism and Fiction*"); most of the original series is reprinted, with commentaries and a useful bibliography, in Edwin H. Cady, *William Dean Howells as Critic* (London: Routledge and Kegan Paul, 1973), pp. 73–212, ("The Editor's Study," 1886–92).

10. William Dean Howells, *Criticism and Fiction* (New York: Harper, 1891), pp. 3, 6, 7, 10, 15–16, 60, 63–64, 73–77, 98–99, 103–4, 123, 145.

11. Ibid., pp. 15–16, 59–60, 82–83, 105–7, 187.

12. Ibid., pp. 147–62, 123, 128–29. For a discussion of the context of these statements, see Cady, *Howells as Critic*, pp. 89–90.

13. See Howells, *Criticism and Fiction*, pp. 184–85, 188: "Neither arts, nor letters, nor sciences, except as they somehow, clearly or obscurely, tend to make the race better and kinder, are to be regarded as serious

interests; they are all lower than the rudest crafts that feed and house and clothe, for except they do this office they are idle; and they cannot do this except from and through the truth." See also Donald Pizer, "The Evolutionary Foundation of W. D. Howells's *Criticism and Fiction*," in his *Realism and Naturalism in Nineteenth-Century American Literature* [1967] (New York: Russell and Russell, 1976), pp. 37–52 (also pp. 67–87).

14. See Cady, *Howells as Critic*, pp. 112–20, 202–12, 397–405, 257–62, 232–42.

15. Ibid., pp. 268–91, where his "Interview" and his essays on Bellamy and Veblen are printed side by side (p. 288 for quotes).

16. *Howells and James: A Double Billing* (New York: The New York Public Library, 1958); pp. 8–10, 14–15. This pamphlet includes "Novel-Writing and Novel-Reading" by Howells, ed. William M. Gibson, and "Henry James and the *Bazar* Letters," ed. Leon Edel and Lyall H. Powers.

17. Ibid., pp. 16–17, 20–21. Howells expressed here, as elsewhere, a dislike for the love story, telling how he and James tried to "eliminate the everlasting young man and young woman" (p. 19).

18. Ibid., pp. 22–24.

19. See Cady's *Howells as Critic*, pp. 206–12 (see pp. 51–55 for Howells's 1880 review of James's *Hawthorne*); Richard Ruland, ed., *A Storied Land* (New York: Dutton 1976), pp. 188–92, for Howells's essay on Mrs. Humphrey Ward.

20. Howells, *Criticism and Fiction*, pp. 135, 142–43, 137, 131; Cady, *Howells as Critic*, pp. 238–42 (pp. 337–51 for Howells's 1901 appraisal of Twain).

21. See Edward H. Goold, Jr., "Mark Twain on the Writing of Fiction," *American Literature*, 26 (1954): 141–53, where most of the references are given; the basic texts are in Ruland, ed., *A Storied Land*, pp. 126–46 (also for what follows).

22. Ruland, ed., *A Storied Land*, pp. 126–28 (and pp. 131–32, 136–46, for what follows).

23. Ibid., pp. 122–23.

24. Ibid., pp. 154–58 (and pp. 145–53 for Boyesen's previous essay).

25. Ibid., pp. 219–21 and 225–26.

26. Hamlin Garland, *Crumbling Idols: Twelve Essays on Art Dealing Chiefly with Literature, Painting and the Drama*, ed. Jane Johnson (Cambridge: Harvard University Press, Belknap Press, 1960), pp. 49–50, 53–54, 59–63. See also chapter 7, below.

27. See Frank Norris, *The Responsibilities of the Novelist* [1903] (New York: Hill and Wang, 1967; American Century Series), published together with Howells's *Criticism and Fiction*, and chapter 8, below.

7.
NATURALISM, VERITISM, AND IMPRESSIONISM

—•—

I

THE COMMON TERM "extreme realism" was one of the names given to French *Naturalisme*. Its theoretical significance was superbly defined by Zola in his *Le roman expérimental* (1880). Zola's idea was that the novelist should go about his work like a research scientist carrying out an experiment. In other words, he should seek to discover the laws that govern human life and society with all the detachment required by laboratory testing. "What I care most about," Zola had written, "is to be purely naturalistic, purely psychological. Instead of principles (monarchy, Catholicism) I shall have laws (heredity, atavism)." The laws were, in fact, those of biological and environmental determinism. The novel was to be "une expérience 'pour voir' "—to *see*, establish, and reveal how those laws operated on the individual and in the social context. As he put it in two major statements: [1]

> I judge that the question of heredity has a great influence on man's intellectual and emotional manifestations. I also attach great importance to environment. . . . This is what constitutes the experimental novels: to master the phenomena of man, to show the ravages of intellectual and sensual manifestations as explained by physiology, under the influence of heredity and environmental circumstances, and then to show man living in the social *milieu* which he himself produced, which he modifies every day, and within which he in turn is continually transformed.

This strategy implied or favored the study of the processes of degeneration, both on the physiopsychological and on the social levels. The "experimental" novelist was to pursue, analyze, and illustrate both individual passions and social diseases. In the background, of course, loomed the Darwinian theory of evolution, which fascinated as well as frightened much of the century. Since, moreover, the "laws" of Social Darwinism and environmental determinism implied the prevalence of the strongest—including the ruthless and the unscrupulous—and the conditioning of brutal forces of avarice and greed, blind competition and conflict—the principle of the *homo homini lupus*—the illustration of those laws could be turned into a denunciation of the ideological and social evils besetting contemporary society. The "survival of the fittest" and man's dependence on surrounding conditions that were imposed on him implied processes of "impersonal" violence and submission that it was the novelist's task to expose. All this meant that the novel had a purpose—that it was, to use the French term, a *roman à thèse*—exposure and denunciation of personal and social evils were part of its purpose. It also meant that an insistence on biological and social determinism gave a different perspective to the whole issue of personal guilt and moral responsibility: To what extent was man to be held responsible, if under the sway of impersonal, brutal, and overpowering forces in battleground or prison conditions outside his control? These elements accounted for the uneasiness and sometimes open hostility that naturalism caused.

As much as Zola was read and discussed, comparatively little theoretical attention was given to these theories in England. It was mostly a question of disclaimers; adherence was partial and carefully qualified. English and American theories of naturalism were obviously derived from France, were heatedly debated, and were then rather quickly left to cool. In most cases, they were expressions of compromise. More often than not, naturalism was simply dismissed to bring it down to size, to adapt it to forms more suitable to Anglo-Saxon balance. Thus, the more interesting definitions were often in negative terms, resulting from disputes or refutations, and they often led to different emphases and results. George Moore and George Gissing are two representative and well-known cases; they were early converts to the cause of naturalism and yet dealt with it in idiosyncratic ways.[2]

In 1885 Moore criticized the hypocrisies and the restrictions of the fictional market in his pamphlet *Literature at Nurse, or Circulating Morals,* where he attacked Mudie's circulating libraries for exercising a stifling form of indirect censure. There he also advocated the inclusion of fact in fiction and set forth a number of naturalistic principles: "To analyze, you must have a subject; a religious or sensuous passion is as necessary to a realistic novel as a disease is to a physician. The dissection of a healthy subject would not, as a rule, prove interesting." The novelist must be granted "the right to probe and comment on humanity's failings"; the century "should possess a literature characteristic of its nervous, passionate life," which was by its very nature impossible to reconcile with young girls. Moore wrote of his interest in French naturalism in *Confessions of a Young Man* (1888), where he also expanded on his interest in decadentism and aestheticism, subjects that he took up in various essays as well. The novel was for him an artistic endeavor; it should aim at organic form, logical development, and rhythmic inevitableness. "Art is not nature. Art is nature digested," he wrote; the impersonality of the artist was an illusion.

Gissing also believed in a "novel with a purpose," in the social implications of fiction, which had to deal with actuality and to interpret life (including the hidden mechanism of the human heart) with "scientific" accuracy. He was one of the first, and one of the few, to treat the "netherworld" in fiction. Yet, as early as 1883, he wrote that he was addressing those who loved art for its own sake and that he did not believe in the impersonality of the novelist. His essay "The Place of Realism in Fiction" (1895) identified realism and naturalism with sincere treatment and unconventionality:

> Let the novelist take himself as seriously as the man of science; be his work to depict with rigid faithfulness the course of life, to expose the secrets of the mind, to show humanity in its eternal combat with fate. No matter how hideous or heart-rending the results; the artist has no responsibility save to his artistic conscience.

But he then ended by extolling the art, rather than the "purpose," of fiction. Discarding even the abused term *realism*, Gissing wanted to judge a work of fiction entirely on the basis of sincerity and craftsmanship. Reality had a different meaning in art than in science. He maintained that the writer's vision of reality must be filtered subjectively, and he felt attracted by what he called the recent method of "simply suggesting," of telling a story as in real life by hints and guesses. He favored the dramatic rather than the illustrative method of presentation and eschewed documentation. There was no "science of fiction" (another period term for naturalism) in Gissing's opinion, then; the novelist, moreover, "must recognize limits in every direction."

In his "Limits of Realism in Fiction"—an essay that in 1890 he could get published only in an American magazine, *Forum*—Edmund Gosse, a pundit of the age, analyzed with balanced care the issue of naturalism, only to conclude that it was on the wane. "The naturalistic school is really less advanced, less thorough, than it was ten years ago," he wrote and then went on to list its weak points. Life was elusive, and one could make a portrait of one corner of it in an imaginative, not a photographic way; the "disinterested"— that is, detached—attitude was in practice a snare and led to a contemplation of crime and frailty. By trying to "draw life evenly and to draw it whole," the naturalists had introduced "such a brutal want of tone as to render the portrait a caricature"; they had "pushed away with their scientific pitchfork the fantastic and intellectual elements." Gosse acknowledged that they had produced a huge and durable work of fiction, that realism had done the novel a great deal of good, but felt that the "experimental" school was in decline and was turning more and more to psychology and mysticism. Naturalism had been a phase, perhaps necessary, but certainly "surmountable" in the history of the novel. "The limits of realism have been reached," he concluded. No novelists would now adopt the experimental system; they would rather aim "to the human instinct for mystery and beauty." Gosse was prophetic here, for such a trend would indeed characterize the turn of the century. But, in his essay "The Tyranny of the Novel" (1892), he upheld Zola's mastery over the mechanisms of society, his grasp of the modern masses in their incessant movement, and he acknowledged the "experiments" of Moore and Gissing.[3]

Gosse referred to a period of open hostility to naturalism, which coincided with the late 1880s and early 1890s, when it came under attack for its "beastliness" and immorality, for its treatment of sex and its "intrusive and unmanly" analysis of morbid states, and for its social philosophy. Those who led the attack declared that it no longer presented man as lord of his fate but as a being physiologically and socially "determined." Free will and individual moral responsibility were thus jeopardized. Naturalism was branded as "the conquering anarch of our time." The opposition reached its peak with the two trials (1888 and 1889) of Zola's publisher in England, Henry Vizetelly, who was fined in the first and sentenced to three months' imprisonment in the second. A cautious reversal in attitude then followed, with essays such as Edmund Gosse's (and Vernon Lee's "The Moral Teaching of Zola," 1893) offering a more temperate reconsideration of the issue.[4] Still, when the *New Review* held a symposium on "The Science of Fiction" in 1891, most respondents rejected the scientific claims of naturalism as pretentious.

II

A representative, and for our purposes conclusive, case was provided by Thomas Hardy, the writer whose novels seemed to come very close to embodying some of the basic tenets of naturalism: man as "determined" by family and social circumstance, the "sport of fate" over human actions, the depiction of "low life" and elementary psychologies, the use of dialect (evident, for instance, in *Tess of the d'Urbervilles,* 1891). In his contribution to "The Science of Fiction" symposium, Hardy recognized "the codified law of things as they are," the need for a "comprehensive and accurate knowledge of realities," but only as a starting point. "The exercise of Art" was of greater importance, in his opinion. He discussed Zola's *Le roman expérimental* but repudiated "such conformation of storywriting to scientific processes", in that "the Daedalian faculty for selection and cunning manipulation" remained essential. "The phantasmagoria of experience" could hardly be reproduced in its entirety; only the "illusion of truth" could be captured. Hardy admitted that he was sympathetic toward the hyperbolic claims made on behalf of a realism of substance and contours, but he dismissed the method of photographic copying in favor of "what cannot be discerned by eye or ear, what may be apprehended only by the mental tactility that comes from a sympathetic appreciativeness of life in all its manifestations." Here and in other writings, Hardy insisted in the reproduction or projection of impressions, rather than on fidelity to facts.

In a notebook entry of 1892, he specified that "in getting at the truth, we only get at the true nature of the impression that an object, etc., produces on us." Two years earlier he had written that "art is a changing of the actual proportions and order of things, so as to bring out more forcibly than might otherwise be done that feature in them which appeals most strongly to the idiosyncrasy of the artist." Art had to increase the sense of *vraisemblance;* yet, it was also a "disproportioning—(i.e., distorting, throwing out of proportion)—of realities"; hence, " 'realism' is not Art." The novelist thus had to rely on his own eyes and on what appealed to his individual temperament and idiosyncrasies, on his "seeing into the *heart of a thing,*" or on what Matthew Arnold had called "the imaginative reason." Fiction for Hardy, in other words, was not objective mimesis but an expression of personal impressions. As he so often stated, it had to do with "seemings," appearances, and "provisional impressions only" (in his Preface to *Jude the Obscure,* he said that his novel presented "a series of seemings, of personal impressions," while in his Preface to *Tess* he warned that the book was an impression, not an argument). As a realist, therefore, Hardy was early attracted by the possibilities of fictional impressionism, and he saw in fiction an intensification of the actual world, a revelation of the secret essence of things, of their golden halo, of the unseen light. As early as 1886 he claimed in a note that novel writing, having reached the analytic stage, must now transcend it "by rendering as visible essences, spectres, etc., the abstract thoughts of the analytic school." He envisaged "abstract realisms to be in the form of Spirits, Spectral figures, etc. . . . The Realities to be the true realities of life, hitherto called abstractions. The old material realities to be placed behind the former, as shadowy accessories."[5]

Hardy grafted, as it were, his version of realism and penchant for naturalism onto a fictional strategy of presentation that was impressionistic, personal, and idiosyncratic. He tried to reconcile objective reproduction with subjective expression. Insisting on a basis of *vraisemblance* and realism, he felt that the best fiction was more "true than history or nature can be." Thus the Hardy novel emphasized the dimension of tragedy and exploited symbolic potentialities. It was left to writers like H. G. Wells—who embodied the passage from the nineteenth- to the twentieth-century novel, in theory as well as in practice—to extol social partisanship in fiction, the novel not only "with a purpose" but as a vehicle for the discussion of social problems and intellectual debate, where great historical and social movements substituted individual characters as protagonists.[6] "The new structural conception," Wells wrote, "was the grouping of characters and incidents . . . about some social influence or some far-reaching movement of humanity." Valuable novels would display "a group of typical individuals at the point of action of some great social force, the social force in question and not the 'hero' and the 'heroine' being the real operative interest."

This was a development, more than a revival, of naturalistic, "scientific" theories of the novel at the turn of the century. For most British novelists involved in the debate over naturalism in the 1890s, the answer, as we have seen, pointed to forms of compromise, to an attenuation of the "extreme" aspects of realism, to a reconciliation with more traditional, artistic, and "personal" kinds of writing. Two features, in particular, were crucial in England in modifying the pure form of the theory, so to speak: a stress on the necessary subjectivity of vision on the part of the writer; and an emphasis on personal, individual, often impressionistic renderings. Both contributed to the theoretical advancement and development of naturalism in America.

A dialectical relation between naturalism and impressionism ought not to be surprising. Far from being mutually exclusive, these two trends developed almost simultaneously. Impressionist painting began as a reaction against illustrative realism (the very method of naturalism); yet it derived from the same matrix—the application of scientific premises to art. Originally, it was an attempt to apply to painting the new optical discoveries about the nature of colors, the decomposition and recomposition of light on the retina. Impressionist painters and writers ended up by breaking the ideal of photographic realism that naturalism had pursued to its extreme consequences. But their starting point was similar, and points of contact were more numerous than those of disagreement. Zola himself was an early admirer and supporter of impressionist painting. Maupassant, Turgenev, and James tended strongly toward a kind of selective—and far from a merely documentary or illustrative—realism that naturally anticipated literary impressionism (indeed, for James fiction was "a direct, personal *impression* of life").

Literary impressionism may have been linked in some ways to aestheticism and art for art's sake. Its critical premise has often been identified in Walter Pater's celebrated passage about the smile of the Gioconda and in his conclusion to *Studies in the History of the Renaissance* (first edition, 1873, but omitted in the second): "While all melts under our feet, we may well catch at any exquisite passion, or any contribution to knowledge that seems, by a lifted horizon, to set the spirit free for a moment, or any stirring of the senses, strange dyes, strange flowers, and curious odours, or work of the artist's hand, or the face of one's friend." It might have drawn inspiration from James Whistler's polemical *nocturnes*. Yet it was far from being a product of decadentism, and far from merging with elusive, diffuse, or purely atmospheric attitudes of dreamlike evasion, as for instance in Maurice Maeterlinck. Its proper theoretical formulation, as we shall see in a moment, was provided first by Joseph Conrad, in his 1897 Preface to *The Nigger of the "Narcissus,"* then by Ford Madox Ford in a series of twentieth-century essays and critical statements. These authors saw in impressionism a method for, and a support of, a truthful representation of life, an aid to *vraisemblance,* a condition for a realistic approach to portraiture that relied on the personal view of the author. This view gave depth and foreshortening to the picture, fragmented its aspects, and juxtaposed them in order to re-create and allow for a global vision.

Even the French writers who were connected with the naturalist school—the Goncourt brothers, Daudet, Flaubert, Pierre Loti—broke up illustrative realism from the inside. In a study on *Romanciers français de l'Instantané au XIXe siè- cle,*[7] Jacques Dubois has shown that an *instantanéiste* tendency in these writers led them to fragment narrative moments, to reproduce directly personal impressions, and to capture and present the instants of vision or perception, the fleeting aspects of life. For Dubois, these writers applied to their novels the principles of pictorial impressionism:

> What [impressionist painters] apply to the canvas, these writers introduced into the duration of the novel. It is at first a form of fragmentation [*une mise en forme fragmentiste*] that can be observed in Manet and Degas as well as in the Goncourts and Vallès. . . . It is the beginning of an immediate rendering which, both in the case of writers and painters, consists in emphasizing certain details, analyzing certain impressions, so as to recapture the *données* of the first grasp . . . they show a predilection for instantaneous subjects.

Contemporary writers were aware of these analogies. Dubois himself reminds us that as early as 1879 the French critic Brunetière had written an article on "L'impressionisme dans le roman," which he significantly reprinted in his book entitled *Le roman naturaliste* (1893).

III

I chose to dwell briefly on these historical relations because they provide the background and at least a partial explanation for what otherwise would appear as startling: the ease with which American writers such as Hamlin Garland, Stephen Crane, and Frank Norris seemed to combine, at the end of the century, naturalist with impressionist theories. While they accepted the scientific premises of naturalism (evolutionism, the burden of heredity, social determinism), they insisted on the writer's right to his own view of phenomena, and on personal impressions or the subjective angle of vision from which facts, characters, and events were to be presented. In the case of Norris, we witness a complete reversal in which he passed from naturalism to a new kind of inspired romance.

In his *Crumbling Idols* (1894), a collection of "Twelve Essays on Art Dealing Chiefly with Literature, Painting and Drama," which for the most part were published in various periodicals from 1890 to 1893, Hamlin Garland attacked what he called the worn-out literary and artistic traditions, dependence on European, feudal, and romantic narrative models (the "crumbling idols" of his title), and propounded his theory of *veritism*. This term does not appear in either the *Shorter Oxford Dictionary* or *Webster's New Collegiate Dictionary*. Although no evidence is available, it might have been suggested by the Italian word *verismo*, which in Italy was used in preference to "naturalism." The term "veritism" was not invented by Garland; it circulated in the pages of the Boston *Arena* and the New York *Forum*, the two leading periodicals of the new literature. As Benjamin O. Flower used it, for instance, it meant "that which is real, or, if ideal, is in perfect alignment with the eternal verities as found in life."[8] Garland employed the term in a similar way (including the implicit connotations of spiritual potentialities): veritism involved looking at life with open eyes and in all of its range. Garland expressed a belief, not only in the poetry of the new, but also in the truth of domestic dramas; not only in social evolution, but in environmental determinism. The novel was the highest form of expression in the contemporary age. "Fiction commands the present," he wrote, for it

is "the most modern and unconventional of arts," superior
to both poetry and drama. It expressed the average personality and democratic individualism, not romantic falseness.
As already intimated in Chapter 6, it relied heavily on, or
merged with, localism; it was a re-creation of the beautiful
and the *significant*. In Garland's opinion, it must above all
be true to life and authentic. The veritist's art was art for
truth's sake—nor for art's sake. It was to be based on firsthand knowledge and direct experience; in short, on proper
documentation. It did not seek effects but fidelity to the
present, to recognizable places, to the writer's own life.

Veritism was synonymous with realism or, better still, with
truth-saying: the veritist must learn and state the truth. Put-
ting aside all models, he must "consciously stand alone before nature and before life." Garland wrote: "This is, I believe, the essence of veritism: 'Write of those things of which
you know most, and for which you care most. By so doing
you will be true to yourself, true to your locality, and true
to your time.'" Or again: "The surest way to write for all
time is to embody the present in the finest form with the
highest sincerity and with the frankest truthfulness." Further on we read: "The novel of the slums must be written
by one who has played there as a child. . . . It cannot be
done from above nor from the outside. It must be done out
of a full heart and without seeking for effect." Garland insisted that "life is the model, truth is the master, the heart
of the man himself his motive power. . . . To the veritist,
therefore, the present is the vital theme."[9]

There are echoes of Zola in these essays, quick references
to Taine, to Herbert Spencer, and to Charles Darwin. In
Garland's view, the theory of evolution shed a splendid light.
Here and there, one also finds references to the principles
of social determinism: they concern the development of literary kinds in particular sociohistorical situations (the epic,
the drama, the novel), just as they concern the definition of
literary characters or the developments of the story line. The
novel, like the drama, must have, for Garland, a strong so-

cial purpose. He energetically defended Ibsen's social partisanship (in the essay on "The Influence of Ibsen") as well as his influence on contemporary American dramatists (like James A. Herne, for instance, in his "The Drift of the Drama"). He also insisted that veritism, although opposed to "literalism"—to the minute gathering of small details of down-to-earth realism—implied not only an adherence to truth but also the possibility of verifying it, of referring constantly to facts as guiding principles. For the publication of these essays in book form, he toned down some of the references to literary evolutionism and social commitment; but he was firm in his opposition to the ghost of romance, to the persistence of European "courtly" influences, and to the southern chivalric tradition.

Yet, as one looks closer at these essays, it becomes gradually clear that these premises allow for particular developments. In the first place, veritism is identified with the cause of western fiction, which was to deal with the West and the big cities of the frontier: "for forty years an infinite drama has been going on in those wide spaces of the West—a drama that is as thrilling, as full of heart and hope and battle, as any that ever surrounded any man." The lesson of Walt Whitman (to whom Garland referred in an inspired page) was at work here, together with the wish to move away from the influences of the East so as to discover the new, regional, and even provincial American reality:

> in writing upon Pacific-Coast literature, undoubtedly I shall once more be stating the cause of veritism; for the question of Pacific-Coast literature is really the question of genuine American literature. The same principles apply to all sections of the land.

Turning to the West for inspiration meant specifically that—facing the question of regionalism and local color, which Garland discussed in the two essays "Local Color in Art" and "The Local Novel." Veritism called for the spontaneous perception of local facts; regionalism lay at the heart of genuine American literary expression. We saw that for Garland "local color in fiction is demonstrably the life of fiction. It is the native element, the differentiating element." He insisted that local color "means that the writer spontaneously reflects the life which goes on around him. It is natural and unstrained art." He also wrote: "The genuine American literature, in the same way, must come from the soil and the open air, and be likewise freed from tradition."[10]

In regard to subject matter, then, veritism ran the risk of being confused with the picturesque sketch or with the healthy poetry of the land. In fact, in protean fashion Garland's veritism embraced moralism and didacticism; it embraced the tendency that in those years took the opposing name of idealism. It would exalt and console, move and make dream, welcome in utopian and messianic strains. It would foster optimism rather than pessimism:

> This literature will not deal with crime and abnormalities, nor with deceased persons. It will deal, I believe, with the wholesome love of honest men for honest women, with the heroism of labor, the comradeship of men. . . .
>
> Because the fictionist of to-day sees a more beautiful and peaceful future social life, and, in consequence, a more beautiful and peaceful literary life, therefore he is encouraged to deal truthfully and at close grapple with the facts of his immediate present. . . . The realist or veritist is really an optimist, a dreamer. He sees life in terms of what it might be, as well as in terms of what it is. . . . He aims to hasten the age of beauty and peace by delineating the ugliness and warfare of the present; but ever the converse of his picture rises in the mind of the reader. . . .
>
> . . . The test of a work of art is not, Does it conform to the best models? but, *Does it touch and lift and exalt men?*[11]

These quotations ought to suffice to establish the soft underside of Garland's theory. As Jane Johnson rightly suggested, and as Garland himself later recognized in his *Roadside Meetings* (1930), veritism, realism, Americanism, and idealism came to mean much the same thing for him. There were unmistakable echoes and traces of Howells's genteel and optimistic form of realism in Garland's stance. Yet a further development in the latter's theory led him to equate veritism with impressionism.

IV

Eugène Véron's *L'estétique*, published in Paris in 1879 and translated into English the next year, is the only work on aesthetics that Garland quoted in *Crumbling Idols*. Véron's book stressed the individual and moral character of artistic vision, the personal, impressionistic quality of artistic rendering, which was stimulated by the perception of single objects and events regardless of their representative value. Garland accepted and developed these ideas. More than once he insisted on the importance of the artist's individuality and wrote that "this *theory* of the veritist is, after all, a statement of his passion for truth and for individual expression." Or again: "Art, I must insist, is an individual thing,—the question of one man facing certain facts and telling his individual relations to them. His first care must be to present his own concept." According to Garland, poetry was an "*impassioned personal outlook on life,*" and he was quite ready to apply this Jamesian definition of art to his general conception of veritism in the novel as well.

In an essay from the same period, Garland defined veritism as "the truthful statement of an individual impression corrected by reference to the fact": the two poles of his conception (reference to fact and individual impression) are handsomely joined together. In a central essay of *Crumbling Idols*, "Literary Prophecy," he wrote that the fiction of the future would grow "more democratic in outlook and more individualistic in method" (again the two sides of his notion) and proceeded to define fictional impressionism in a crucial way: [12]

> Impressionism, in its deeper sense, means the statement of one's own individual perception of life and nature, guided by devotion to truth. Second to this great principle is the law that each impression must be worked out faithfully on separate canvases, each work of art complete in itself. . . . The higher art would seem to be the art that perceives and states the relations of things, giving atmosphere and relative values as they appeal to the sight.

These ideas correspond rather closely to Conrad's definition of literary impressionism in his Preface to *The Nigger of the "Narcissus,"* including the fact that the appeal was made to the reader's perception. In this manifesto of literary impressionism, Conrad had stated that fiction

> if at all aspires to be art—appeals to temperament. . . . Such an appeal to be effective must be an impression conveyed through the senses. . . . All art, therefore, appeals primarily to the senses, and the artistic aim when expressing itself in written words must also make its appeal through the senses. . . . It must strenuously aspire to the plasticity of sculpture, to the colour of painting, and to the magic suggestiveness of music—which is the art of arts.

The writer was to convey to the reader the terseness and arresting quality of the sense impression, to capture the fleeting image of life:

> My task which I am trying to achieve is, by the power of the written word to make you hear, to make you feel—it is, before all, to make you *see.* . . .
>   To snatch in a moment of courage, from the remorseless rush of time, a passing phase of life, is only the beginning of the task. The task approached in tenderness and faith is to hold up unquestioningly, without choice and without fear, the rescued fragment before all eyes in the light of a sincere

mood. It is to show its vibration, its colour, its form; and through its movement, its form and its colour, reveal the substance of its truth—disclose its inspiring secret: the stress and passion within the core of each convincing moment. . . .

. . . And when it is accomplished—behold!—all the truth of life is there: a moment of vision, a sigh, a smile.

For Garland, the novel, "like impressionism in painting, will subordinate parts to the whole. It will teach . . . not . . . by direct expression, but by placing before the reader the facts of life as they stand related to the artist. This relation . . . will address itself to the perception of the reader." Even when writing about social drama, Garland emphasized that a "work of art is an individual thing,—a relation of one human soul to life, emotionally expressed." The artist's "only obligation is to be true to life as it seems to him from his personal angle of vision"; veritism "deals with life face to face . . . from the individual artist's standpoint"; indeed, the "force that flowers is the individual, that which checks and moulds is environment."[13]

Garland devoted section IX of *Crumbling Idols* to a long essay (it seems first to have been a lecture) on "Impressionism," which deals with the impressionist painters at the Chicago Exhibition, and competently equates them with the veritists: "these men are veritists in the best sense of the word," he wrote, and went on to describe their method of juxtaposing primary colors on the canvas in a way that would apply very well, for instance, to the literary impressionism of Stephen Crane. A picture should be "a unified impression"; a complete, momentary concept of the sense of sight; it should be "the stayed and reproduced effect of a single section of the world of color . . . a single idea impossible of subdivision without loss." Impressionists select some center of interest, generally that of a very simple character, and work on it with care, letting all else fade away into a blur (as in life). They paint with nature's colors directly placed on the canvas side by side, thus leaving the eye to mix them.

One could easily multiply quotations from Garland's view of impressionism. But what is important is his stress on the *individual* perception of the artist and on the single impression reproduced and juxtaposed with others both on the page and on the canvas so that a composed, unified, and *atmospheric* effect would result. In this way Garland relegated to the background not only the concept of *scientific* naturalism but also the very concept of objective truthfulness and *vraisemblance* that seemed so central to his idea of veritism. In a letter he used the terms "impressionism" and "veritism" interchangeably: [14]

> In truth I was an impressionist in that I presented life and landscape as I personally perceived them, but since I sought a deeper significance in the use of the word, I added a word which subtended verification. I sought to verify my impression by comparing impressions separated by an interval of time.

In that it sought and purported to offer *verification,* veritism was in line with "scientific" naturalism; but it was also in line with Ford Madox Ford's later theory of literary impressionism that sought (once again) to respond to the need for *vraisemblance.* "We saw that Life did not narrate, but made impressions on our brains," Ford wrote of his collaboration with Conrad: "We in turn, if we wished to produce on you an effect of life, must not narrate but render . . . impressions." This was an attempt to reconcile objectivity of presentation with subjectivity of vision, and Henry James was as much behind it as Conrad was. But a significant element—that of selection—was reintroduced by such theories into the fairly nebulous concept of the "slice of life," which the naturalist writer was supposed to cut without too much personal tampering. A further important theoretical development was implied, which would be stated and discussed a few years later by Henry James in his Prefaces and which would become of paramount importance in the new century: the opposition of the comparative values of "telling" and "showing." At this stage, however, the growth of fictional impressionism out of the bosom of veritism amounted to a major contribution to a theory of the novel that made the most of its realist foundations, while at the same time emphasizing the importance of the writer's personal perceptions and artistic application. It would be tempting here to analyze twentieth-century developments, those in which the novel moved toward fragmentation and the *instantané*, toward the breaking up and montage of impressions, the stress on stylistic "texture" as fictional "structure"; but then one would have to discuss Virginia Woolf and James Joyce who, it must be said, came from the same matrix that produced H. G. Wells and Arnold Bennett. The end of the century was indeed such a breeding ground of attitudes and theories, concepts and practices, that we too quickly tend to label as typically "modern." Here, for our purposes, it is sufficient to point out how a theorist like Garland, so closely identified with the realistic movement, managed to open what he himself called "the other side of realism," and how this "other side" was developed in close connection with the realistic matrix.

What I am trying to stress is that such theories of fictional impressionism had nothing in common with forms of evasion, atmospheres of vagueness and dreaminess, pale and ghostly appearances, which we tend to associate with fin de siècle decadentism and aestheticism. Such tendencies, which did indeed raise their heads in these very years, will be touched upon in the next chapters, where I will discuss the contemporary forms of the "new romance." Particularly in America, impressionist theories of the novel were closely linked with the realities of the new continent—with regionalism, urbanization, the western frontier, the growth of industrialism—all new areas of life and human activity that waited to be captured by appropriately created fictional forms. This much is borne out by an instinctive writer (certainly not a theorist) like Stephen Crane and by the convinced naturalist Frank Norris who ran the whole gamut, from realism back to romance.

V

In his fiction, rather than in his few theoretical statements, Stephen Crane shows a marked combination of naturalistic and impressionist elements, quite similar, for instance, to their coexistence in Garland's collection of stories, *Main-Travelled Roads* (1891). This characteristic combination has been analyzed elsewhere.[15] Yet, even in his few (and rather implicit) formulations, Crane confirmed the dialectical relation between the two concurring theories. In a letter written in 1892 to Lily Brandon Munroe, he said that he had renounced "the clever school in literature" (largely influenced by Rudyard Kipling) in order to develop a "little creed in art," which he soon found "identical" with that of Howells and Garland; that is, that fiction is man's substitute for nature and should come as close as possible to it, for there lies the truth:

> in this way I became involved in the beautiful war between those who say that art is man's substitute for nature and we are the most successful in art when we approach the nearest to nature and truth, and those who say—well, I don't know what they say. They don't, they can't say much but they fight villainously and keep Garland and I out of the big magazines. Howells, of course, is too powerful for them.

In dedications that he inscribed in various copies of *Maggie: A Girl of the Streets* (1893), he announced that he tried "to show that environment is a tremendous thing in the world and frequently shapes lives regardless." This was a crucial tenet of naturalism, and Crane was aware of its moral and social implications. He felt that the reader might be "greatly shocked" and that, if this theory was proved, one made room in heaven "for all sort of souls (notably an occasional street girl) who are not confidently expected to be there by many excellent people." In his dedication of the same book to Howells, he attributed to the latter the readjustment of point of view of which he spoke in the letter quoted above. At this point in his career, he repeated almost verbatim to Howells his insistence on truth and faithfulness to life as requisites for the novelist. In a letter of 1895 to the editor of *Leslie's Weekly*, he specified that "the nearer a writer gets to life, the greater he becomes as an artist." His ambitious goal was that of realism: Tolstoy and Zola were the writers he most admired—Zola in particular for his brand of "scientific" realism.[16]

In both *Maggie* and *George's Mother*, Crane applied the naturalistic principles of biological and environmental determinism, scientific detachment, and representative value; in both cases he dealt with the processes of degeneration on the psychological as well as the social level. We know now that this was only part of his inspiration. Maggie is a product and a victim, not only of the social environment, but of the false morality and the perverted moral values imposed on that environment and on her family.[17] Yet at the time Crane was hailed as a "pure naturalist" by both Howells and Garland and included in the ranks of "narrative radicalism"; he would become a "documentary" writer, he would live in the slums, rub shoulders with the poor of New York so that he could write from experience (as he did in various celebrated Bowery sketches and tales) and "get at the real thing." As he put it in a letter to John N. Hilliard (1897?), he offered the reader a slice of life (a typically naturalistic idea) in perfect detachment, leaving him free to draw the moral lesson: "Preaching is fatal to art in literature." Crane did stress, though, that he was an "independent writer," engaged in writing about whatever he found interesting under the sun, and that in most cases he would write of "imagined" rather than "experienced" reality. This seems to be the case with *Maggie*, the first draft of which he had written before he went to New York where he eventually lived in the Bowery; and it is certainly the case with *The Red Badge of Courage* (1896), which he wrote without any direct experience of battle (although one would never have guessed it). Crane delighted in this paradox: "They all insist that I am a veteran of the civil war; whereas . . . I never smelled even the powder of a sham battle." At the same time, he emphasized that his novel "was an effort born of pain—despair, almost; and I believe that this made it a better piece of literature than it otherwise would have been. It seems a pity that art should be a child of pain, and yet I think it is." He also called his little masterpiece "a psychological portrait of fear."[18]

The stress was now on "felt" rather than "observed" life—on impressions rather than notions of reality. Notions were to be thrown to the wind like sand to the sea breeze, according to an early record of his conversation: "Forget what you think about it. . . . You've got to feel the things you write if you want to make an impact on the world." The novelist had to get emotionally involved in his subject; presentation was not to be illustrative or documentary but built up through quick, sensitive, impressionistic renderings based on sense perception. Unfortunately, Crane never elaborated a theory of fictional impressionism *as such,* except perhaps within *The Red Badge of Courage* itself, where we read that Henry Fleming's "mind took a mechanical but firm impression, so that afterward everything was pictured and explained to him." Crane did practice it, however, and in such an intense and constant way that after the publication of his novel he was hailed as "the chief impressionist of the age" by Edward Garnett and as "the impressionist by excellence . . . the *only* impressionist" by none other than Joseph Conrad—two writers who, as it were, personified the new school. An analysis of the texture of his writing bears this out quite conclusively.[19] A fragmented kind of writing made up of flashes, which makes its appeal to and through sensuous impressions, would break and reverse its realistic premises from within. The sought-for slice of life becomes a phantasmagoria of sensations; a manner of writing or a stylistic mode acquires structural relevance, thereby bringing about a new way of perceiving and organizing reality in the novel.

This was the path that would lead eventually to Virginia Woolf's reversal of referential and representational realism into interior monologue, to the dissolution of the data of experience into a welter of sensations and a turmoil of impressions. In other words, it was the path that negated the very concept of illustrative, surface realism (see Virginia Woolf's well-known attack on Arnold Bennett, for instance). Crane was most likely unaware of the implications and the disruptive force of his mature method and would have rightly claimed its realistic foundation, its links with naturalism. But the dissolution of a nineteenth-century concept of realism that is implicit in his method, if not in his theoretical statements, found confirmation in the forms of fin de siècle opposition to realism that emphasized artificiality of approach and a return to romance, in England as well as in America. Here the call was eventually for a kind of Great American Novel that would rely on new romantic, psychological, and symbolic modes.

NOTES

1. See *Anthologie des préfaces de romans français du XIXe siècle,* ed. Herbert S. Gershan and Kernan B. Whitworth, Jr. (Paris: Julliard, 1964), pp. 272–73.

2. For George Moore, see Kenneth Graham, *English Criticism of the Novel, 1865–1900* (Oxford: Clarendon Press, 1965), pp. 59–60, 74–75, 118–20; for George Gissing, see *Selections, Autobiographical and Imaginative,* ed. A. C. Gissing (London: Cape, 1929), pp. 217–21.

3. Edmund Gosse, "Limits of Realism in Fiction" (1890), in *Questions at Issue* (New York: Appleton, 1893), pp. 146–54; William C. Frierson, "The English Controversy over Realism in Fiction, 1885–1895," *PMLA,* 43 (1928): 533–50 (also for what follows).

4. Frierson, "The English Controversy," pp. 543–48: Arthur Waugh and Hugh Crackenthorpe in the first and second issues of the *Yellow Book* recognized the new climate of opinion.

5. Thomas Hardy, "The Science of Fiction" (1891), in *Personal Writings,* ed. Harold Orel (Lawrence: The University Press of Kansas, 1966), pp. 134–38, 32–33; Florence Emily Hardy, *The Life of Thomas Hardy: 1840–1928* [1928] (London: Macmillan, 1962), pp. 247–48, 228–29, 147, 177; also Lawrence E. Jones, "Imitation and Expression in Thomas Hardy's Theory of Fiction," *Studies in the Novel,* 7 (1975): 507–25. For a contemporary modification of realism, through philosophy and "the comic spirit," see E. Arthur Robinson, "Meredith's Literary Theory and Science: Realism versus the Comic Spirit," *PMLA,* 53 (1938): 857–68. Meredith, who in 1887 had defined the novel "the natural history of man," evolved an elaborate theory that used the principle of evolution to show that man was moving away from his brutish condition—hence the need to investigate in the novel man's spiritual, rather than animal side, his complex inner reality.

6. See, for instance, H. G. Wells, "The Novels of George Gissing" (originally in *Contemporary Review,* 1897), in *George Gissing and H. G. Wells: Their Friendship and Correspondence,* ed. Royal A. Gettmann (London: Hart-Davis, 1961), pp. 242–59; E. A. Bennett, "H. G. Wells and His Work" (originally in *Cosmopolitan Magazine,* 1902), in *E. A. Bennett and H. G. Wells: A Record of a Personal and Literary Friendship,* ed. Harris Wilson (London: Hart-Davis, 1960). For the period see Paul Goetsch, *Die Romankonzeption in England 1880–1910,* Anglistische Forschungen, 94 (Heidelberg: Carl Winter, 1967).

7. (Brussels: Palais des Académies, 1963). Here and in what follows I have drawn from my "Naturalism and Impressionism in Stephen Crane's Fiction," in *Stephen Crane: A Collection of Critical Essays,* ed. Maurice Bassan (Englewood Cliffs, N.J.: Prentice-Hall, 1967), pp. 80–94, and from my *Vie della narrativa americana* (Turin: Einaudi, 1980), chaps. 5 and 6, to which the reader is referred for a discussion of, and further documentation on, the relation between naturalism and impressionism. They had a common epistemological matrix in the idea that science would provide a new basis for perception; the artist should have a fresh, detached, unimpassioned outlook on life; their outcomes were different—naturalism tending to forms of impersonality and heavy documentation, impressionism to individual vision and coloristic renderings. Their connection had already been posited in Eugène Véron's *Aesthetics* (trans. W. H. Armstrong, 1879). On this issue see also Donald Pizer, *Realism and Naturalism in Nineteenth-Century American Literature* [1966] (New York: Russell and Russell, 1976), where Véron is quoted to the effect that "the manifestation of individual impressions" is the best form of art and that "TRUTH

and PERSONALITY: these are the alpha and omega of art formulas; *truth as to facts*, and the *personality* of the artist" (pp. 91–92).

8. Hamlin Garland, *Crumbling Idols*, ed. Jane Johnson (Cambridge: Harvard University Press, Belknap Press, 1960), p. xxii; Johnson's Introduction is very valuable for information and critical *aperçus*.

9. Ibid, pp. 23, 30, 38, 44, 50, 61, 64–65.

10. Ibid., pp. xii, 14, 17, 49, 52, 135.

11. Ibid., pp. 25, 43–44, 133.

12. Ibid., pp. 21, 30, 64, 42; Hamlin Garland, "Productive Conditions of American Literature," *Forum*, 17 (1894): 670, quoted ibid., p. xxi.

13. Joseph Conrad, *The Nigger of the "Narcissus"* (New York: Penguin Books, 1963), pp. 11–14; Garland, *Crumbling Idols*, pp. 43, 73, 76, 144; for the essay on "Impressionism," pp. 97–101.

14. For a valuable study of these and related matters see Donald Pizer, *Hamlin Garland's Early Work and Career* [1960] (New York: Russell and Russell, 1969), and his "Hamlin Garland and Stephen Crane: The Naturalist as Romantic Individualist," in *Realism and Naturalism*, pp. 88–98, where the conclusion is offered that "in *Crumbling Idols* Garland stated an aesthetic system in which evolutionary ideas served as the intellectual foundation, impressionism as the artistic method advocated, and local color as the end product in various arts" (p. 93). For Ford Madox Ford's ideas of literary impressionism discussed further on, see *Critical Writings of Ford Madox Ford*, ed. Frank MacShane (Lincoln: University of Nebraska Press, 1964), part II: "Impressionism and Fiction," pp. 33–103.

15. See notes 7 and 14 above, and James B. Stronks, "A Realist Experiments with Impressionism: Hamlin Garland's 'Chicago Studies,' " *American Literature*, 36 (1964): 38–52.

16. See Stephen Crane, *Letters*, ed. R. W. Stallman and Lillian Gilkes (New York: New York University Press, 1960), pp. 31–33, 14 and 19 for the dedications, p. 78 (and note 7 above).

17. See Donald Pizer, "Stephen Crane's *Maggie* and American Naturalism," in *Realism and Naturalism*, pp. 121–31 (but also pp. 95–98), and Stephen Crane, *Maggie: Text and Context*, ed. Maurice Bassan (Belmont, Calif.: Wadsworth, 1966).

18. Crane, *Letters*, pp. 158–59, 78–79; and John Berryman, *Stephen Crane* (New York: Sloane, 1950), p. 25 (for the testimony below).

19. See my "Naturalism and Impressionism in Stephen Crane's Fiction"; a heavy reliance on verbs of perception and color touches allowed Crane to provide individual views and impressionistic renderings of impersonal forces at work (social and psychological determinism, war, primordial fear).

8.
THE NEW ROMANCE

I

REACTIONS to realism were stronger in England than in America. An extreme but symptomatic case is provided by Oscar Wilde, for whom truthfulness or *vraisemblance* was anathema. So was the idea of a "living" character. Though not specifically dealing with the novel, Wilde's essay "The Decay of Lying" (1889) offers a paradoxical and polemical repudiation of all realistic premises. Art is for "Vivian" (Wilde's mouthpiece) an artifice—it is made up, contrived. It "competes" with life only in that it denies it, for fiction is antithetical to reality. Real people are those who never existed; the mask matters more than the face, not for what it hides, but for what it is in itself. Far from copying nature, art is imitated by it. An abstract, artificial pattern or design is the supreme form of art. All accepted ideas are reversed:[1]

the more we study Art, the less we care for Nature. What Art really reveals to us is Nature's lack of design, her curious crudities, her extraordinary monotony, her absolutely unfinished condition. . . .

. . . . modernity of form and modernity of subject-matter are entirely and absolutely wrong. We have mistaken the common livery of the age for the vesture of the Muses, and spend our days in the sordid streets and hideous suburbs of our vile cities when we should be out on the hillside with Apollo. . . .

. . . . Romance, with her temper of wonder, will return to the land. . . .

. . . . Art never expresses anything but itself. It has an independent life, just as Thought has, and develops purely on its own lines. . . .

. . . . All bad art comes from returning to Life and Nature. . . . As a method Realism is a complete failure, and the two things that every artist should avoid are modernity of form and modernity of subject-matter. . . .

. . . . Life goes faster than Realism, but Romanticism is always in front of Life. . . . Life imitates Art far more than Art imitates Life. . . .

External Nature also imitates Art. . . . Lying, the telling of beautiful untrue things, is the proper aim of Art.

These concepts nourished and reflected the fin de siècle spread of aestheticism. Although they were applied to fiction only incidentally, they were bound to influence its disaffection with the idea of mimesis, representational value, referential accuracy. Art turned its back on actual life and chose, instead, to pursue a winding, artificial path. Fiction did not reflect the visible but sought out the invisible, the abstract, the symbolical. The best expression of the new artistic aim of the novel (of its combining an attachment to reality with the pursuit, discovery, and revelation of the hidden aspects of life, of the mysterious sources of humanity, of the fleeting moments of existence) can be found in the Joseph Conrad of the 1890s. His theory, as we have briefly seen, required that the novel render the highest form of justice to the visible as well as to the invisible world. Conrad propounded an almost magical or mystical view of the novelist's task. In its baffling way, fiction captures the very essence of the world, is instrumental in rescuing its fragments and giving it form; it is perhaps the only way to save reality from disruption and dissipation. But all this remains quite elusive, because while the novel can, and does, have free play with life, it can convey only a vibration, a glimpse, a momentary impression of it. Even this is due, finally, to the symbolic potentialities and connotations that reality possesses.

The symbolic, as opposed to the realistic, capabilities of the novel were extolled at the very end of the century by Arthur Symons in his highly influential book, *The Symbolist Movement in Literature* (1899). According to him, "Without symbolism there can be no literature" (not to speak of language). By its very nature, symbolism is approximative, arbitrary, and conventional; it aims at unseen reality: "the visible world is no longer a reality, and the unseen world no longer a dream" for it. After the age of science, of material things, or representational realism, after the Goncourts, Taine, and Zola, suggestion takes the place of saying. Art returns to the one pathway leading to eternal beauty; mystery is now welcomed. In brushing aside the accidents of daily life, in revolting against exteriority and materialism, symbolic writing (for Symons as well as for Conrad) hoped to reveal the very soul of things, "to disengage the ultimate essence, the soul, of whatever exists." The best example of this could be found in the work of Joris Karl Huysmans, for whom the novel preserved the precision of detail characteristic of the language of realism, but also grappled "with the within and the after" so as to create "a spiritual Naturalism." Psychology could now be carried "far into the darkness of the soul"; the novel could now compete with poetry. As Symons tellingly put it: "The novel, which, after having chronicled the adventures of the Vanity Fairs of this world, had set itself with admirable success to analyse the amorous and ambitious and money-making intelligence of the conscious and practical self, sets itself at last to the final achievement: the revelation of the sub-conscious self, no longer the intelligence, but the soul." Once the novel was "purged of the distraction of incident, liberated from the bondage of a too realistic conversation," it could be "internalized to a complete liberty" and become a new form—"at once a confession and a decoration, the soul and the pattern."[2]

Symons was here heralding in the new novel of the twentieth century, internalized to mirror the obscure and fragmentary movements of the subconscious, what would soon be termed the stream of consciousness. In between Wilde's artificiality and Symons's symbolism of the subconscious, the last decade of the century placed emphasis on a peculiar form of opposition to realism: a full-fledged return to romance.

Writing on "The Present State of the English Novel" in 1888, an influential critic like George Saintsbury maintained that the contemporary novel was genetically weakened and leveled by scientism and evolutionism. This explained "the return to the earliest form of writing, to the pure romance of adventure," and the reversion "to the simpler instead of the more complicated kind of novel, trusting more to incident, less to the details of manner and character," which appeared to Saintsbury right and wise. Monotony and lack of freshness had inevitably overtaken the novel of contemporary life, whereas the romance appealed to universal and, ultimately, immutable passions and actions:

> For the romance is of its nature eternal and preliminary to the novel. The novel is of its nature transitory and is parasitic on the romance. . . . The novel has nothing to do with any beliefs, with any convictions, with any thoughts in the strict sense, except as mere garnishings. Its substance must always be life not thought, conduct not belief, the passions not the intellect, manners and morals not creeds and theories.

Charged with treating the appearances of social existence, the novel was exhausted. And given the increase of the reading public, the circulating libraries, and the spread of journalism, the novelist was the only artist whose métier was "liable to be confounded with the simple business of the ordinary tradesman." Novel producers took the place of novelists, and the development of novel writing, so compressed in terms of time, accounted for such superficial results. Better, then, the romance, in Saintsbury's opinion, for at least it remained much the same through the ages, disengaged from contingency as it was, and could still depict the eternal and never-changing qualities, the very essence of man—although unfortunately, as he complained, "many of our best proved writers continue to write the novel and not the romance, or to treat the romance as if it were the novel."[3]

A stronger plea for romance was made by H. Rider Haggard in his essay "About Fiction." "The love of romance is probably coeval with the existence of humanity," the first line ran; it was, like the passions, "an innate quality of mankind." Romance writing was perhaps the most difficult art, and it was extolled and evoked not only against the dreariness of French naturalism or the analytic studies of the Americans but as the expression of an ideal of cold and statuesque beauty, of a world of pure fantasy. Rider Haggard went on to attack the lack of action, the extended soliloquies, and the dissection of petty feelings in American novels, where the heroines "are things of silk and cambric" and the men "emasculated specimens of an overwrought age" (the reference here was obviously to Henry James), just as he violently criticized the brutality, carnality, and filth so prominent in the naturalists. What becomes, he asked, "of the things that are pure and high—of the great aspirations and the lofty hopes and longings?" The answer was that new romances had to express "a higher ideal," in spite of the fact that the age was not a particularly romantic one. "Art in the purity of its idealized truth should resemble some perfect Grecian statue. It should be cold but naked"—like the Venus of Milo, "not an obscene photograph taken from the life." For Rider Haggard, then, romance was a way to express ideal beauty and to write not of externals but of the inner life—of hopes and pains, aspirations and personal sufferings. It thus differed widely from manufactured books.[4]

For Hall Caine, the romance spoke to the heart; it revealed passions and motives rather than facts; it confronted the unusual and the sensational. As with Wilde, the stress was placed on the lying (rather than the truthful) character of fiction, which was neither history nor a substitute for facts but a poetic and pathetic fallacy. In his "The New Watchwords of Fiction" Caine wrote in favor of idealism in literature: if realism gave importance to the real facts of life, idealism was "the doctrine of the superiority of ideal existence" over them. His stance was at least partly ethical: painting life "as it is" resulted in showing a preponderance of evil in the world, while "it is only the eye of the imagination, the eye of faith, that sees the balance of good and evil struck somewhere and in some way." Realism resulted in cynicism, while "the true consort of imagination is enthusiasm." Caine wanted the principles of "poetic justice" and moral uplift restored to the novel: this was more easily achieved if fiction took a romantic turn. Romance was the natural vehicle for great conceptions; conversely, "Idealism claims Romance as her handmaiden."

In Caine's view (as later on in Frank Norris's), romance was not restricted to "the loveliest spots" or "exclusively to the past"; it existed "within the four-mile radius at the present hour." Fiction writing should not be confused with the historian's task:

> To condemn all forms of romance, as the Zola manifesto tried to do, to banish from fiction all incidents that are out of the common, all effects that are startling and "sensational," all light and colour that are not found in every-day life, is to confound the function of the novelist with that of the historian. To the historian fact is a thing for itself, it is sacred, it dominates all else. To the novelist fact is only of

value as a help towards the display of passion; he does not deliberately falsify fact, but fact—mere fact—has no sanctity for him, and he would a thousand times rather outrage all the incidents of history than belie one impulse of the human heart.

The mere recording of contemporary life narrowed the range of imaginative art. If the function of the novelist was that "of proposing for solution by means of incident and story a problem of human life," Caine was driven by this particular idea of a "novel with a purpose" to emphasize the role of passion and the revelation of the mysteries of life entrusted to fiction. The novelist would seek that solution of which human nature is capable when at its best; he would seek heroism and romanticism. Quoting Francis Bacon and Robert Burton, Caine saw fiction as no mere handmaid of history, but as correcting it, showing life as it should be. This craving for idealism and for moral rather than factual truth led him to stress, as did Oscar Wilde, the fallacious side of fiction: *"Fiction is not nature, it is not character, it is not imagined history; it is fallacy, poetic fallacy, a lie if you like, a beautiful lie, a lie that is at once false and true—false to fact, true to faith"* (Caine's italics). In following this poetic fallacy, English fiction had the liberty not of realism but of romanticism, "of all great and healthy passions." Romance was not a "backwater" but the new trend:

> On every side, in every art, music, the drama, painting, and even sculpture, the tendency is towards Romance. Not the bare actualities of life "as it is," but the glories of life as it might be; not the domination of fact, but of feeling. . . . The cry of the stage to-day is Romance, the cry of fiction is Romance, the cry of music is Romance.

"The watchwords of fiction for the next twenty years at least," Caine concluded, were going to be *"Romanticism and Idealism."* [5]

A strong moral bias lay behind Caine's defense of romance. For others, romance was the best form of popular fiction, and it was fraught with the best consolatory value (Anthony Hope): it led people to dream what they could be if unfettered by time, fate, or circumstances, and to feel better after the dream. In most cases, the urge was to turn one's back on reality, escape into another realm, face other worlds. There was a sense of weariness caused by too much exposure to realism, a strong wish for illusion and evasion, a willingness to dream. Were it not for a barely hidden strain or an overt admission, it would hardly be worth discussing here, except perhaps in merely descriptive terms, so much fin de siècle attention to the escapist, idealistic, and consolatory value of romance—a genre that would indeed become a consumer's staple in the next century. Romance allowed for a vision of the human heart, the sounding of deep and obscure passions, the investigation of psychological processes, the analysis of the soul. This role or potentiality, as we have seen, had been recognized at least since the time of Hawthorne. It now acquired new emphasis and a new impetus on two accounts: the analytic school had dealt with the minutiae of character analysis, the winding and devious paths of human motives, inner contradictions, and compromises; the naturalistic movement had led to the investigation of abnormal states and conditions, of degenerative processes in psychic as well as physical terms. Fiction had become bolder and a new consciousness was stirring: Freud was just around the corner. Writers such as James or Meredith, Hardy or Dostoevski, had shown undreamed-of ranges of fictional glimpses into the human soul. The psyche was increasingly identified with the reality of man and with the realm of fiction. Romance stepped boldly into that new consciousness—between, as it were, the first tentative moves in that direction of nineteenth-century realism and the engulfing experience of the stream-of-consciousness novel in the new century.

Fiction could still be written from the inside out, rather than from the outside in: the novel of external facts and incidents, of social experience and exposure, was if only temporarily renounced (Joyce would restore the continuity of the two sides). This note struck a deep and familiar chord in America—a stronger chord, indeed, than in England— owing to historical precedents, a deep-seated tradition, the difficulties involved in embracing wholeheartedly the novel of manners or of contemporary life, with its complexities and nuances—a realm in which the New World was still ill at ease. On this side of the Atlantic, then, we find the romance proposed and propounded with even stronger conviction than in England: first for its escapist and entertaining qualities, then as the highest form of committed and responsible fiction—indeed, of the "novel with a purpose"— and of psychological investigation.

II

An expatriate writer and the author for the most part of historical romances and narratives of cosmopolitan life, Francis Marion Crawford devoted in 1893 a short book to *The Novel: What Is It*, where the theory of the novel/romance as entertainment and escape is set forth in its pure form. A novel, for Crawford, is first of all

> a marketable commodity, of the class collectively termed "luxuries," as not contributing directly to the support of life or the maintenance of health. It is of the class "artistic luxuries" because it does not appeal to any of the three material senses—touch, taste, smell; and it is of the class "intellectual artistic luxuries," because it is not judged by the superior senses—sight and hearing.

As such, it must appeal to the intellect, satisfy the requirements of art, and be of no practical use, but only "conduce to peace of mind and delectation" during hours of idleness. Its first object "is to amuse and interest the reader." If it is a "novel-with-a-purpose" (what the Germans called *Tendenz-Roman*), it serves two masters and violates the implicit contract between writer and reader. A moral lesson appears to be incompatible with an artistic luxury, and if we buy a plaything we do not want "somebody's views on socialism, religion, or the divorce laws." The purpose novel was for Crawford an odious attempt to lecture and therefore a fraud: granting that a novel may educate the mind and purify the heart, extol what is noble and honest, it has no right to tell "what its writer thinks about the relation of labour and capital" or to set up a scheme for salvation. A "guide to morality" is antithetical to fiction; the novelist had better be an amuser of the public rather than a prophet. Crawford went to great length to keep the role of the novelist down to its elementary level of entertainment.[6]

As such, the novelist is opposed to realism ("red pepper and stimulants" instead of "bread and milk"): "Zola's shadow, seen through the veil of the English realistic novel, is a monstrosity not to be tolerated." Not only does realism provide photographs instead of pictures, catalogues instead of descriptions, it is (as for Hall Caine) "better suited to the exposition of what is bad than what is good." The kind of fiction that Crawford exalted "must deal chiefly with love," because of our interest in that passion; it must be clean and sweet; though it can combine three-dimensional realism with the romance of the human heart, it must aspire to transcendent idealism, "not measured to man's mind, but proportioned to man's soul." Its religion must be of "grand and universal span." Although writing that the element of romance need not shut out the element of realism, for both are part of everyday life, Crawford's theory ended up by emphasizing the new form of romance: "Art, if it is 'to create and foster agreeable illusions,' as Napoleon is believed to have said of it, should represent the real, but in such a way as to make it seem more agreeable and interesting than it actually is." The novel, as Crawford insisted on calling it, is, or ought to be, a "pocket-stage" that we can carry around with us; and "A play is good in proportion as it represents the more dramatic, passionate, romantic, or humorous sides of real life." (Language was the tool, but not dialect that, lacking dramatic interest, "is colour without form or outline." The impression to be created in the reader must be "widely felt," while dialect—like puns—was "of a particular local character.")[7]

Crawford had little to say of interest about methods, except that all sorts of knowledge were now required of the novelist, and that he must resist, if anything, the demands of too much scientific knowledge. All these detailed and discursive points tended to strengthen the idea of the superiority of romantic fiction: "anything which fixes the date of the novel not intended to be historical is a mistake, from a literary point of view"; describing dresses is to be discouraged, so that the narrative does not become "dated." Characters must be drawn with consistency, but they must be invented rather than taken from real life or from people who actually lived. Even the historical novel is not written for the sake of the history it contains, but rather for its dramatic interest and the depiction of character. Ancient drama and the epic dealt with subjects considered to be historical; consequently, the modern writer can do his " 'sensation work' with tragic facts widely known." Yet, "in treating of history, where the personages are great and the events are of stupendous import," the distance that separates the sublime from the ridiculous is very small. Historical facts are limitations, just as the details to which the novelist is bound in realistic fiction are: it is only in romance that true inventive freedom can be exercised. We are then brought back to the central question—"the realist proposes to show men what they are; the romantist tries to show men what they should be"—and Crawford knew very well where his preference lay: "For my part, I believe that more good can be done by showing men what they may be, ought to be, or can be, than by describing their greatest weaknesses with the highest art."[8]

Of the three qualifications for novel writing—native talent, education, and industry—the second was for Crawford of paramount importance, in that it involved firsthand experience of men and women, direct knowledge of life, love, and suffering in their various forms and phases. But the qualifications were typical: the writer is "to know and understand, so far as he is able, men and women who have been placed in *unusual* circumstances" (my italics). He must appeal, not so much to the emotions, as to the heart (Crawford wrote of the "religion of the heart"); further,

> What we call the heart in each man and woman seems to mean the whole body of innate and inherited instincts, impulses, and beliefs, taken together, and in that relation to one another in which they stand after they have been acted upon throughout the individual's life by the inward vicissitudes and the outward circumstances to which he has been exposed. When all this is quiescent I think we call it Self. When roused to emotional activity we call it the Heart. But whatever we call it, it is to this Self or Heart that everything which is ethic and therefore permanent must appeal.

The foundation of fiction is, therefore, ethical, and its appeal is emotional—addressed "to the constant element in human nature." Moreover, as opposed to playwrights, fiction writers can "appeal entirely to the imagination . . . can call up surroundings which never were and never can be possible in the world;" they can use "impossible characters . . . and make them do impossible things . . . can conceive a tale fantastic beyond the bounds of probability" and transport readers into fairyland. This was the mark of romance—creating for the moment "something almost like belief" and appealing "to the heart almost directly." Crawford was afraid that a touch of frivolity might be perceived here; in fact, the drift of his argument led to the acknowledgment of the value of sentiment and emotion (but not sentimentality) in fiction. Lives filled with emotion, and therefore necessarily exceptional lives, offer the proper subjects for romantic fiction, and Crawford's rationalization here is of some interest: "The great emotions are not every-day phenomena, and it is the desire to experience them vicariously which creates the demand for fiction and thereby and at the same time a demand for emotion. This is felt more particularly nowadays than formerly."[9]

Indeed, Crawford identified rather well the historical foundation and motivation for such a trend. After a century of artificiality and convention in literature,

> The French Revolution seems to have introduced an emotional phase into social history, and to it we must attribute directly or indirectly many of our present tastes and fashions. With it began the novel in France. With it the novel in the English language made a fresh start and assumed a new form.

Fiction writing belonged to a climate of "emotional habit" subsequent to the very high pressure put on lives during the French Revolution and the Napoleonic Wars, and it provided the kind of vicarious experience that was emotionally needed but without actual consequences: "There was a general desire felt to go on experiencing without dangerous consequences those varying conditions of hope, fear, disappointment and triumph in which the whole world's nervous system had thrilled daily during so many years and at such fearful cost." After that, "sterner, rougher stuff" was in demand—the name of which, needless to say, was romance. Even in the world of modern civilization and easy (often evil) communication, emotions played a considerable part, "and being real, of the living, and of superior interest to those who feel them, reflect themselves in the novel of today, diverting the course of true love into very tortuous channels and varying the tale that is ever young with features that are often new." This was, according to Crawford, true of southern Italy as well as of North America: "the prime impulses of the heart are, broadly speaking, the same in all ages and almost in all races"—they come "from depths

not reached by civilizations nor changed by fashions." Crawford's final plea was thus for a kind of fiction that struck at
the heart, investigated the depths of the psyche and of the
passions: "Those deep waters the real novel must fathom,
sounding the tide-stream of passion and bringing up such
treasures as lie far below and out of sight—out of reach of
the individual in most cases—until the art of the story-teller
makes him feel that they are or might be his."[10] Faithful to
his title, he used the term "novel": in fact, all his formulations and the trend of his argument connoted very clearly
the kind of romance that was getting the upper hand, at
least theoretically, in the 1890s.

In particular, the idea that romance would fathom the
unsounded depths of the human heart and pursue the
winding ways of our subconscious moods and motives
emerged with considerable frequency in these years. Magazine articles still facing the old question of the Great American Novel found that the analysis of what would soon be
called depth psychology might constitute its distinguishing
mark. An anonymous writer in the *Dial* (1896), beginning
with Hawthorne, noticed once more the absence of a novelist "really representative of American society" in the sense
that Balzac, Thackeray, or Turgenev could be seen as representative, respectively, of French, English, and Russian
society. Prophesying the arrival of the "G.A.N.," this writer
saw it coming by stealth and unnoticed, puzzling reviewers
with its originality, being borne to fame "by a strong under-
current of intelligent appreciation." As to what it would be
like, being American "it must needs reflect the democratic
principle"; unable to use the artificial distinctions of older
civilizations for its characters, it "must fall back upon the
distinctions of mind and heart that are inherent in human
nature. In other words, it must command a deeper psychology than the European novelist needs to give interest to his
book." A *"deeper psychology"* was the telltale sign of the new
romance, in spite of—or because of—its democratic bias. (At
the end of his short article, the author quoted Emerson's

motto for his essay on "Culture" about "the semigod whom we await," "musical / Tremulous, impressional" who "Shall into the Future fuse the Past"—the adumbrated hero of the most typical American romance.) Bliss Perry, in his already quoted *A Study of Prose Fiction* (1902), wrote that realistic fiction appeared more suitable to democratic society, owing to its leveling conformity to common models. But our sense of wonder in the face of external things and the developments of industry would soon cease; soon there would be no more unexplored corners in the world. It was precisely this that would make us turn into ourselves in order to discover the marvelous; the "wonders of Cathay" would be within us. Hence, psychological fiction would thrive on the assumption or recognition that the inner world was the reign of wonder. Writing in *The Critic* in 1897, William B. Chisholm admitted that "if the picture of national life and manners in the closing years of the century is to be handed down with faithful coloring it must be through romance."[11]

These three writers, while writing of possible romances, stressed the actual basis of fiction, its constant and necessary reference to fact, its complex links with contemporary society. For the anonymous contributor to the *Dial,* "the political motive must figure among the leading motives of the Great American Novel"—thereby touching "one of the most responsive chords" of the national consciousness. "Such a novel," he continued, "is under bonds to be an epic of individualism"—a significant recognition that would coincide with Marxism ideas. For Bliss Perry, as we have seen, it was essential that fiction in its present historical phase adhere to real life and actuality. As for William B. Chisholm, who was uneasy about the cosmopolitan tendencies of American fiction *and* its dialect stories, the novel of the future "must throw vividly upon the camera the types of social and political leadership" (the American politician had never been "written up," except in caricature). The "restless progress" of the age of steam, telegraph, and daily papers had to be taken into consideration; moreover, the new novel "must grasp the significance of great popular movements" and emphasize "the life of the people as affected by rapidly changing conditions and an imperious business system." It should "keep abreast with every phase of national discontent." If all this dictated that the novel adhere to reality and develop not "upon legendary or romantic lives," Chisholm insisted more than once on what he called "the special character of the coming American *romance*" (my italics). He did not seem too eager to make a neat distinction between the novel and the romance. One thing in particular, however, is worth noting at this stage: in his important revaluation of romance, which closes a century of theoretical discussion most aptly, Frank Norris started precisely from there—from a recognition of the socially committed dimension and realistic bias of fiction.

III

In his young years, Norris had thrived on exoticism and medievalism (witness, for instance, his narrative poem *Ivernelle*, on feudal France). In the 1890s he appeared as the most convinced theorist and practitioner of naturalistic fiction. In both his representative novels *Vandover and the Brute* and *McTeague*, he drew documentary studies of degeneration of individuals brought about by heredity and social determinism. He had meditated on Zola perhaps more than any other contemporary; he turned to the West to write an (unfinished) epic trilogy on the wheat industry—from agricultural product to consumers' staple. But in the West Norris also looked for local color, and he ended up by finding romance. This inborn propensity to romance subsumes and breaks up his realistic allegiance, and he cannot help combining the two aspects. As he expressed it in an article in *The Wave*, naturalism became for him a sort of romance where everything was extraordinary, fantastic, even grotesque.

The duality of his interests and the way in which such opposite theories closely blended are exemplified by the essays, written mainly in the 1890s, that were posthumously collected in the volume *The Responsibilities of the Novelist* (1903). Norris is one of those who, in this age, disclaimed caring about style and asserted the superiority of life over literature. The novel for him was the best expression of modern life: "To-day is the day of the novel. In no other period and by no other vehicle is contemporaneous life so adequately expressed," he wrote. The novel is necessary, even essential to "the civilization of the twentieth century," better than architecture, painting, poetry, or music. Moreover, "It is an instrument, a tool, a weapon, a vehicle." It reflects, but can also condition or change, contemporary society. It addresses itself to, and is inspired by, "the People," who provide its frame of reference and, in the last analysis, "pronounce the final judgment." The novel must, therefore, seek after Truth, because the People "have a right to the Truth as they have a right to life, liberty and the pursuit of happiness. It is not right that they be exploited and deceived with a false view of life." This is why the novelist has responsibilities and the novel must be "with a purpose" (two essays are devoted to these ideas). The novel with a purpose is the best class and the highest form in that it "proves something, draws conclusions from a whole congeries of forces, social tendencies, race impulses." It deals with "type-men, men who are composite pictures of a multitude of men" and with the social forces expressed or embodied by them. Of course, even if this is "the all-important thing," the purpose is to the novelist's story "what the keynote is to the sonata"—"only a note to which his work must be attuned," something that simply coordinates his music. In spite of the sympathy he feels as a man for his fellow sufferers, the novelist is mainly concerned with his craft. The artist's attitude, Norris seems to suggest, remains rather detached. Yet, "purpose" is essential to fiction: "Take this element from [it], take from it the power and opportunity to prove that

injustice, crime and inequality do exist, and what is left? Just
the amusing novels, the novels that entertain." The novel
represents, then, a committed kind of literature. It is en-
gagé; it has an aim and provides guidance. It deals truth-
fully with the present, with economic and social conflicts,
with elementary forces and moving themes, not only showing or telling us something about them, but proving something about them. In sum, the Muse of Fiction is for Norris
a teacher, keeping pace with the great march of the People.[12]

Further on, in the essays on "An American School of Fiction" and "Novelists of the Future," Norris sees the Muse of
American Fiction as "no chaste, delicate, superfine made-
moiselle of delicate poses and 'elegant' attitudinizing, but a
robust, red-armed *bonne femme,* who rough-shoulders her
way among men and among affairs, who finds a healthy
pleasure in the jostlings of the mob." She is "a Child of the
People," with a new heaven and a new earth in her face, the
tan of the sun in her cheeks, the dust of the highway thick
on her shoes, her robe torn, who "will lead you far from the
studios and the aesthetes, the velvet jackets and the uncut
hair . . . straight into a World of Working Men." As Norris
insists elsewhere in the book, of all the difficult things that
a writer has to learn, the most difficult to acquire "is the
fact that life is better than literature . . . it still remains true
that all the temperament, all the sensitiveness to impressions, all the education in the world will not help one little,
little bit in the writing of the novel if life itself, the crude,
the raw, the vulgar, if you will, is not studied." Beauty is
simple, "of an almost barren nudity." Norris has "no pa-
tience with a theory of literature . . . that claims the Great
Man belongs only to the cultured few" and has no interest
in the way in which the fictional game was played in former
times. "It is the people, after all, who 'make literature' ": the
United States at the end of the century "does not want and
does not need Scholars, but Men." In more than one place
Norris exalts populism and invites a healthy plunge into life:

A literature that can not be vulgarized is no literature at all.
. . . The things that last are the understandable things—understandable to the common minds, the Plain People, understandable, one is almost tempted to say, to the very children. . . .

If the modern novelist does not understand the Plain People, if he does not address himself to them intelligibly and simply, he will fail. . . . How necessary then for him—of all men—to be in the midst of life! He can not plunge too deeply into it. Politics will help him, and Religious Controversies, Explorations, Science, the newest theory of Socialism, the latest development of Biology.[13]

In the opening and closing essays, Norris makes the novelist not only a mirror of the times but a reflector of contemporary customs, movements, and ideas. The novel will deal with politics and imperialism, social contrasts and clashes, racial differences, wars among nations. The frontier has "gone at last" (as the title of one of the essays runs), industrial exploitation has supplanted rural values. Owing to the spread of democracy, the Plain People, as Norris insists on calling them, have become the objects as well as the subjects of artistic concern. *"In the last analysis the People are always right"* (Norris's italics), he writes toward the end of the book. His becomes, then, the most genuine formulation of socially committed fiction and of some tenets of naturalism, with their insistence on truth and truthfulness, the social role and the direct engagement of the writer on contemporary problems. This included, as we saw, a characteristic reliance on regionalism as the proper source of national literary expression, or indeed of the Great American Novel ("such a novel will be sectional. The United States is a Union, but not a unit, and the life of one part is very, very different from the life in another. . . . It is only possible to make a picture of a single locality").[14] Avoiding regionalism, going too deep into the lives of the people of one community to find what they have in common with other lives miles away would result in a nonnational (or supernational) kind of fiction.

But all this is only one side of the coin, one half of Norris's theory. One soon realizes that for him—as for James or Crane—it is the *personal* perception of the novelist that allows for an accurate and colorful presentation of reality. The filter provided by the writer's own vision is essential even to truthfulness. Second, although he starts from a naturalistic reliance on "typemen," Norris tends to avoid representative cases and to emphasize, rather, abnormal cases, what he calls "variations from the type of normal life." As had been the case with Zola, the naturalistic formula becomes interesting in that it allows for a higher level of romance, for being visionary rather than documentary. Finally, according to a deep-seated American bias, that formula and that attitude are extolled because they favor the exploration of man's soul and consciousness, the plunge into the dark regions of the mind and heart, the revelation of psychological complexities and depths.[15] Naturalistic premises—scientific detachment and objectivity, the dispassionate presentation of outward reality and social forces at work—end by being reversed. Significantly enough, the central essay of Norris's book is devoted to "A Plea for Romantic Fiction"—a plea for romance, not in its popular form or sense, but as the summa and the crown of realism. These three aspects are worth examining in some detail.

The eye of the novelist, Norris notes, "never once should wander to the gallery, but be always with single purpose turned *inward* upon the work." At first, he wants the writer to "go out into the street and stand where the ways cross and hear the machinery of life work clashing in its grooves." But then he enjoins him:

> Shut yourself in your closet and turn your eyes inward upon yourself—deep *into* yourself, down, down into the heart of you; and the tread of the feet upon the pavement is the sys-

tole and diastole of your own being—different only in degree.

Given that "life is not always true to life—from the point of
view of the artist,"

> How shall the writer guide himself in the treatment of a piv-
> otal, critical scene, or how shall the reader judge whether or
> no he is true? Perhaps, after all, the word "seem," and not
> the word "true," is the most important. Of course no good
> novelist, no good artist, can represent life as it actually is . . .
> here we are dealing not with science, but with art, that in-
> stantly involves the personality of the artist and all that that
> means. . . .
> The point is just this. In the fine arts we do not care one
> little bit about what life actually is, but what it looks like to
> an interesting, impressionable man. . . . His accuracy cuts
> no figure at all.

These last sentences are from the essay called "A Problem
in Fiction," which distinguishes the "accurate" from the
"true" and considers the idea itself of fictional accuracy as
false to life, in almost the same terms that we find stressed
by Ford Madox Ford a few years later. Elsewhere, Norris
seems almost to foreshadow Ford's central idea of the fictional importance of what Ford called *progression d'effet:* "And
it seems as if there in a phrase one could resume the whole
system of fiction mechanics—preparations of effect." Norris
is in fact aware of the artificial (one could say, Jamesian)
method of constructing a novel not "in one continued fine
frenzy of inspiration" but considering

> each chapter as a unit, distinct, separate, having a definite
> beginning, rise, height and end, the action continuous. . . .
> Each chapter thus treated is a little work in itself, and the
> great story of the whole novel is told thus as it were in a
> series of pictures, the author supplying information as to what

has intervened between the end of one chapter and the beginning of the next by suggestion or by actual *résumé*. As often as not the reader himself can fill up the gap by the context.[16]

Norris, then, seems to focus on a view of fiction as experimentation. Moving away from naturalism, he is ready to maintain that true realism is to be found in romance, not in minute accuracy or in detailed depictions of life. Romance is not sentimentalism, he writes in "A Plea for Romantic Fiction": "Romance, I take it, is the kind of fiction that takes cognizance of variations from the type of normal life. Realism is the kind of fiction that confines itself to the type of normal life." Romance, therefore, "may even treat of the sordid, the unlovely" (as in Zola). Realism, instead, "stultifies itself. It notes only the surface of things"; it is without dimension and depth, a mere outside; it does not go far enough; "it is the drama of a broken teacup, the tragedy of a walk down the block." Just as realism is limited, minute, skin-deep, so romance is free to roam and soar. Far from being "a conjurer's trick-box full of flimsy quackeries"—or from being restricted to the Middle Ages—romance has a contemporary, everyday connection and relevance. There is as much romance in Michigan Avenue, Allen Street, and Mulberry Bend as there is realism in King Arthur's court.

Romance is therefore an extension and an intensification of realism. It is a serious business. If realism takes you to pay a formal visit to your neighbor's house and bows on the doormat, telling you "That is Life," Romance takes you into the front parlor—and does not stop there, either. "She would be off upstairs with you, prying, peeping, peering into the closets of the bedroom, into the nursery, into the sitting-room; yes, and into that little iron box screwed to the lower shelf of the closet in the library; and into those compartments and pigeon-holes of the *secretaire* in the study." She—because Norris has ended by personifying Romance—takes you *inside* and *upstairs*, and reveals the heartache between the pillows of the mistress' bed, the secret in the master's box, the hope, perhaps even the intrigue or the affair of the young lady in the house. In brief, whereas realism is illustrative, romance is revealing, scrutinizes mysteries, breaks down reticence, brings to light secrets, repressions, deceits. Above all, romance, as Norris sees it, allows the writer to roam widely, not only in the world, but within the soul of man in a way that is denied to realism.

Norris had already postulated "not the Realism of mere externals (the copyists have that), but the realism of motives and emotions." In the opening and final statements of his "Plea," he identifies romance with a strong power of psychological, indeed psychoanalytic insight that is denied to realism and in which resides instead the interest of the modern writer. We read at the beginning of the essay: "Can we not see in it [romance] an instrument, keen, finely tempered, flawless—an instrument with which we may go straight through the clothes and tissues and wrappings of flesh down deep into the red, living heart of things?" And, at the conclusion of the essay:

> Let Realism do the entertainment with its meticulous presentation of teacups, rag carpets, wall-paper and haircloth sofas, stopping with these, going no deeper than it sees, choosing the ordinary, the untroubled, the commonplace.
>
> But to Romance belongs the wide world for range, and the unplumbed depths of the human heart, and the mystery of sex, and the problems of life, and the black, unsearched penetralia of the soul of man.[17]

The mystery of sex, the black penetralia of the human heart: with a remarkable leap, given his premises, Norris joins here with Conrad and James in postulating a totally new realm for the novelist.

IV

It is tempting to close this study of American theories of the novel in the nineteenth century with Norris's personification of Romance as a daring young girl taking us into the secret places of life and the recesses of the human soul. It is a fitting conclusion, which brings us back, after half a century, to Hawthorne's and Melville's conceptions of a higher, deeper, and broader task for fiction. It is fairly obvious that such a recurring insistence builds up into a tradition—a tradition that has often been recognized as typical of American literature and its theoretical expression. Yet, differences and qualifications are of crucial importance here. The late-nineteenth-century revival of romance, as exemplified by Frank Norris and others, stems out of, and takes into full account, the long battle for realism and its theorization. It is strictly connected with, and dependent on, the achievement of a realistic conception of the novel. Romance is seen as not only broadening the scope and range of the artist's view; it appears imbued with all the sustaining power of life in all its aspects.

For Hawthorne, and sometimes for Melville (as we saw), romance was a *pis aller,* a shortcut out of, and a compromise with, the difficulties that America posed to the novelist. They made the most of a postulated weakness, though finding in romance the perfect vehicle for symbolic investigations. For Norris and his contemporaries, romance was a way of exploiting the full potentialities of fiction and literary insight—of human life as well as of human sympathy. It is significant that a consideration of American theories of the novel in a crucial span of years should offer two symmetrical conclusions—one at midcentury, the other at the turn of the century—both inscribed under the name of romance. Yet, the paths leading to these symmetrical vindications of its value are widely different. If in the first instance romance was conceived as a response to the negative conditions, restrictions, and shortcomings of a new country and a new culture, in the second instance a full appreciation of contemporary conditions went into the conception of a heightened form of romantic fiction. In other words, the full body of theoretical formulations that in the second half of the century characterized the novel in realistic terms contributed as much as anything to this revival of romance. If romance, then, is seen and presented in the closing years of the century (and in the final pages of this study) as a kind of "supreme fiction," this is because it subsumes and embodies the full recognition, envisaged by James and carried out by his followers, that the novel can do anything, go anywhere, eschew nothing. It is the highest form of rival, as well as incremental, creation. It takes off from our actual, everyday world but brings us back to face it with renewed confidence and awareness.

The final recognition that romance is the privileged form for sounding and exploring depth psychology represents a grand opening on the new century. The conquests of James Joyce and stream of consciousness are around the corner; Virginia Woolf or William Faulkner would not take long to appropriate the idea and take up the challenge. Yet, in all these cases, the exploration of the complexities and tortuousness of the psyche and of the inner life is closely combined with a strong sense of physical, outward, tangible reality. This strong sense of the actuality of life has also been theoretically appropriated to fiction as an integral, inescapable part of its bearing.

My conclusion is therefore somewhat removed from the current idea that romance constitutes the sustaining tradition of an American theory of fiction and of American literature in general. Its revival at the turn of the century represents the crowning effort of a conception of the novel that stresses its realistic purport and aspects. One might say, rather, that as long as the discussion concerned mainly a theory of the *American* novel, romance became prominent as an escape from, and a way out of, postulated difficulties; when the discussion focused and developed on American theories of the novel as such, romance combined with realism in asserting the ways, values, and potentialities of fiction. Since the very beginning, romance may have drawn American theories into a greater appreciation of the necessity and value of psychological analyses on the part of the fiction writer. This tendency appears fairly consistently throughout the century; it colors and qualifies most of its formulations—from Brockden Brown to Hawthorne to James and to the debate over the analytic school. Yet, at least in theoretical terms, realism and romance came gradually to share the spotlight, to contend for equal status—to offer, not mutually exclusive, but complementary alternatives. Romance is never really severed from its realistic foundation; realism is constantly qualified and modified, challenged and enhanced, by a recourse to romantic or symbolic modes.

Theories of the novel in nineteenth-century America are thus characterized, not by a uniform drift, but by a twofold, delicately balanced, constantly readjusted recognition that the demands of reality and the lure of imagined worlds are complementary; both are part of the novelist's burden and task. Both came to be seen as essential to the life of fiction, just as the form of the novel, after initial suspicions, came to be recognized as essential to a representation of America, of modern times, of human life in all its possible aspects.

NOTES

1. Oscar Wilde, "The Decay of Lying," in *The Artist as Critic,* ed. Richard Ellmann (New York: Vintage Books, 1970), pp. 290–320 (pp. 290–91, 300, 301, 318–20 for quotes). Wilde referred to Robert Louis Stevenson, Rider Haggard, Hall Caine, Marion Crawford (for whom see below) as well as to the realistic novelists.

2. Arthur Symons, *The Symbolist Movement in Literature* (London: Heinemann, 1899), pp. 3, 6–7, 9–10; pp. 142, 144–45.

3. George Saintsbury, "The Present State of the Novel: I," *Fortnightly Review,* 42 (1887): 410–17; "The Present State of the Novel: II," *Fortnightly Review,* 43 (1888): 112–23 (reprinted in *Miscellaneous Essays* [London, 1892], and in *The Collected Essays and Papers, 1875–1920* [London, 1923], 3 vols.).

4. H. Rider Haggard, "About Fiction," *Contemporary Review,* 51 (1887): 172–80.

5. Hall Caine, "The New Watchwords of Fiction," *Contemporary Review,* 57 (1890): 480–88; and Kenneth Graham, *English Criticism of the Novel: 1865–1900* (Oxford: Clarendon Press, 1965), chap. 2, p. vii (for what follows).

6. F. Marion Crawford, *The Novel: What It Is* (New York: Macmillan, 1893), pp. 8–9, 11–12, 16–17, 22. If the novel is like a play, it is not like a miracle play (p. 27); as for the question of young readers, Crawford discussed it in a devious way, hoping for "a little more liberty," but the core of his attitude was, "if we do not write for the young girl, who will?" (p. 30). He also discussed the frequent danger of "writing oneself out"— "for the romance of romancing soon disappears" (p. 35); in fact, the worn-out novelist should adopt the tenets of realism (p. 37).

7. Ibid., pp. 39–41, 43–44, 45–46, 49–50, 52–55.

8. Ibid., pp. 64–65, 68, 72–73, 75–77.

9. Ibid., pp. 79–81, 83, 85–86, 88–89, 97–98.

10. Ibid., pp. 101–3, 106–8.

11. For ease of reference, both articles are in Richard Ruland, ed., *A Storied Land* (New York: Dutton, 1976), pp. 222–25 (pp. 223 and 225 for quotes) and pp. 225–28 (p. 226 for quote); Bliss Perry, *A Study of Prose Fiction* (Boston and New York: Houghton Mifflin, 1902), chap. 13. The anonymous writer of the *Dial* specified that the "G.A.N." "must give to social phenomena their true ethical rating, and exalt . . . 'that which one is' above that which he possesses. . . . It must make the reader feel how far the true aristocracy of heart and intellect overshadows all the sham aristocracies of wealth and of social position" (Ruland, ed., *A Storied Land,* p. 224). Unconscious elements of romance crept in here.

12. Frank Norris, *The Responsibilites of the Novelist* (New York: Hill and Wang, 1967; Norris's book is published together with W. D. Howells's *Criticism and Fiction*), pp. 195–97 ("The Responsibilities of the Novelist"); pp. 203–6 ("The Novel with a 'Purpose' ").

13. Ibid., pp. 278, 288, 292 ("Simplicity in Art"); pp. 298, 301, 308–9 ("Salt and Sincerity").

14. Ibid., pp. 317, 229.

15. For these and related aspects see Alfred Kazin, *On Native Grounds* (Garden City, N.Y.: Doubleday, 1942), pp. 74–79 and 91; Larzer Ziff, *The American 1890s: Life and Times of a Lost Generation* (New York: Viking, 1966), chap. 12, pp. 250–74; Richard Chase, *The American Novel and Its Tradition* (Garden City, N.Y.: Doubleday, 1960), chap. 9, pp. 185–204.

16. Norris, *The Responsibilities of the Novelist,* p. 198 ("The True Reward of the Novelist"); pp. 214–15 ("The Need of a Literary Conscience"); pp. 283–84 ("A Problem in Fiction"); p. 309, pp. 253–54 ("The Mechanics of Fiction").

17. Ibid., pp. 279–82 ("A Plea for Romantic Fiction"); p. 199. For fur-

ther documentation see *The Literary Criticism of Frank Norris,* ed. Donald Pizer (Austin: University of Texas Press, 1964); *Frank Norris of "The Wave,"* introduction by Oscar Lewis (San Francisco: The Westgate Press, 1931); George W. Johnson, "Frank Norris and Romance," *American Literature,* 33 (1961): 52–63. For Norris's view of naturalism as a transcending synthesis of realism and romanticism, see Donald Pizer's "Frank Norris's Definition of Naturalism" and "The Significance of Frank Norris's Literary Criticism" in his *Realism and Naturalism in Nineteenth-Century American Literature* [1966] (New York: Russell and Russell, 1976), pp. 33–36 and 99–107.

HENRY JAMES IN THE TWENTIETH CENTURY

I

IN THE ESSAYS he wrote at the beginning of the new century, James went back to his cherished masters—Zola, Flaubert, above all Balzac—and stressed the factual basis of fiction, the novelist's reliance on actuality, fidelity to detail, and saturation with life. Writing of Zola, he saw fiction as a capacious vessel and "the only form for which such a claim can be made. All others have to confess to a smaller scope. . . . The novel has nothing to fear but sailing too lightly. It will take aboard all we bring in good faith to the dock." Of course, "If you insist on the common, you must submit to the common"; science and *vérité* illuminate only as we apply them; the game of art must always be played. Yet, what seemed important in Zola was the realization of a *"totally represented world,"* a world "more founded and established, more provided for all round, more organized and carried on" than any other, with the possible exception of

Balzac—whose quality of scale and assimilation was extolled in three essays. "[W]hen I think . . . of the nature and the effort of the Novelist, I think of something that reaches its highest expression in him," James wrote. Balzac was seen as the first and foremost of his craft, "the father of us all"; his way of dealing with facts and details confirmed the value of social specification. An obsession with the actual and an appetite for facts, viewing the subject in the light of science as well as in regard to "the bearing of all its parts on each other" were the marks of an "attack on life" that was combined with free observation and personal experience.[1]

The ideal convincingly realized was to "reconcile such dissemination with such intensity, the collection and possession of so vast a number of facts with so rich a presentation of each." There lay the lesson of Balzac, which was detailed in a lecture-essay of that title (1905), which updated the views expressed in "The Art of Fiction." If the lyrical poet expressed life directly, James maintained, novelists are lovers of the *image* of life: "The most fundamental and general sign of the novel, from one desperate attempt to another, is its being everywhere an effort at *representation*." A "respect for the liberty of the subject," quantity *and* intensity, "a reproduction of the real on the scale of the real" leading to a multiplication of values—all were signs of a mature possession of the prerequisites of fiction. So was the power of identification with the subject (getting, as Balzac had done, "into the constituted consciousness, into all the clothes, gloves, and whatever else, into the very skin and bones, of the habited, featured, colored, articulated form of life" that one wished to present). Balzac's lesson was in the art of "complete representation," in the evocation of the medium, in the distillation of the natural and social air, in the great part that was assigned to the *conditions* of the characters; in his showing "how we are placed and built-in for being so. What befalls us is but another name for the way our circumstances press upon us." As James put it in a later essay on Balzac (1913), the French writer proved exemplary for "his having felt his fellow-creatures . . . as quite failing of reality . . . unless their social conditions, to the last particular, their generative and contributive circumstances, of every discernible sort, enter for all they are 'worth' into his representative attempt."

To this was added, however, "an all-inclusive form, a form without rift or leak, a tight mould, literally, into which everything relevant to a consideration of the society surrounding it . . . might be poured in a stream of increasing consistency." This fusion of all the elements was of exemplary value, again, in a period in which, according to James, the novel had ceased to be artistically interesting and had become an object of easy manufacture, an article of commerce, no longer handmade but showing the stamp of the machine. Now that fusion of elements was achieved by overcoming the compositional difficulties that beset the novel mainly through the use of foreshortening—a device that imposed meaningful compression and a perspective on the wealth of vicarious experience that was an important asset of the novelist but that constantly threatened (as in Tolstoy) to overthrow his formal balance. This involved the creation of an atmosphere, the capacity to present the lapse of time—that is, the duration of the subject—with authority, the alternation of illustrative parts with the controlled use of dialogue and "scenic" moments. In other words, by the very nature of his work the novelist was forced into the constructive office. He had indeed to learn the cost of structure, and that "there is no convincing art that is not ruinously expensive." And structure was achieved by the operation, once more, of "the mystic process of the crucible, the transformation of the material under aesthetic heat," of which James wrote at the beginning of his 1905 essay,[2] and on which he insisted in various other essays of the period on Flaubert, Gabriele D'Annunzio, Shakespeare's *The Tempest,* "The New Novel."

To put it briefly, James's mature concept was that the novel depended on a strong, almost overpowering sense of reality, on a saturation with life, which had to be combined with artistic sensibility and formal control. Quite understandably, at this stage he wavered between the two poles. After extolling so repeatedly a saturation with facts, in his essay on Flaubert (already quoted) he not only wrote of "the fertilization of subject by form" but maintained "that expression is creation, that it *makes* the reality, and only in the degree in which it *is*, exquisitely, expression; and that we move in literature in a world of different values and relations, a blest world in which we know nothing except by style, but in which also everything is saved by it, and in which the image is thus always superior to the thing itself." Likewise, in the essay on D'Annunzio, he insisted that there is "no complete creation without style any more than there is complete music without sound."[3]

II

This attitude and this conviction underlie James's comprehensive view of the "Art of the Novel"—as the Prefaces he dictated for the New York Edition of his novels and tales (1907–9) rightly came to be known. Here we find his greatest plea for art and discrimination, an impassioned exaltation of the artistic value and dignity achieved by the novel. But we also find a proper appreciation of the links that tie novels and novelists to our world and our reality. It is too often overlooked that at the very end of his painstaking analysis of all the possible aspects, problems, and implications of novel writing (which are here of course only touched upon in passing), James chose once more to exalt "the vast example of Balzac," to whom is owed "our richest and hugest inheritance of imaginative prose." James's wavering between the values of life and those of art is, however, best expressed, for our purposes, in the statement that "Art deals with what we see, it must first contribute full-handed that ingredient; it plucks its material, otherwise expressed, in the garden of life—which material elsewhere grown is stale and uneatable. But it has no sooner done this than it has to take account of a *process*. . . . The process, that of the expression, the literal squeezing-out, of value is another affair." Experience (i.e., "our apprehension . . . of what happens to us as social creatures") must be organized; fiction has to do with, indeed has to establish, relations: "the painter's subject consisting ever, obviously, of the related state, to each other, of certain figures and things." James maintained that "the novel is of its very nature an 'ado,' an ado about something"; but it must be given "deep-breathing economy and an organic form," and achieve "unity and quality of tone."[4]

Of course, we can see "the grave distinction between substance and form in a really wrought work of art signally break down." But a basic dichotomy—which may indeed become dialectic—is here perceived and emphasized by James. While life is "all inclusion and confusion," art is "all discrimination and selection." A picture of life founded on "reserves and omissions and suppressions of life" has no chance, and a plea for the novelist's freedom of subject, for his affronting the whole of human life, was neatly expressed. Yet in the Prefaces, more than anywhere else, much of the discussion is devoted to the conditions that allow the art of fiction to perform its selective, organizing, *representational* role, to accomplish its constructive and creative function, to assert itself as "the great extension, great beyond all others, of experience and of consciousness." It was a difficult attempt and achievement. First, "clearness and concreteness constantly depend, for any pictorial whole, on some *concentrated* individual notation of them." This was done, according to James's well-known image, through the window of literary form:

> The house of fiction has in short not one window, but a million. . . . The spreading field, the human scene, is the "choice of subject"; the pierced aperture . . . is the "literary form"; but they are, singly or together, as nothing without

the posted presence of the watcher—without, in other words, the consciousness of the artist.

Second, "the value of composition" must be constantly sought. James developed his most characteristic theories in this connection. One way was that of illustrative, processional, and panoramic presentations of the subject; here the form is looser and wider, the control less tight. There is the possibility, indeed the advantage, of what James termed the "going behind"—that is to say, of psychological analysis, of searching into the souls and minds of the characters for motivations, urgings, implications. Generally speaking, this was the pictorial form. The "scenic form," instead, which was based more on the dialogues and the conduct of characters, on direct presentation of actions and gestures, aimed at a tighter structure, at architectural composition: "The dramatist has verily to *build,* is committed to architecture, to construction at any cost." Here the value was the value of "guarded objectivity," depending on "the imposed absence of that 'going behind', to compass explanations and amplifications" and on the fact that the "presented occasion" is made to "tell all its story itself." In the scenic form, more than in the pictorial form, an attempt must be made to achieve foreshortening—"the art of figuring synthetically" that "particular economic device" that allows the novelist to control expansion and to avoid looseness of form:

> To give the image and the sense of certain things while still keeping them subordinate to his plan, . . . to give all the sense, in a word, without all the substance or all the surface, and so to summarise and foreshorten, so to make values both rich and sharp . . .—such a case of delicacy proposes itself at every turn to the painter of life who wishes both to treat his chosen subject and to confine his necessary picture.[5]

Another principle is connected with foreshortening and scenic form: the principle of the narrator and of the limited point of view—that mainstay of James's theory and practice, so often taken as its pivot, which proves instead to be one cornerstone of his elaborate construction. We have seen the novelist standing at one of the many windows of the house of fiction. But a third party is introduced between him and the reader. James had already theorized that "the affair of the painter is not the immediate, it is the reflected field of life, the realm not of application, but of *appreciation*. . . . What a man thinks and what he feels are the history and the character of what he does." (Isabel Archer's meditative vigil in *The Portrait of a Lady* was considered to throw the action forward more than twenty "incidents.") This principle—"that the figures in any picture, the agents in any drama, are interesting only in proportion as they feel their respective situations"—implied that those "vessels of consciousness" became the centers of consciousness, the "reflectors" of the story (James harped on this aspect in more than one place). In other words, a reflective character is interposed between subject and reader, not only to tell or filter the story through his or her eyes, but to live and experience it in his or her consciousness, often as a gradual process of acquisition of knowledge, of painful realization. The drama becomes, then, more and more the drama of consciousness of a character directly or tangentially involved in the action, while the interest is given by his or her particular vision, conception, interpretation of the events. What matters is how the events are seen, felt, or presented by that character. The reader is seated at the window of that consciousness (as James put it) and is made from there to "assist."

According to James, "There is no economy of treatment without an adapted, a related point of view"; and there is "no breaking-up of the register, no sacrifice of the recording consistency, that doesn't rather scatter and weaken." The effect of a fine central intelligence or center of consciousness is, then, to economize and intensify the value as well as to stress the character's relation to itself. The life of fiction is not only in "relations" but in purely internal, psychological relations. The adoption of this principle has at least two important consequences. On the one hand, "the safest arena for the play of moving accidents and mighty mutations and strange encounters" becomes the field "rather of their second than their first exhibition." The apprehension and experience of life is internalized: facts are shown by the way in which they are felt, by the impression they make. The story is made up, not by the accidents, but by "the human emotion and the human attestation of them." On the other hand, the central intelligence becomes a structural principle: by referring facts to one particular point of view, it provides the proper perspective and the limited angle of vision through which foreshortening and dramatic intensity are achieved. More and more James tends to give the whole situation only through what might pass before, appeal to, touch, and affect the character involved. Thus, the device becomes functional, not only for the field of reflected vision, but for the organizing play of the scenic form. It limits the vision, allows for muddlement, confusion, and ambiguity; but it also selects and foreshortens. It gives the view and the appreciation of facts often in a limited, confused, tantalizing way. But the field of reflected vision and of the second exhibition restores to the novel that "thickness" and saturation with life that the process of formal selection might have jeopardized and that a reliance on mere externals would have compromised: "with its 'objective' side too emphasized the report (it is ten to one) will practically run thin . . . and we get the thickness in the human consciousness that entertains and records, that amplifies and interprets it."[6]

We reach here the clue to James's mature theory of a novel in which subjectivity of point of view combines with objectivity of dramatic presentation, psychological diffuseness with clarity of outline, the drama of consciousness with the picture of life. The novel needed "the particular attaching case *plus* some near individual view of it." In the same way, although originally opposed to each other, scenic form and picture could be combined, not only in arranged alternation, but in disguised symbiosis (as James emphasized about his later novels, where "everything that is not scene . . . is the fusion and synthesis of picture"). In his Prefaces virtually every aspect of the art of fiction and its poetics is faced, debated, and discussed: how "germs" of subjects operate on the writer's consciousness and characters spring up at him; how to define or suggest setting and locale; preparations of effects and the use of *ficelles;* consistency of dialogue and adumbration; freedom of choice, variety of experiment, and "make believe"; first- and third-person narrative; the *nouvelle* and the distinction between novel and romance ("The only *general* attribute of projected romance . . . is the fact of the kind of experience with which it deals—experience liberated, so to speak; experience disengaged, disembroiled, disencumbered . . . operating in a medium which relieves it . . . of the inconvenience of a *related,* a measurable state"); finally, "the perfect dependence of the 'moral' sense of a work of art on the amount of felt life concerned in producing it"; and so on.[7]

Two final points are worth stressing here. In the first place, James insisted not only on the "crucible of the imagination" that performs the necessary artistic fusion but on the predominance of the aesthetic vision over the facts of life—"that odd law which somehow always makes the minimum of valid suggestion serve the man of imagination better than the maximum," or "the operative irony" that "implies and projects the possible other case, the case rich and edifying where the actuality is pretentious and vain." In the second place, James came to the realization that, in spite of his well-rounded, organic, and totalizing view of the novel, its form was by its very nature elusive and ever changing, constantly breaking its confines and limitations. He acknowledged "its power not only, while preserving that form with closeness, to range through all the differences of the individual relation to its general subject-matter, all the varieties of outlook on life . . . but positively to appear more true to its character in proportion as it strains, or tends to burst . . . its mould." All this would lead to his final, elated vindication that "the Novel remains still, under the right persuasion, the most independent, most elastic, most prodigious of literary forms."[8]

III

This view was resumed and made the central point of James's last essay on the novel ("The Younger Generation," in the *Times Literary Supplement*, March–April 1914, expanded as "The New Novel" in *Notes on Novelists*), and during the controversy it stirred with his fellow novelist H. G. Wells. Here James saw contemporary fiction threatened by indiscriminate quality and "rough-and-tumble" output, by the refusal of selective and comparative principles, and by its democratization. The new novel was characterized by what he termed "value by saturation"—saturation with facts and outward details, with social notation and external appearances. This "documented state" (exemplified by Wells and Arnold Bennett) seemed to James, however, to constitute only one half of the novelist's authority: "the other half being represented of course by the application he is inspired to make of them." The question of "application" and the treatment of the theme, in order to counterbalance the prevailing "disconnection of matter from manner," seemed to James of crucial importance. To establish a center, a relation, and an interest appeared much more essential to the art of fiction than the loose "expression of life," the multiplication and flow of facts. He opposed to the novel of saturation the need of "the touch of the hand of selection"; he argued that "there being no question of a slice upon which the further question of where and how to cut it does not wait, the office of method, the idea of choice and comparison, have occupied the ground from the first." Or, as he had put it in his 1912 essay on "The Novel in 'The Ring and the Book' ":

Call a novel a picture of life as much as we will; call it, according to one of our recent fashions, a slice, or even a chunk, even a "bloody" chunk, of life, a rough excision from that substance as superficially cut and as summarily served as possible, it still . . . has had to be selected, selected under some sense for something. . . . If the slice or the chunk, or whatever we call it, if *it* isn't "done" . . . the work itself of course isn't likely to be.

There was for James no sense in, or indeed possibility of, an amorphous slice: he was all for "an extracted and related state" in the novel. Against ungoverned verbiage and discursive and rambling examples of novels saturated by the personality of the author, by his outbursts and opinions, James saw the novel as an exercise in objective presentation, organization of elements, and formal control: "We take for granted by the general law of fiction a primary author . . . that we forget him in proportion as he works upon us, and that he works upon us in fact by making us forget him." He stressed once more that the proper field for the novel was the field of reflected vision and the multiplication of aspects. In opposition to drama, which lived on the thing said, the novel lived on the report of it:

The order in which the drama simply says things gives it all its form, while the story told and the picture painted, as the novel at the pass we have brought it embraces them, reports of an infinite diversity of manners, gathers together and gives out again a hundred sorts, and finds its order and its structure, its unity and its beauty, in the alternation of parts and the adjustment of differences.

James's tackling directly the question of the contemporary novel at this late stage of his career testified to his unrelenting interest in the vital questions of the form and exalted status of fiction. The controversy stirred by his essay and Wells's reply led to James's final pleas for the artistic nature of fiction, in which he extolled the supremacy of art over life in a way that does away with his previous checks and balances. The novel needed the "fulness of life and the projection of it"; fictional "interest may, *must* be, exquisitely made and created." The fine thing about the fictional form was "that it opens such widely different windows of attention," he wrote; "but that is just why I like the window so to frame the play and the process!" He held Wells's distinction "between a form that is (like) painting and a form that is (like) architecture for wholly null and void." His final words, so often quoted, summarize his impassioned view of the supreme value of the art of fiction: "It is art that *makes* life, makes importance, for our consideration and application of these things, and I know of no substitute whatever for the force and beauty of its process."[9] James's valediction was a legacy to modernism, just as his nineteenth-century formulations summarize the case for a novel that, in spite of its grandiose pretensions, remains a vehicle for the reflection and the representation of human life and human reality.

NOTES

1. Henry James, *Notes on Novelists* (London: Dent, 1914), pp. 23, 42, 44–45 ("Emile Zola," 1902); pp. 86–89, 103, 108 ("Honoré de Balzac," 1902).

2. Henry James, *The Question of Our Speech and The Lesson of Balzac: Two Lectures* (Boston and New York: Houghton Mifflin, 1905), pp. 75, 78, 89, 92–93, 103–4.

3. Ibid., pp. 103–4, 105–12, 101–2; James, *Notes on Novelists*, pp. 118 and 115 ("Honoré de Balzac," 1913); pp. 78–79 and 81 ("Gustave Flaubert," 1902); p. 202 ("Gabriele D'Annunzio," 1902). See also James's essay on Shakespeare's *The Tempest* (1907), in James E. Miller, Jr., ed., *Theory of Fiction: Henry James* (Lincoln: University of Nebraska Press, 1972), p. 284.

4. Henry James, *The Art of the Novel: Critical Prefaces*, with an Introduction by Richard P. Blackmur (New York: Scribner's, 1934), pp. 343, 312, 64, 3, 5, 48, 84, 97.

5. Ibid., pp. 115, 120, 286, 29–30, 69, 46, 109–11, 158, 181–82, 278, 87–88, 14.

6. Ibid., pp. 65–66, 57, 62, 15–16, 37, 51, 276–77, 145, 300.

7. For quotes see ibid., pp. 31–34, 45, 328, 298, 322–23. For two meaningful classifications of these and related points, see Blackmur's Introduction to James, *The Art of the Novel,* and Miller's Introduction to *Theory of Fiction.*

8. James, *The Art of the Novel,* pp. 161, 222, 45–46, 326.

9. James, *Notes on Novelists,* pp. 253–54, 258–59, 271–72, 275, 280, 313–14, and Leon Edel and Gordon N. Ray, eds., *Henry James and H. G. Wells* (London: Hart-Davis, 1958), pp. 262–63 (James's letter of 6 July 1915); p. 267 (letter of 10 July 1915); and pp. 178–215 (for the original text of James's essay, "The Younger Generation").

INDEX